'We A[r
Creolization and Moderni[

CEDLA – Amsterdam

The Editorial Board of the CEDLA Latin America Studies (CLAS) series:

C.W.M. den Boer, CEDLA
Pitou F.F.M. van Dijck, CEDLA
Kathleen Willingham, CEDLA

Jan M.G. Kleinpenning,
    Katholieke Universiteit Nijmegen
Antonius C.G.M. Robben,
    Rijksuniversiteit Utrecht

The Centre for Latin American Research and Documentation (CEDLA) conducts and coordinates social science research on Latin America, publishes and distributes the results of such research, and assembles and makes accessible documentary and scholarly materials for the study of the region. The Centre also offers an academic teaching programme on the societies and cultures of Latin America.

El Centro de Estudios y Documentación Latinoamericanos (CEDLA) realiza y coordina investigaciones sobre la América Latina en el campo de las Ciencias Sociales, edita publicaciones, divulga sus resultados y colecciona documentos y materiales de carácter académico, accessibles al público interesado. El Centro ofrece, además, un programa académico de enseñanza sobre las sociedades y culturas de Latino América.

Hans Siebers

'We Are Children of the Mountain',
Creolization and Modernization
among the Q'eqchi'es

A CEDLA Publication
Centrum voor Studie en Documentatie van Latijns Amerika
Centro de Estudios y Documentación Latinoamericanos
Centro de Estudos e Documentação Latino-Americanos
Centre for Latin American Research and Documentation

Keizersgracht 395-397
1016 EK Amsterdam
The Netherlands / Países Bajos

Fax: +31 20 625 5127
E-mail: secretariat@cedla.uva.nl

© 1999 CEDLA

ISBN 90 70280 17 5

No part of this publication may be reproduced or transmitted in any form or by any means, electronic or mechanical, including photocopy, recording, or any information storage and retrieval system, without permission from the copyright owner.

NUGI 659

Contents

Preface vii

List of Tables xi

Maps xii

Chapter one: In Search of a Perspective that Holds:
A Theoretical Prologue 1

Chapter two: History and Life-worlds of the Q'eqchi'es 17

Chapter three: The Religious Field:
Intervening Churches and Local Specialists 39

Chapter four: The Religious Field:
Practices and Meanings of the Q'eqchi'es 63

Chapter five: Q'eqchi' Religion and Modernization 99

Chapter six: The Economic Field:
Intervening Agencies and Local Leaders 109

Chapter seven: The Economic Field:
Practices and Strategies of the Q'eqchi'es 123

Chapter eight: Q'eqchi' Economy and Modernization 149

Chapter nine: Conclusions, Considerations and Reflections 157

Note on Methodology 173

Notes 177

Bibliography 183

Glossary 189

Index 193

Preface

In the present globalizing world, social actors are increasingly confronted with flows of people, capital, goods, symbols, information and images stemming from distant corners of the globe. It is not just cosmopolitan business people, journalists or scientists in trade centres, offices, conference rooms or airports and connected by internet who take part in these flows. Even indigenous peoples who live in parts of the world that were considered as remote and isolated until recently are increasingly faced with the new and unknown. One wonders whether there is any space left beyond the Coca Cola frontier.

Actors faced with these flows feel encouraged, or even compelled, to answer to new impulses, to rework their representations and practices, to redefine their identities and to modify their ways of dealing with the ever expanding outside world. The resulting processes of social change raise important questions which involve some of the basic issues of social sciences such as modernity and modernization. While paying due attention to the particular characteristics of each case and avoiding the trap of portraying history as the outcome of development laws, we may ask whether these processes have some basic features in common which point into a modern direction. Are these actors trading in pre-modern characteristics for modern or even post-modern ones? Has the literature on modernity and post-modernity any relevance at all to the ways in which actors deal with global flows? Is a homogeneous modern or post-modern world the outcome to be expected from globalization or is its corollary, processes of localization, encouraging increasing local and regional diversity which escapes modern frameworks?

The Q'eqchi'es, living in northern Guatemala, make up such a group of social actors who are increasingly immersed in global flows. At first sight they do not appear to be an obvious case for studying the impact of globalization processes. They live rather far away from national and international communication centres and have access to only very poor infrastructure. Within the Guatemalan context they are renowned for their reservation regarding external influences and they stress their own specific characteristics such as their language and dress.

However on closer inspection, it becomes clear that they are very much involved in global flows. They produce cash crops such as coffee and cardamom that are consumed in North America, Europe and the Arab world. They face the influences of churches whose headquarters are in various parts of the world and many of their traditional or customary practices have a European Catholic origin. Thus, precisely because of the relationship between their specific characteristics and external influences, they present an excellent case for studying the impact of globalization processes. Moreover, there is a scientific interest involved because, so far, little research has focused on them.

I conducted the fieldwork for this study at the invitation by the Bishop of the diocese of Verapaz, Mgr. Gerardo Flores Reyes, and several diocesan officials. The boundaries of the Bishopric of Verapaz encompass the majority of Q'eqchi'es though other ethnic groups are also included in this bishopric and considerable numbers of Q'eqchi'es live in the adjacent bishoprics and diocese-like units of El Quiché, El Petén and Izabal. In this study I have not focused on the minorities of Q'eqchi'es in Belize and Mexico.

These diocesan officials were anxious that after almost five centuries of pastoral work in the region, the church should become more sensitive to the Q'eqchi'es' way of life and begin to play a more positive and stimulating role among them. They expected the research to provide greater knowledge about the religion and development strategies of the Q'eqchi'es and about the impact of the development and religious efforts of the Catholic church. With support from the Rafael Landívar University, the AVANCSO research institute and the Department of Social Pastoral Work of the diocese of Verapaz, I carried out the fieldwork during 1991 and 1992 in Verapaz and the other areas where Q'eqchi'es live.

After overcoming physical hardship, I set out to analyze my data and write this book at the Catholic University of Nijmegen, the Netherlands. The book has nine chapters. The opening chapter provides a theoretical perspective from which to approach the Q'eqchi'es; it discusses the relevance of the concepts of modernity and modernization in a globalizing world. In the second chapter some general lines of the history of the Q'eqchi'es and some basic aspects of their life-worlds as well as the four villages that play a central role in my analysis are presented.

Next, religion and economy, two of the main aspects of Q'eqchi' reality which together encompass a large part of their social and cultural world, are discussed. Two clusters of three chapters are dedicated to each of those aspects; the first cluster deals with religion, the second with economy. Each of these clusters starts with a chapter (Chapter Three and Chapter Six) focusing on the relevant agencies and actors such as churches and the ministry of agriculture, that intervene in the life-worlds of the Q'eqchi'es. These are actors and agencies which transmit global flows to the Q'eqchi'es. In the second chapter of each cluster (Chapter Four and Chapter Seven), the practices and representations of the Q'eqchi'es themselves are discussed. The last chapter of each cluster relates the analysis presented in the preceding two chapters to the conceptual framework of Chapter One. In the final chapter (Chapter Nine) the central research questions are answered and some final reflections are presented on the issues of globalization, modernization and creolization. The latter term is used to characterize the ways Q'eqchi'es deal with problems of modernization.

As a result of this style of argumentation, the chapters vary considerably in character, style and idiom. Some are rather descriptive whereas others concentrate on relating empirical material to theoretical questions and issues. However, they all stay within the boundaries of social sciences. Consequently, I should warn the reader to draw no easy theological conclusions from my work because it was not meant to produce such conclusions. The discussion of the various "persons" in the universe of the Q'eqchi'es in Chapter Four, for example, is not suitable as a basis from which to draw any conclusion as to the monotheistic or polytheistic character of Q'eqchi' religion.

The material I collected to write this book stems mainly from 1991 and 1992. As a consequence, I do not discuss specific developments which occurred after that time, such as the impact of the peace treaties between the government and the guerrilla movement with ex-soldiers reinterpreting their arms as tools for ordinary criminal activities, the resettlement of refugees from Mexico in the Q'eqchi' region, the missionary work of the so-called *sacerdotes mayas* among the Q'eqchi'es and latest chapters of the story of internal conflicts within the Catholic church.

Because this book deals with a specific group in Guatemala which has its own language, the use of several words and expressions that are foreign to English has been unavoidable. These words and expressions are written in italics only the first time they appear and most of them have been listed in a glossary at the end of the book. Words in Q'eqchi' or other Guatemalan Indian languages have been written in accordance with the official indigenous orthography as established by the *Academia de Lenguas Mayas*. The exceptions to this rule are the names of indigenous groups in their plural form. They have been Castilianized because in the indigenous languages these nouns have no plural form. For example, the word Q'eqchi'es as such does not exist in the Q'eqchi' language; in this language the plural form of Q'eqchi' is *eb' li Q'eqchi'*.

Of course, in many ways this book is the result of teamwork. As the author of this book I am very aware that the whole research project would have been impossible without the invaluable support of many persons and institutes to whom I owe a debt of gratitude. To begin with, I want to thank all the villagers of those communities in which I worked for months and who allowed me to share some of their food, water, shelter, confidence and time and who were so willing to tell me about what they do and think, about their hopes and fears. My assistants and interpreters (Fidel, Cándida, Elvira, Eric, Jorge) also deserve mention especially because of helping me to communicate with the villagers, conduct interviews and solve many intercultural problems. The information, help and institutional backup I received from Mgr. Gerardo Flores Reyes, the priests, religious women, friars and ministers in the region as well as the friends and *compañeros* of the Department of Social Pastoral Work of the diocese of Verapaz (especially Drs. Fons Huet) were absolutely crucial. I owe all of them a great deal. The Rafael Landívar University (especially Dr. Guillermina Herrera) and the AVANCSO research institute (especially Dr. Clara Arenas and Dr. Edgar Gutierrez) were also very kind in offering me their institutional backup and intellectual feedback. In addition to this institutional support all those warm, friendly people whom I contacted in Cobán, Guatemala City and other places deserve special mention (especially Juan-José, Juan, María).

In the Netherlands I want to express my gratitude first to Prof. Dr. Arie de Ruijter who helped me through the darkest hours and whose analytical assistance has been crucial. I also feel indebted to my colleagues and frieds at the Third World Centre of the Catholic University of Nijmegen (especially Drs. Luuk Knippenberg and Dr. Frans Schuurman), the Free University of Amsterdam (especially Prof. Dr. André Droogers, Drs. Barbara Boudewijnse, Drs. Marjo de Theije, Dr. Frans Kamsteeg, Drs. Els Jacobs) and at the Centre for Latin American Research and Documentation CEDLA in Amsterdam (PhD research group). I appreciate the fact that the authorities of the Nijmegen Institute for Comparative Studies in Development and Cultural Change and the Third World Centre of the University of Nijmegen enabled me to do my research. I am very grateful to Dr. Jean and Zella Carriere for correcting my English text. And, last but not least, the warm and understanding support of my personal friends during the whole process of research and writing has been invaluable. Without them this book would not have come about. I want to thank all of those mentioned here and those whom I may have missed out.

Finally, my thoughts go back to one who gave her life to inform us about what has happened to those whose cries have not been heard, to write down the cruel experiences of those who cannot write. The regime thought it necessary to silence her and with her all those on her side. Myrna Mack.

Hans Siebers
Nijmegen
1 November 1998.

List of Tables

Table 3.1:	number of evangelical churches in three departments in 1980 and 1987	51
Table 7.1:	average land use patterns at household level in four villages in manzanas and percentages)	124
Table 7.2:	labour forms practised in clearing land, planting maize and harvesting maize in four villages in percentages of respondents	128
Table 7.3:	average production, sale and purchase of maize per household and average maize consumption per capita in four Q'eqchi' villages (in quintales)	130
Table 7.4:	gross product and net income per household and per main activity or product in four villages (in quetzales and percentages)	132
Table 7.5:	gross product per capita in four villages (in quetzales and US dollars)	137
Table 7.6:	spread of maize consumption per household in four communities (in number of respondents and percentages per category)	139
Table 7.7:	spread of net income of households in four communities (in number of households per category)	140
Table 8.1:	average net income of committee members and community members in four villages in quetzales	155

Map 1. Guatemala, Q'eqchi' Region and Departments

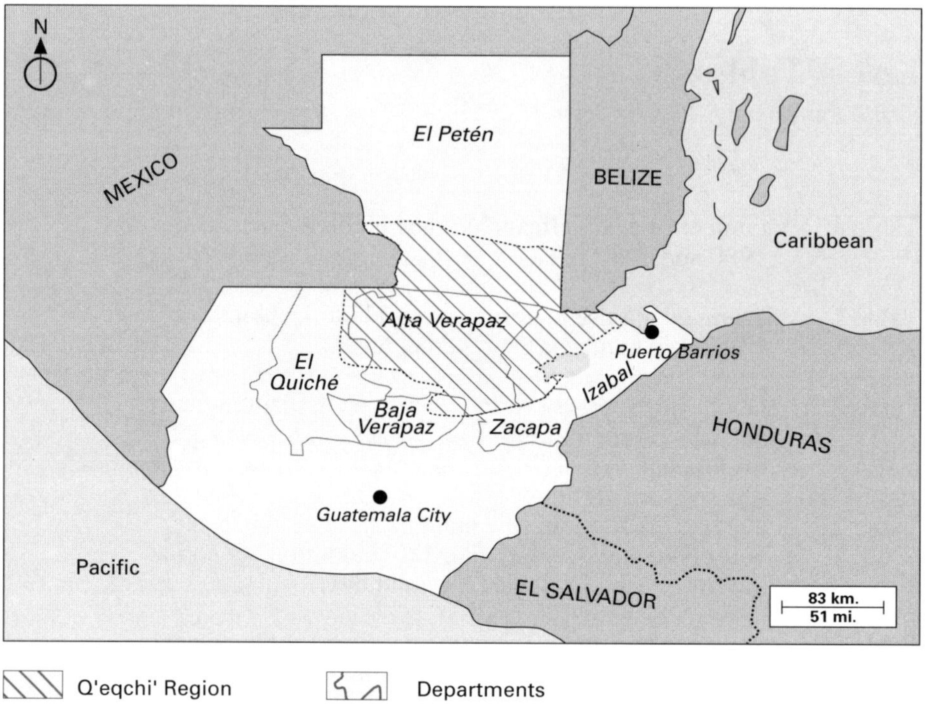

Map 2. Q'eqchi' Region, Main Rivers and Mountains

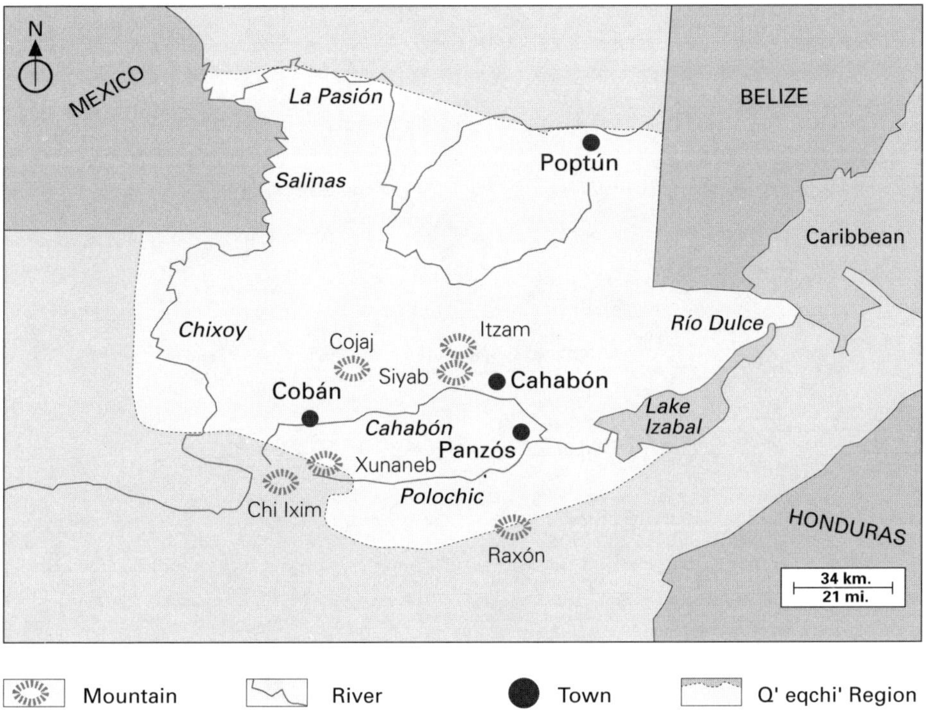

Map 3. Q'eqchi' Region, Roads and Main Towns

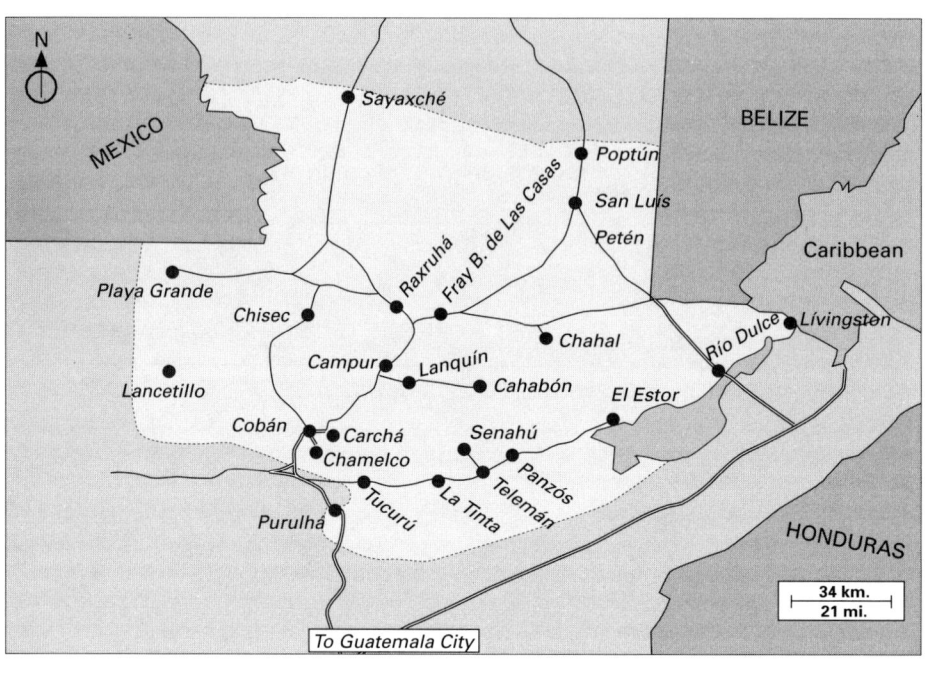

| Dirt Road | Paved Road | ● Town |

Q'eqchi' Heartland:
Cobán, Carchá, Chamelco, Lanquín, Cahabón, Purulhá, Tucurú

Ixcán:
Playa Grande, Lancetillo

Franja Transversal del Norte:
Lívingston, Río Dulce, Chahal, Fray Bartolomé de Las Casas, Raxruhá, Chisec, Playa Grande

Polochic Valley:
El Estor, Panzós, Telemán, La Tinta, Tucurú

1

In Search of a Perspective that Holds:
A Theoretical Prologue

In one of the many buses I took in the Q'eqchi' region, I had the following conversation with *Qawa' Manu*, an old Q'eqchi' gentleman, who sat next to me. He was in a cheerful mood.

- 'Where do you come from?' he asked me after some chatting.
- 'From the Netherlands,' I replied.
- 'Where is that? That must be far away, mustn't it?'
- 'Oh yes, very far indeed.'
- 'How many days on foot?'
- 'Forget it, you can't go there on foot.'
- 'Aha, but how many hours would this bus need to get there?'
- 'A bus would not make it across the sea; there is a big sea between here and the place I live. I took an aeroplane to come here.'
- 'Hum...'
- 'But to give you an idea, the distance is about ten thousand kilometres. If you take the bus to Guatemala city round trip and do that 25 times you have gone more or less that distance.'
- '*Putchica*! Then you must feel very lonely over there,' he responded and smiled.

Here we have Qawa' Manu interviewing me, as it were. He interpreted my information about distance in his framework based on his own experiences and local conventions about distance. He thinks about distance in terms of remoteness from a central town, and usually in the Q'eqchi' region the farther you go from a central town the sparser the population gets. But then again, he smiled at me while he was apparently impressed by our loneliness in Holland. Was he just joking?

Intercultural communication is always an awkward endeavour. One can never be sure about conclusions which are based on information provided by someone from a different cultural background. Here I am writing a book about the Q'eqchi'es of Guatemala and pretending to say something significant about them; but who am I to assume that I am not making the same mistakes Qawa' Manu made about the Netherlands? Nor can I guarantee that my frame of references does not make the same errors in processing information about and from the Q'eqchi'es that Qawa' Manu made about Dutchmen. I cannot pretend to be error proof.

It seems hard to resist a post-modernist temptation to say that any story one tells about someone else is arbitrary. If you go to the Q'eqchi'es to write a book about them and someone else does the same, you always end up with two different stories. The relationship between what one tries to say about social reality and that reality itself is always problematic. So why not do away with the whole idea of social reality and accept the metaphor of various free-floating stories next to, on top of, beside, or through each other?

Well, of course this book is coloured by the cultural frameworks that inspire the meanings I attribute to what I have experienced and the information I have gathered, and the limitations of my capacity to understand the Q'eqchi'es severely condition its content. However, these considerations do not turn this book into fiction. To be sure, it is highly problematic to speak about social reality because it is impossible to distinguish reality "out there" from our understandings of it, but still the fact cannot be denied that one story about the Q'eqchi'es is more plausible than another. One cannot say just anything about them. An assertion such as 'all Q'eqchi'es have three legs' is simply not true, as I can assure the reader. Granted that science is just one way of looking at the Q'eqchi'es alongside others, the application of the methodological rules of the game does distinguish between scientific accounts that are more or less plausible. They point to the possibility of knowledge as a construction that is valid 'in principle' and 'until further notice' (Giddens 1990: 39, 48-49).

Some of the methodological requirements that have been met in my research on the Q'eqchi'es and the kind and the reach of statements that can reasonably be made in line with the applied methods will be discussed in Chapter Two and in the Note on Methodology. Before that, my perspective on the Q'eqchi'es will be made more explicit using concepts such as modernization and globalization.

Multiple perspectives to choose from

The acceptance of science as one way of looking at the Q'eqchi'es, alongside poetry or other genres, and defined in terms of a set of rules is just one step forward. It still leaves open a variety of theses and disciplines that could potentially serve as a perspective from which to approach them. This perspective guides the kind of knowledge this book is intended to produce.

One possible perspective is offered by the popular resistance approach highlighting the struggle against capitalist exploitation and political oppression. Another possible perspective is opened up by the cultural imperialism thesis. Non-Western areas and cultures - such as Q'eqchi' culture - would be invaded by Western culture which would destroy local cultural identities and replace cultural particularism with cultural synchronization.[1] All these approaches have been influential among scholars studying Guatemala, but for various reasons I do not think they shed much light on what the daily life of most Q'eqchi'es is all about (See Chapter Two and Chapter Nine).

The approach which served as a starting point at the moment I began my fieldwork among the Q'eqchi'es, is the development approach linked to sociology and anthropology of religion. I started my work among the Q'eqchi'es requested to do so by the Bishop of Verapaz and other ecclesiastical institutions who expressed their desire to enlarge their knowledge and to deepen their insights into the relationship between their development efforts (economic, education and health care projects) and their religious work. Consequently, I focused on the interrelations between religion and development and subdivided the development part into economics, education and health care as I went ahead.

Trouble soon crossed my path. The concept of development turned out to useless for analytical purposes because of its ambiguous character. On the one hand it refers to a "real" process of social change: its positive or substantive side. On the other hand, not just any process of social change qualifies as development. The concept of development has a normative character as well: it supposes that the actors concerned are becoming "better off" and that in the end their situation has "improved".[2] As a result of this confusion of substantive and normative aspects, it is difficult to work out a sound and consistent definition of development. As regards social change as such, the positive or substantive side, one can consult the social scientists' understanding of modernity, as development theorists have always done. This understanding of modernity has played the role of - often implicit - presuppositions of the various paradigms of development.

The normative side of development has made the concept liable to all kinds of desires and wishes. Based on political, ideological, moral, humanistic, and other considerations and interests it has been claimed that development should legitimate the entry of Western capital in developing countries; that it ought to bring us a step closer to socialism; that it should alleviate poverty; that it ought to be sustainable; that it should contribute to closing the social inequality gap; that women in particular should benefit; that it ought to fit in the ecological context, and so on.

To be sure, many of these qualifications might be very desirable, the problem is: 'Who speaks?' Are these qualifications relevant in the case of the Q'eqchi'es or are there other priorities and who is supposed to answer that question? Of course, the Q'eqchi'es themselves ought mainly to decide, but that leads to the problematic assumption that they would speak with one voice. Moreover, the act of asking the Q'eqchi'es may involve others and what if these others define development problems that most of the Q'eqchi'es themselves do not consider to be a problem? The mix of positive and normative aspects within the concept of development severely limits its analytical value in case studies. Moreover, as long as speakers at the international level - development agencies, Western and other governments and international agencies dominated by these governments - have a strong voice in defining the normative side of development it remains difficult to escape from an ethnocentric framework while using this concept.

Faced with these problems I continued my fieldwork among the Q'eqchi'es and I did not lose sight of the ways in which the Q'eqchi'es work out their aspirations and desires to improve their situation. Meanwhile I continued to look for another perspective from which a more fruitful analysis of the Q'eqchi'es as well as of the agencies that intervene in their lives might be made. The alternative, doing away with the whole idea of a perspective, did not appear to be very attractive because that would result in a lack of analytical focus in my study. Moreover, that would mean giving up my objective of contributing to a deepening of our understanding of more general contemporary processes of social change based on my case study. Without underestimating the value of detailed ethnographic research, I did not want to become prey to the temptations of diffusion and consequent relativism which, in the end, frustrate any attempt to reach at such an understanding. They lead to particularism as the alfa and omega of the case study.

The globalization and modernization perspective

> One morning in 1991 when the inhabitants of the Q'eqchi' town of Campur woke up, haze was hanging between the mountains in the surrounding landscape. A few hours later, when I arrived in the town, the priest told me that several Q'eqchi'es had expressed their anxiety that this haze might be smoke because there was a new war. The radio had told them the night before that the Gulf War had broken out.

At the end of the present century the world has reached a stage in which even in remote and relatively isolated towns such as Campur messages from the other side of the world come through; but in the course of global communications the meanings of messages are easily modified within the local and particular context. Meanings flowing through global communication and becoming transformed within local contexts are highlighted in the present-day literature on globalization.

The globalization perspective sheds light on the compression of the world. New transportation and communication systems allow social relations and interactions to increasingly span the globe. Flows of people, technology, capital, images and ideas take on global dimensions (Appadurai 1990 and 1996). Distant localities are linked in such a way that local happenings are shaped by events occurring many miles away and vice versa (Giddens 1990: 64). One is increasingly confronted with aspects of different cultures that stem from many parts of the polycentric world. Globalization not only refers to processes; the world as a whole is adopting systemic properties in which characteristics of each particular entity have to be understood within the framework of the world as a whole (Friedman 1995; Robertson 1992).

The global system and globalization processes cannot exist without their corollary, i.e. processes of localization. The latter refers to the incorporation of meanings and elements from global flows into local processes of meaning-making (Hannerz 1992: 217-267). It points to the particularization and fragmentation of individual world-views and moral frames of references (Bauman 1991: 12-14, 185-187; Bauman 1993: 195-197). It emphasizes the increasing need for every individual and group to search for new identities in the face of the questioning or relativization of pre-existing cultural frames of references in the globalizing framework.

Globalization and localization are involved in constant interplay (Robertson 1995: 30). On the one hand, universal aspects or elements that belong to global culture may be adapted to particular local circumstances. The production of Mexican or Brazilian soap operas presents a case in point. On the other hand, definitions of local particular identities may legitimize themselves in global and universal terms and may become global movements. The movements of indigenous peoples appealing to international laws and conventions and creating networks among each other exemplify this trend

Is all this just another way of saying that the world is becoming ever more homogeneous; is this the cultural imperialism thesis redefined in other terms? No, it is not. Of course, global communication presupposes at least some standards of communication and culture, such as the mastering of international languages; but next to homogenizing tendencies the globalization perspective also points to heterogenizing trends towards multiculturality both at the global and the local level. There are various images of world order competing to define the global circumstance, and cultural particularities increasingly try to enter the global scene (Robertson 1992: 77-83).

Another way of stating the homogeneous-heterogeneous problem is to define it in terms of modernity. The meanings that are flowing globally, the institutions that are spreading all over the globe, the cultural particularities that are becoming transformed: can all these phenomena be classified either in modern or post-modern terms and what about pre-modern features in a globalizing context? Does modernity monopolize the scene and require a minimum level of standardization of institutions and cultural frameworks or is a basic degree of diversity guaranteed because globalization incorporates and recovers pre-modern and post-modern elements? Then again, is modernity itself a coherent phenomenon encouraging homogenization?

The debate on globalization has led to a renewed interest in the issue of modernity but there is quite some controversy in the literature on the relationship between both phenomena. Giddens and Robertson exemplify the basic opposites in this respect. Giddens positions the decisive discontinuity in the transition from pre-modern to modern or post-traditional society and conceives of globalization as just the enlargement of modernity. Driven by the modern dynamics of time and space separation[3], the disembedding of social relations[4] and the reflexive or explicit ordering of social relations in the light of continual inputs of knowledge, globalization means the spread of modern institutional dimensions all over the globe. These dimensions, i.e. capitalism, industrialism, surveillance capacities and control over the means of violence, adopt a global shape in the forms of the world capitalist economy, the international division of labour, the nation-state system and the world military order (Giddens 1990: 4, 52-56, 63, 70-71). By contrast, in Robertson's view globalization is something qualitatively different from modernity. He holds the radical claim that globalization rather than modernity should be the essential *explanans* in contemporary social sciences. In criticizing Giddens he even maintains that globalization predates modernity, so how can the former be the enlargement of the latter?[5]

In my view, there is more rhetoric than substance to this controversy. Giddens' and Robertson's positions do not need to rule each other out. On the one hand, Giddens' argument that modern institutions made globalization possible is simply illustrated by the fact that without *modern* technology of communication and transport the present degree of compression of the world would have been impossible. On the other hand, Robertson's point that contemporary processes of modernity developing strongholds all over the world take place within the context of globalization, which leaves strong marks on these processes, makes sense as well. Given the fact that modernity refers to a wide range of issues, I advocate the view that globalization can be conceived as an increasingly important element of modernity.

The positioning of globalization and localization within the wider framework of (pre- or post-)modernity opens up the possibility of reaching a more integral and comprehensive approach to both phenomena. The debate on globalization and localization has remained quite sectoralized without much interrelation between the various sectors. There is Wallerstein *cum suis* focusing on economic matters within the framework of the capitalist world-economy (see Hopkins, Wallerstein 1982); there is Meyer and his colleagues writing about the world political system (see Beyer 1994: 21-26); and there are the authors discussing globalization in the cultural sense. The latter want to complement Wallerstein's and Meyer's work, but do not work out an interdisciplinary approach on globalization and localization.

Globalization and localization may be understood as two components of contemporary modernity,[6] but not without considerable qualification. To begin with, we need to acknowledge the fact that modernity itself is a far from homogeneous phenomenon. There are no Great Unifiers in modernity and it is not a mono-causal phenomenon; instead, it is marked by paradoxes, disjunctures and different internal logics that can enter into conflict with each other (Arnason 1990: 220, 227; Appadurai 1990: 297-301; Giddens 1990: 5-6; Therborn 1995: 128-129). Consequently, modernity often remains very incomplete; it may take centuries or just a few years to come about and reversals and deviations may mark its operation. The coming into being of modernity is no singular, linear or all-encompassing process.

Next, the use of the concept of modernity should not entail a revival of the Grand Narrative of progress, evolutionism and optimism (see Therborn 1995: 137). If they were ever there, the times for such narratives are over. The debate involves concerns about authenticity, about the fear of social disorder and chaos and about the dark and destructive side of modernity. After all, the holocaust is intimately linked to the severe ethical regimes of states in the modern era (Bauman 1989). Totalitarianism, the destruction of the material environment, the massive devastating capacity of military power and the threat of personal meaninglessness are all possibilities created by modernity (Giddens 1990: 8, 9, 111). Already three of the founding fathers of modern sociology - Durkheim, Weber and Marx - were certainly not very impressed by the blessings of modernity. They saw threatening dangers of anomy, social disintegration, the loss of values and meaning of life, the locking of man within the iron cage of bureaucracy, brutal exploitation and *Verelendung*.

Of course, vis-à-vis these three founding fathers some claim that modern times have passed away and that we have moved into post-modernity (See Lyotard 1984). In line with what I have written above about the epistemological conditions of knowledge and doubtful of post-modernists' claims that we have entered into a radically a new era, I follow Giddens who holds that the issues post-modernist authors point to not necessarily constitute a profound rupture with modernity but a new condition within it (Giddens 1990: 38, 50-51). I will call this condition "contemporary modern" in which these issues as well as the themes raised by the globalization debate will be included.

The distinction between two conditions of modernity, an original and a contemporary one, presupposes a third condition, called "pre-modern". These conditions refer to a specific type of society or culture and as such these concepts have a synchronic character. A diachronic perspective might be opened up by using the term "modernization" suggesting processes of social transformation from pre-modern characteristics to originally and contemporary modern features. It is the objective of this book to relate the theories on modernity and modernization that can be found in social science literature, to my ethnographic material on the Q'eqchi'es. On the one hand I will try to evaluate to what extent these theories help us to deepen our understanding of basic aspects of the life of the Q'eqchi'es. On the other hand I want to see what such an understanding tells us about these theories themselves. Without trying to revive portrayals of modernity or modernization as a master universalizing narrative it does make sense to raise the question whether social actors in various parts of the world, making meaning and developing practices within the context of globalization, have something in common. If their experiences do express some common denominators, it may be useful to see whether the various elements that the theories on modernity and modernization point to reflect this common ground. Against this background I want to raise the question to what extent the experiences of the Q'eqchi'es reflect these elements and whether they are experiencing a process of social change that can be classified in terms of modernization.

At this stage, several clarifications have to be made. Whether there is a diachronic process of modernization taking place among the Q'eqchi'es remains an open question which will be answered in the final chapter. In addition, in using the term modernization it is essential to question all kinds of connotations that stem from "modernization theory". This specific theory has drawn on the discussions on modernity in a distorted and simplistic way within the context of the cold war and assuming a single process, a single direction and a given end provided by the Western example (see for example Rostow 1960). It has been used as an ethnocentric prescription for social transformation in non-Western areas. While rendering the term modernization operational I want to discard these assumptions of "modernization theory".

Moreover, I want to stress that the theories on modernity and modernization should be conceived as ideal-typical models of social reality. They try to interrelate various aspects and elements of this reality in order to enhance our understanding of the latter. To be sure, these theories have been developed with mainly Western historical experiences in mind, but they do not provide exact historiographical descriptions of any specific development. Consequently, in trying to relate the theories on modernity and modernization to my material on the Q'eqchi'es, these two levels should not be confused. For example, based on the literature urbanization and wage labour can be classified as basic elements of a modern condition, the historical fact that there were cities and people who worked for wage in the Middle Ages or earlier is irrelevant to that argument. Classifying phenomena in pre-modern, originally modern and contemporary modern terms is one step, to see whether these terms can be applied to the experiences of the Q'eqchi'es is another step. Both steps will be made in this book, starting with the first one in this section.

Modernization made explicit

The vocabulary of modernity and modernization covers a wide variety of items and issues, there is a wide range of different or even contradictory approaches in the literature and each sheds its light on specific aspects. As a result, any attempt to make the concepts of modernity and modernization explicit shows interpretative, selective and even eclectic marks. Nevertheless, in the following pages I will try to work out a balanced overview of modernity and modernization, rendering contradictions as explicit as possible.

Disembedding

As a starting point for discussing modernization Tönnies (Tönnies 1957) *Gemeinschaft* and *Gesellschaft* theme remains fruitful. In a pre-modern context primordial and all-encompassing social units such as the local community and kinship systems mainly circumscribe social relations and communications. Within a process of modernization social relations are "lifted out" of the local context of interaction.[7] A dialectical process of individualism and collectivism, of individualist and associative action has its way. On the one hand the individual can no longer take local social relations for granted. He or she is immersed in a process of individualization stressing individual achievement, competition and ambitions. On the other hand, society offers the individual a number of networks and institutions to associate with, such as trade unions, bureaucratic organizations and enterprises which emphasize collective action and common goals.[8]

Social relations are increasingly inscribed within the framework of modern society as a whole, which coalesces with the nation. To each individual the nation, as an "imagined community"[9], becomes a predominant reference point of identity construction. Moreover, the nation becomes linked to a specific state. The state extends its administrative control over the territory over which it claims sovereignty and appropriates a monopoly on the means of violence (Giddens 1990: 57). The state has an interest in promoting cultural homogeneity within its borders.[10] This culture either serves national social integration or works as an ideology legitimating or veiling class interests, depending on whether one takes a Durkheimian or a (neo-)Marxist position.

Within the present phase of globalization the importance of the nation-state is seriously challenged. Disembedded communication no longer halts at national borders, and individuals increasingly draw on images and identity constructions of groups in other parts of the world. On the one hand, relatively new dimensions of identity constructions at the international and global level are coming to the fore. The champions of Human Rights and international law claim there is something like humankind embodying universal values (see Robertson 1992: 75*ff*). On the other hand, intermediary groups such as ethnic groups increasingly claim a specific identity and special rights, including territorial ones. These groups disrupt schemes of national culture and identity and may easily cross national borders. Ethnicity can no longer be relegated to a pre-modern condition (Appadurai 1990: 303-306; Hall 1991: 22-26).

In short, there is an increasing variety of levels of identity construction and socialization both beneath and above the national level. Moreover, the nation-state increasingly loses its capacity to intervene in economic matters and even its monopoly of the means of violence within its borders cannot be taken for granted any more. Of course, in many parts of the world reality has never come close to the concept of the nation-state. Nevertheless, Stuart Hall's distinction between two phases of globalization is convincing. The first phase is characterized by such phenomena as classes, nation-states and colonialism, whereas in the contemporary phase these phenomena give way to increasing social and cultural fragmentation and multiculturality (Hall 1991: 33).

Differentiation

In the wake of modernization society becomes increasingly complex. In a pre-modern condition there is a relatively low-level of division of labour. Each household or community develops more or less the same basic activities. Economics, social relations, politics and religion are inextricably intertwined: the social actors concerned do not make a distinction in these terms, and from an analytical point of view a pre-modern action cannot be neatly classified into one of these categories. Pre-modern society is mainly organized in terms of a hierarchy of different strata and status-groups among which status, wealth and power are unequally distributed. Basically, the ruling strata's aim is to reproduce their status and power, and social inequality is based on ascription. The meaning of an action by a social actor is determined by the question to which status-group this actor belongs.[11]

The increasing complexity of modern society is reflected in an ever more detailed division of labour[12] which not only allows modern society to vastly increase its resources, but also leads to the separation of economics, politics, science, religion, etc. into as many distinct institutions (Godelier 1978: 765). Each of these dimensions of society develops into a specific field or subsystem oriented towards the fulfilment of a specific function - making money (economy), producing knowledge (science) etc. - and is made up of a network of unequal power relations.[13]

At first, when the division of labour has not yet advanced very much there is a considerable level of convergence in the position and culture of large sectors of society and classes and status groups continue to play an important role in social inequality.[14] But as modernization moves ahead social inequality becomes much more individualized and fragmented (Van der Loo, Van Reijen 1993: 104). The action of an individual social actor now receives meaning in terms of how it contributes to the fulfilment of the function that is at stake in a specific field or sub-system.[15] Achievement becomes the basic principle in order to define one's place in society.

This definition is necessarily many-sided because of the fact that any social actor is playing a role in various fields or sub-systems, and achievement can be made in each of these fields. Each actor has a variety of subject positions, plays various social roles in daily life and has a variety of related perspectives from which to look at the world (Hannerz 1992: 64-68; Laclau 1985: 27-42). This plurality of subject positions causes the segmentation or fragmentation of his or her life-world.

The division of labour also entails the differentiation between a corps of specialists on the one hand and laypersons on the other. Pre-modern indigenous knowledge (knowledge based on accumulated experiences, transmitted from one generation to another, which tends to be rich, varied and adapted to the requirements of living in the local milieu) is replaced by scientifically or rationally elaborated knowledge. Giddens talks about deskilling and reskilling (Giddens 1990: 144*ff*). Specialists claim the competence to produce this expertise on which laypersons come to depend. However, their construction of competence entails the construction of incompetence or ignorance considered to be common to laypersons. As a result, relations between specialists and laypersons disclose clear asymmetrical traits (Hannerz 1992: 53-55, 81-84).

Part of the process of deskilling and reskilling is the shift from trust in persons to trust in abstract systems. In a pre-modern setting social actors trust persons who possess special capacities, and essential tasks in the reproduction of life are accomplished by way of direct interactions between persons. For example, personal contacts such as strategic marriages are intended to establish political relations. Hence the "honour", "probity", "friendship" or "love" of the other person need to be confirmed repeatedly to reproduce society (see Beyer 1994: 64; Giddens 1990: 27, 33).

By contrast, the functionality of modern fields or sub-systems depends on trust in abstract things such as professional expertise. For example, going upstairs we trust in the expertise of the architect who designed the building but whom we usually do not know personally, a trust that makes us confident that the building will not immediately collapse. Trust is focused on the expertise rather than on the professionals. Formal education plays a crucial role here in teaching children to respect expert knowledge of all kinds. Institutions take over essential communicative tasks, and within them functional communication sets the standard (Giddens 1990: 26, 33, 80-89).

Rationalization

Rationally elaborated knowledge, fields or sub-systems oriented towards a specific function and functional communication, all these phenomena point to rationalization as another central aspect of modernization. In a pre-modern condition the social actor depends heavily on nature, the community and the kinship line to which he or she belongs. The actor feels part of nature which he or she often views in terms of "persons", gods, and spirits. A more or less pre-fixed identity is handed down to the actor by the common culture of the community and kinship line (see Hannerz 1992: 41-43; Therborn 1995: 131).

Within the process of modernization the world becomes disenchanted and social relations no longer have a pre-fixed character. Consequently, both nature and social relations can become the object of formal rationality: they can be instrumentalized in order to meet the objectives of individuals and organizations (see Van der Loo, Van Reijen 1993: 126-128; and Morrison 1995: 220-223). Usefulness and calculation of means are the catchwords. For his or her part, the logic of formal rationality confronts the individual with an extensive set of requirements. He or she has to be able to live an ordered and disciplined life, to control his or her emotions and behaviour and to plan his or her life. Norbert Elias talks about the transition from *Fremdzwang* to *Selbstzwang* within the modern process of civilization (Van der Loo, Van Reijen 1993: 109, 113, 146*ff*), which is in line with the working of ideology in a capitalist society or with the effects of the moral order or *conscience collective,* if one prefers to follow a (neo)Marxist or a Durkheimian logic respectively. In both cases the individual is pressured to refrain from actions that might disrupt the existing power relations or integration of society.

However, the calculating and disciplined actor as well as ideologies and unifying cultures are highly problematic phenomena. Freud has suggested that passions and sexual desires may easily conflict with the modern requirement to control, plan and discipline one's life. Weber was seriously concerned about instrumental rationality seriously threatening the possibility of moral behaviour and of making sense of one's life in the absence of religion (see Morrison 1995: 121-122; Van der Loo, Van Reijen 1993: 123-134).

In addition, with the increasing fragmentation of the individual's lifeworld and the diversification of roles and perspectives the possibilities of constructing some sort of encompassing and integral identity become very questionable. Moreover, Bauman emphasizes the disappearance of cultural and moral unifiers in society. The state is neither able to produce such unifiers any more, nor do the majority of its citizens expect the state to do so. Cultural and moral choices have been privatized: they have become matters of the individual's decision (Bauman 1990: 143-169; Bauman 1993: 138-140).

In any case, tensions and conflicts between disintegration and integration, fragmentation and merging, individualization and globalization, diversity and uniformity mark the contemporary modern world. An important source of these tensions is the fact that in a global context it is very difficult to claim an absolute identity. Globalization entails the relativization of every identity and worldview. In principle, there are two different stands regarding this relativization: a fundamentalist and a creolizing one.

In the fundamentalist case the reaction is defensive, conserving an absolute set of values one is supposed to have and which organize all spheres of life, rejecting modernization and external influences.[16] In the creolizing case the emphasis is on the crossover, on the selective incorporation of external influences, on the interplay between indigenous and exogenous elements. The endeavour - more or less wilfully - is to create something new out of the merging of inputs stemming from one's own cultural background and from foreign cultures, losing some, winning some. Local cultural entrepreneurs take external influences apart and tamper and tinker with them in such a way that the resulting new forms are more responsive to, and at the same time in part outgrowths of, local everyday life (Hall 1991: 37-39; Hannerz 1992: 261-267; Robertson 1992: 101, 114). Whatever different categories the terms creole[17], hybrid[18], or syncretic[19] refer to, they all point to processes of bringing together, merging and mixing elements or meanings from these different categories.

These concepts have not remained free from criticism. Friedman is highly critical of the concept of creolization (Friedman 1995: 82-84). In his opinion the concept presupposes an essentialist view of culture, as if culture were a "thing" or a "substance" that can be attributed to specific groups and that can be mixed and merged. Instead, Friedman prefers to view culture as a process of meaning-making by social actors in a specific social context. In my view the social actor uses existing meanings from different origins in the process of constructing meaning which present themselves to him or her as given bodies. For their part, the results of his or her meaning-making present themselves as bodies of meaning to the actor him- or herself as well as to others. In short, in my view culture is both a process and the products of this process, which may merge and mix; this means that the concept of creolization remains useful.

Friedman does make sense by paying attention to social actors and contexts. A meaning is not just constructed, it is also communicated and the act of communicating not only includes an exchange of meanings but also an effort to make someone else do something. Consequently, in analyzing creolization the agendas, power relations between them and unequal access to resources of the social actors involved have to be brought in. The results of creolization not only embody difference; they also reflect unequal power relations. They may come closer to the agenda of one group of actors than to the objectives of others.

Secularization

The disenchantment of the world has already been marked as an important element of modernization. In a pre-modern context the world is seen in terms of relations with another world of gods, spirits and invisible "persons" whom the actors try to manipulate. Religion plays an important role in the actors' conceptions of nature, social relations and themselves and can scarcely be distinguished from other spheres of life. Religious modalities provide essential support for issues that in a modern context become functions of specific sub-systems or fields: e.g. religious rituals are indispensable for a good harvest (Beyer 1994: 102; Bourdieu 1971a: 309; Hervieu-Léger 1989: 74).

Within the modern separation of functions of sub-systems or fields, religion develops into one of these sub-systems or fields and becomes subject to professionalization.[20] In Bourdieu's terminology, a religious field comes into being which is specialized in the production, administration and distribution of means of salvation. This field is made up of a corps of religious specialists - clergy, prophets and sorcerers - on the one hand, and laypersons on the other. The specialists claim the right to modify the practices and world visions of the laity who are consequently dispossessed of this right. The power of the specialists to do so not only rests on their capacity to convince the laity, it can be reinforced by coercive power: i.e. to deny the laity the means of salvation or to excommunicate them.[21]

Bourdieu's theory of the religious field has two major shortcomings. First, he ignores the meaning-making capacity of lay actors and portrays them as passive consumers of the religion, which the specialists offer them. It has to be recognized, though, that lay actors maintain a circumscribed but real room for manoeuvre to construct religious meanings themselves and to decide on religious practices. Secondly, in line with his neglect of the meaning-making capacity of lay actors, he identifies the ideological role of religion in a very unilateral way. In his view the specialists offer a religious discourse to dominant groups and classes that legitimizes the power of these classes and groups. To subordinate groups the religious discourse offers a compensation in the hereafter. Based on the recognition of the progressive role of part of the clergy in Latin American political struggles, Otto Maduro has criticised this ideological aspect of Bourdieu's theory. The clergy, he believes, may promote a "collective religious consciousness" among the subordinated classes that makes them autonomous vis-à-vis the ruling classes (Maduro 1979: 191). The ideological role of religion is not unequivocal.

With this religious field the character of religion itself changes considerably. Religion becomes the object of the rationalizing and moralizing work of specialists constructing organized belief systems. Such official religion or theology has a coherent and homogeneous character, emphasizes moral standards and the concept of sin, and makes a claim to universal and eternal validity. Immediate relations to nature and the manipulation of supernatural powers are substituted by rather abstract and long-term goals. God is portrayed as righteous and requires contemplative attention and moral behaviour (Bourdieu 1971a: 303, 309; Bourdieu 1971b: 19-20). However, because the specialists' capacity to influence the laity has its limits, there is always a tension between official and lay religion. The latter, or popular religion,[22] does not need to share the features of official religion.

Within the process of modernization, religion's importance in society and its role in daily life alter, which points to the famous secularization, or the "loss of religion" thesis. Socio-religious bonds are vanishing and society is increasingly functioning in its own terms, subject to human reason, so this thesis holds (Hervieu-Léger 1989: 71, 72; Robertson 1994: 127).

Formulated in these general terms few social scientists would raise objections. Objections have to be made, however, once we look closer at what is claimed here. To begin with, it is asserted that modern religion no longer deals with the ways social actors conceive of nature, social reality and themselves. Religion is seen as retreating to existential, moral and emotional issues.

However, this does not mean that religion would thereby lose its influence on social life. First of all, by dealing with existential questions religion may easily influence the identity construction of modern social actors, and thus interfere in social relations. The acceptance of answers provided by a Pentecostal church to questions concerning the meaning of life may induce a believer to conceptualize social relations in terms of believers and non-believers and act accordingly. Next, official modern religion has a strong moral character, which stimulates religious actors to act in a specific way with specific social consequences. Such consequences are also caused by the fact that religion may maintain an ideological character, either stimulating religious actors to change or to legitimize social reality. Finally, official religion does not exclude rationality. It is based on uncontrollable presuppositions, but its discourse itself may have a rational and systematic character.

Seen from the institutional angle the "loss of religion" thesis holds that the increasing autonomization of the various fields towards one another means that religion's influence on e.g. economy, politics and other fields is diminishing. Each of these fields is ruled by a specific rationality, which makes moral considerations simply irrelevant (Beyer 1994: 82; Hervieu-Léger 1989: 71). However, this argument does not rule out the possibility that moral and religious judgements may be very persistent in referring to problems created but not solved in these fields (Beyer 1994: 80, 97; Hervieu-Léger 1989: 72; Séguy 1989: 9). Examples of this persistence are provided by social inequality created in the economic field and oppression in the political field, judged to be incompatible with God's will, and thus calling for concerted action on the part of believers. In short, the secularization thesis does not necessarily imply the reduction of religion to the private sphere or the loss of religious influence on social matters. Religion adopts new ways of influencing social reality and religious discourse itself may adopt modern rational characteristics.

What is becoming privatized is not religion itself but religious decision-making. Within the contemporary modern framework of reflexivity, relativization and increasing religious pluralism the individual is increasingly impelled to reflect and decide upon the question of which meaning to accept or practice to perform (Beyer 1994: 76). In a society centred on the individual, every religious meaning is constructed by the individual in subjective and do-it-yourself ways. Religion becomes highly atomized, shattered and pulverized, which leads to a conglomerate of indeterminate beliefs, like ungraspable odds-and-ends of reminiscences and dreams.[23] Religion not only adopts a plural, but also a highly fragmented character.

In this context the role of religious specialists becomes very questionable. Any structuration of contemporary shattered religious representations and practices into organized belief systems becomes an almost impossible task. Religious actors selectively take what they like from different religious suppliers without religious institutions being able to control them. Religion will find it increasingly difficult to maintain a field-like character.

Commoditization

As was outlined above, modernization means that economic relations and nature are no longer seen in a personalized way, as relations between visible and non-visible persons. Human activity is no longer conceived of as something given by nature or by divine providence. Instead, in a modern condition human activity is perceived as something socially created. Nature becomes the object of formal rationality in order to maximize economic production and profit. Economy develops into a distinct field and the division of labour reaches ever-higher levels of sophistication.

The transition from a pre-modern to a modern condition includes a shift of emphasis from agricultural to industrial and tertiary activities. In pre-modern society the majority of communities are rural and live primarily on agriculture, while modernity supposes industrialization and urbanization. However, there is agricultural modernization as well, which entails the rise of capitalist production relations. In principle, there are two ways towards the separation of capital and labour and the integration into the market economy: the so-called *Junker*-way and the peasant-way. The former refers to large pre-capitalist estates partially transforming themselves into efficient market-oriented production units hiring large numbers of wage labourers. The latter points to peasants, who improve their cash crop production, gradually enlarge their land holdings and, if necessary, hire wage labourers.

Whatever the road to capitalism, modernization in agriculture includes first of all the shift from subsistence production - i.e. the major part of production is consumed by the same household or local community - to market-oriented production. Secondly, indigenous technology is supplanted by scientifically elaborated technology and other inputs are bought at the market. Thirdly, communitarian ways of land control give way to strictly individual - or household - ownership of and control over the land. Fourthly, economic stratification and differential access to land increase considerably within the local community. Finally, communitarian and group-wise[24] labour disappear: labour is individualized and extra labour is paid for. It becomes abstracted from real persons and freed from extra-economic force, in short, it becomes a commodity (Giddens 1990: 6, 34, 60-62).

Production factors not only become commoditized, within the context of globalization they increasingly move across the globe. Local production becomes integrated into the world economy, which means that in part they can interrelate with these flows of capital, labour and technology, and new markets are potentially opened up. On the other hand, this integration may also result in increased competition and local production may run out of business. Globalization is about opportunities *and* risks, about new horizons *and* dangers, about prosperity *and* poverty.

Three configurations of modernization

On the basis of this outline of processes of modernization the basic characteristics of the three basic configurations within these processes can be summed up: the pre-modern condition or the starting point of modernization, the originally modern condition and the contemporary modern condition.

The pre-modern condition

In a pre-modern configuration i) social life is encompassed in the local community and kinship systems; ii) economics, politics, social relations, religion and other spheres of life are inextricably intertwined; iii) the emphasis is on agriculture and rural life; iv) subsistence production is stressed; v) technology is indigenous; vi) land is controlled in a communitarian way; vii) communitarian and group-wise labour are dominant; viii) the local community has a low level of economic stratification; ix) human activity is conceived of as given by nature and providence; x) religion plays an important role in the conceptions the social actors have of their own identity, nature and social relations; xi) religion has a partial and immediate character in which the manipulation of arbitrary supernatural powers is central; xii) the functioning of society depends on trust in persons and on personal interactions; xiii) society is marked by stratified differentiation.

The originally modern condition

In the early or originally modern condition i) communication is no longer limited to the local context; ii) economics, arts, politics, science, religion etc. are separated and specialize into fields or functional sub-systems and become subject to professionalization; iii) the individual is positioned within a plurality of subject positions; iv) the emphasis is on urban life and on industrial activity; v) production relations are capitalist; vi) production is oriented towards the market and inputs for production are bought in the market; vii) technology is elaborated in a scientific way; viii) there is individual or household control of the land; ix) the emphasis is on individual and wage labour; x) there is considerable economic stratification at the local level; xi) production factors, including labour, are commoditized; xii) the actor increasingly uses external information and knowledge in order to understand and change the surrounding social and natural reality; xiii) actors put their trust in abstract systems, many relations between individuals become functional and organizations and institutions secure the reproduction of society; xiv) there is a process of individualization in relation to the rise of associative structures such as class-based organizations; xv) society is linked to a nation-state; xvi) within national borders cultural homogeneity becomes the rule, promoting national social integration.

Moreover, xvii) religion supports this construction of national culture; xviii) a religious field comes into being with a division of labour between specialists and lay actors; xix) official religion adopts a rational and systematical character emphasizing moral behaviour; it proclaims a universal and absolute validity, formulates abstract and long-term goals and portrays God as righteous and trustworthy; xx) there is a tension between official and popular or lay religion; xxi) nature and social reality are increasingly conceived in profane terms, but religion maintains social influence through its role in identity construction, moral behaviour and the ideology of groups and individuals, and relevant social action oriented at problems created but not solved in other fields; xxii) the ideological role of religion is undetermined.

The contemporary modern condition

In the contemporary modern circumstance most of these characteristics of original modernity remain valid, but some are modified and new features are added. These modified and complemented qualities include i) the extension of communication in global networks; ii) the sophistication of the international division of labour; iii) the increasing importance of tertiary activities; iv) the crystallization of the international system of nation-states; v) the construction of culture and identity not only at the levels of the individual and society but also at the level of the system of societies and human kind; vi) the questioning of the nation-state based on a national culture because states are increasingly marked by cultural pluralism and a national integrating culture or moral order collapses; vii) increasing cultural and religious relativization and pluralism which includes the revival of ethnicity and ethnic groups; viii) the formulation of fundamentalist and creolizing religious and cultural answers to relativization; ix) the fragmentation of life-worlds and views on the world and on one's self on the part of individuals; x) the fragmentation of social inequality; xi) the privatization of religious, cultural and moral choices; xii) the shattered character of religion and the collapse of organized belief systems; xiii) the resulting questioning of the role of religious institutions and specialists and the field character of religion.

Central research questions

After having made explicit the modernization perspective the central research questions that guide this book will be presented. These questions are grouped into two clusters. First of all, can the various aspects of Q'eqchi' social reality be classified into the categories of pre-modern, originally modern and contemporary modern? Is the above outlined concept of modernization useful in order to understand this social reality? Can it serve the purpose of translating my data into the social science vocabulary of modernization? Secondly, if so, how do the Q'eqchi'es interact with pre-modern, originally modern and contemporary modern phenomena in the face of present-day processes of globalization and localization? Does the concept of modernization tell us something about the historical perspective of the Q'eqchi'es? In other words, are the Q'eqchi'es to be found somewhere along the way in a process of modernization, or have they found specific ways to deal with pre-modern, originally modern and contemporary modern elements?

2

History and Life-worlds of the Q'eqchi'es

The geographical unit under scrutiny in this study is the Q'eqchi' region, a term which will be used to refer to those places in which the Q'eqchi'es constitute by far a majority of the population. Very few Q'eqchi'es can be found outside of this region which covers parts of several Guatemalan departments. It includes most of the department of Alta Verapaz except for the municipalities of Tactic, San Cristóbal, Santa Cruz, and Tamahú because a large majority of the population of these municipalities consist of *Poqomchi'es* (see Map 1). A majority of the population of the municipality of Purulhá, which belongs to the department of Baja Verapaz, are Q'eqchi'es. The north-eastern part of the department of El Quiché, known as Playa Grande and Lancetillo, is populated by Q'eqchi'es and the same holds true for the southern part of the department of El Petén and the northern part of the department of Izabal.

The average municipality consists of one central town with anywhere between thirty to several hundred of rural communities surrounding it. These rural communities may be subdivided into fincas, villages and co-operatives. A *finca* is a large estate whose production is market-oriented, it is privately owned and includes a community of permanent land labourers. A rural community which has access to land that is not owned by a landlord and in which individual households have access to a specific piece of land is usually called *aldea*, or village. A co-operative holds its land in collective ownership.

The various sub-regions that can be distinguished include the Q'eqchi' heartland, the Polochic Valley and the *Franja Transversal del Norte* (see Map 3). The heartland covers the areas around the central towns of Santo Doningo Cobán, San Pedro Carchá, San Juan Chamelco and Santa María Cahabón. The Polochic river flows through an area that encompasses the municipalities of Tucurú and Panzós (which includes the areas of La Tinta and Telemán), and parts of Purulhá and El Estor. The Franja Transversal del Norte consists of the strip of land stretching from the Caribbean coast to the northern part of the department of Huehuetenango. The Q'eqchi' areas of the Franja include the northern parts of Izabal and of Alta Verapaz, and the north-eastern part of El Quiché. The latter part is also referred to as Ixcán.

To the Q'eqchi'es the place they live in is not just the landscape and environment, to be easily exchanged for another place. Instead, they identify with the geographical surroundings of their community. The place they live in is the location of their identity and a stage for their religious practices and meanings; it has a sacred character for them (see Chapter Four). Consequently, the term "Q'eqchi' region" points to the places in which the Q'eqchi'es live as well as to the sites with which they have developed a special relationship.

It is here that the Q'eqchi'es interact with one another, but this region is also the site where they interface with non-Q'eqchi' actors and agencies. The

Q'eqchi'es have limited experiences outside of the region including pilgrimages to Esquipulas (see Chapter Four) and incidental trips to the capital to solve land title problems. Communication with the outside world mainly takes place through interfaces with intervening actors and agencies in the region such as churches, radio stations, merchants and government agencies.

This structure of communication is directly related to the isolated character of the region and the very poor quality of the infrastructure. There are only two paved roads into the region (see Map 3) which are connected to a limited number of dirt roads. Buses run on a regular basis to the capital from central towns such as Cobán and Poptún. In most of the municipal towns a bus leaves for or arrives from Cobán or another central town once or twice a day, but from some towns such as Chisec there is no bus connection at all. A large majority of local communities are not connected to any road. Most of the Q'eqchi'es have to walk for hours or even days to reach a road.

In short, the Q'eqchi' region is made up of the aggregate of places the Q'eqchi'es live in, identify with and in which they engage in interfaces with intervening actors and agencies. It points to their life-worlds. The objective of this chapter is to outline some of the aspects of these life-worlds such as their household and community life, their identity constructions and their dealings with intervening agencies and politics. It is these specific aspects of their life-worlds which provided the basis for selecting four local communities that play a central role in this book. Before discussing these aspects a brief outline of the history of the Q'eqchi'es will be presented.

Historical background of the Q'eqchi'es

The peoples living in the areas that now make up the Q'eqchi' region were no easy victims of the Spanish colonizers. The largest group, the Q'eqchi'es, were effectively organized around their supreme commander, the *cacique de los caciques*, the leader of the local leaders (AVANCSO, n.d.(b): 2-3). After several military defeats the Spaniards called this region *Tezulutlán*, or Land of the Warriors. They also decided this area would be a perfect setting for Fray Bartolomé de Las Casas, known for his pleas in favour of human treatment of the *Indios*, to try out his peaceful approach. He accepted the challenge and with three fellow Dominicans he travelled to the region in 1537. To the surprise of many Spanish warriors, he easily managed to baptize the rulers of the *Rab'inal Achi'es*, the Poqomchi'es and the Q'eqchi'es in these areas. Impressed by the Dominicans' success, the Spanish king decided to change the name of this area into *Vera Paz*, i.e. True Peace, to erect the independent bishopric of Vera Paz in 1559 and to install the first Bishop. This ecclesiastical move turned out to be rather optimistic as by 1607 or 1608, the bishopric had already been dissolved and the region was included in the bishopric of Guatemala (AVANCSO n.d.(b): 4-7; Sapper 1936: 7, 8, 27).

For a century and a half the Q'eqchi' heartland in the highlands was the frontier area of Spanish influence. The jungle covered lowlands to the east and the north were sparsely populated by wandering groups of *Ch'oles, Lakandones, Akala'es, Maya-Mopanes* and *Itza'es*. Supported by the Q'eqchi' leaders, the Spaniards tried several times to invade these areas but only succeeded in 1696 when they celebrated their final victory over the Itza'es and

Lakandones. The Akala'es died out at the end of the Seventeenth century and the Ch'oles suffered the same fate two centuries later (Sapper 1936: 40-46).

The effects of conversion and colonization should not be overestimated. The Dominicans were mainly concerned with the administration of sacraments and the collection of revenues, while the Q'eqchi'es maintained their religious beliefs and practices (Sapper 1936: 23, 24, 29). In political terms the changes introduced by the Spaniards were not very radical either. The Spaniards confirmed customary laws and the authority of the caciques in the villages. The cacique de los caciques was integrated in the colonial administration and was even granted the right to imprison Spaniards suspected of crimes (AVANCSO n.d.(b): 10, 12, 16; Sapper 1936: 8).

The economic effects of colonization were relatively limited as well. Q'eqchi' communities maintained access to most of their community lands. Only the Dominicans and the crown possessed lands, not individual Spaniards (AVANCSO n.d.(b): 22; Van Oss 1986: 77; Woodward 1990: 69). Neither were individual Spaniards involved in the collection of tribute as the Spanish crown, represented by the *Alcalde Mayor* of Cobán, gathered tribute directly. The infamous *encomienda* system granting individual Spaniards the right to collect tribute from a certain number of Indians was not applied. In many ways the tribute to the crown was an extension of the goods and services which the Q'eqchi'es had to pay to their caciques before the Spanish conquest. The Dominicans even made sure that no slavery existed in the Q'eqchi' area and that women were exempted from labour services (AVANCSO n.d.(b): 2-22).

The Spanish policy of concentrating the population into towns, the so-called *reducciones*, was not very successful either among the Q'eqchi'es. In 1571 there were 2,364 tribute paying families registered in the six Q'eqchi' towns. However, to cite just one case, the houses of San Pedro Carchá were deserted for most of the year because its inhabitants lived in their fields. There was a constant movement of Q'eqchi'es fleeing from the towns and looking for a piece of land in outlying areas (Sapper 1936: 23, 24, 28).

The epidemics which recurrently afflicted the population had more serious consequences. For example, according to Spanish sources the number of tribute paying families in the whole of Verapaz diminished from over 7,000 to 3,135 in the years after 1561, a drop which they attributed to illness (Sapper 1936: 29). Yet, these sources do not allow us to conclude that the effects of epidemics were worse after the arrival of the Spaniards than before that time.

In short, the limited historical evidence available does not support the Martínez Peláez thesis (Martínez Peláez 1971) which emphasizes a rupture between pre-conquest Maya culture and colonial Indian culture, the latter being the result of colonial relations of production imposed by the Spaniards. Instead, the Q'eqchi' region clearly illustrates the limits to colonial rule in the Indian highlands. In these areas colonial administration was carried out almost exclusively through three religious orders: the Dominicans, the Franciscans and the Mercedarians. They accounted for almost the entire Spanish presence in these areas because they successfully claimed that these Indian areas had to maintain their missionary status. As long as Indians remained different from the colonizers in culture and language, then the orders were able to legitimize their presence in the Indian highlands. This presence was contested by the secular clergy and the Spanish state who wanted to expand their influence over these areas (Smith 1990b: 14, 15; Van Oss 1986: 51*ff*, 77, 128, 144).

The orders were not interested in the hispanization of the Indians and kept many of these areas isolated from the influence of other Spaniards. Their key position guaranteed the Indian population of Guatemala an important level of continuity in economic, social and religious terms. To be sure, the Indians were subjected to all sorts of levies which added up to considerable amounts of money and goods. However, to be able to collect these levies the friars had an interest in the maintenance of the Indians' economic base (Lutz, Lovell 1990: 41; Van Oss 1986: 112, 155-157, 183).

In addition, the friars did not try to supplant the existing social and religious hierarchies within the Indian communities. They preferred to use these structures to organize their practices, thereby reinforcing these same structures. The rapid spread and success[1] of the *cofradías* is a good example of this continuity. Existing hierarchies within the communities were used to organize these confraternities which were dedicated to the worship of a specific saint, the maintenance of a church, mutual aid and the organization of funerals (Van Oss 1986: 17, 21, 77, 89, 109*ff*). The rapid spread of cofradías is not an unequivocal indication of the success of Catholic penetration in the Indian highlands. The Indians accepted Catholicism, but during the whole colonial period Spanish sources complained about the superficial nature of conversion and the continuation of ideas and practices which they labelled as paganism and idolatry (Van Oss 1986: 21, 36, 149, 150). The Indian communities maintained a relatively autonomous position vis-à-vis the colonial church and state (Smith 1990b: 13).

The Liberal Reform

At first, independence from Spain in 1823 had no significant consequences for the Q'eqchi'es. However, serious consequences did emerge from the final victory of the liberal creole elite in their struggle with the conservatives at the time of the so-called Liberal Reform of 1871. First, it meant the expansion of the coffee economy requiring large amounts of land and forced labour from the Q'eqchi' communities. Secondly, the liberals significantly increased the repressive capacity of the state and thirdly, they virtually destroyed the presence of the church and the protection which the Indian communities enjoyed thanks to the religious orders. Fourthly, the *ladino*-Indian contradiction that has been ravaging Guatemalan society to the present day, came into being as a result of the liberal transformations. Finally, Q'eqchi' religious institutions such as the cofradías recovered an increasing autonomy.

One of the points of disagreement between the conservatives and the liberals was whether the new opportunities for coffee production and export had to be seized. Yet, already under conservative governments in the 1850s and 1860s, the first steps towards the creation of privately owned large coffee fincas had been taken. In 1862, 75 such fincas owned by Guatemalan citizens, were registered in the Q'eqchi' municipalities of Cobán, Carchá and Tucurú (Woodward 1990: 69). The main impetus for the expansion of coffee fincas came after 1871 when the liberal government invited Germans to settle in the region, set up fincas and develop the infrastructure. They were very keen to maximize their commercial performance. They started by buying an existing finca, optimizing its coffee production while getting hold of new lands. They invested heavily in infrastructure including a cart road, a railroad and a steamship line linking the central highlands around Cobán along the Polochic valley and Lake Izabal, to the sea ports of Santo Tomás and Lívingston (see Map 3) from where the coffee was exported (Wagner 1991: 173-226).

The expansion of the coffee fincas had very serious consequences for land ownership in the Q'eqchi' region. On the eve of the first world war 32 registered German finca owners owned 2,100 square kilometres of land, or 24.17 per cent of the territory of the department of Alta Verapaz.[2] A map drawn by the German geographer Karl Sapper in 1900 shows that the present pattern of large landownership in Alta Verapaz had, by and large, been established by that time (Wagner 1991: 205).

Those who provided these lands were the municipal governments, the Dominicans and the Q'eqchi' communities. The latter lost the rights to their lands, but this does not mean that in practice these communities completely lost access. Fincas needed labour and the Q'eqchi'es were certainly not very willing to work on fincas. Moreover, labour was relatively scarce since the population of the whole department only just surpassed 100,000 in 1893. To make the Q'eqchi'es work on the fincas a carrot-and-stick approach was applied. On the one hand, the finca owners' treatment was rather modest. They bought large areas of land not just to grow coffee but also to allow their labourers to cultivate a piece of land on the finca and grow food crops. As a reward for this access to land and a small wage, the Q'eqchi'es were required to work a limited number of days on the finca: about six days a month at the end of the Nineteenth century (Wagner 1991: 173, 181, 182, 193).

The state, on the other hand, took a much tougher position. It decreed and implemented several laws which forced the Indian population to work for both the finca owners and the state. The *habilitación* system was the most infamous of all. Workers received payment in advance and paid off their debt with interest by their work and debts were handed down from parents to children. In 1934 this debt peonage was abolished by law but was soon replaced by the vagrancy law obliging every male Indian to carry a booklet in which the number of days he had worked for a finca owner or for the state was recorded. When he was unable to show that he had worked a minimum number of days - over a hundred days a year were often required - he could be put to work or immediately sent to jail (Adams 1990: 141-142; Cabarrús 1979: 116).

Next to Indian communities the church became another "supplier" of land to the coffee economy. Tensions between the state and especially the religious orders were reinforced by liberal intentions of creating a secular state, to integrate the indigenous population into a national entity and to confiscate the lands belonging to the Indian communities and the church. The massive attack on the church included confiscation of ecclesiastical property - the church was the largest landowner in the country - and the expulsion of the archbishop and all male religious orders. Religious ceremonies outside church buildings were prohibited, the seminary was closed and education was secularized. The church virtually disappeared from the Indian highlands. In 1924 there were only 85 priests to look after church life in the whole country. Most of them were very old and lived in the capital (Samandú, Siebers, Sierra 1990: 25-26).

The Liberal Reform and the expansion of the coffee economy gave rise to one of the most severe contradictions in Guatemalan society: the one between Indians and ladinos.[3] A structural differentiation between "redressed" Indians, *mestizos* and others who did not lead an Indian way of life on the one hand, and Indians on the other, emerged after 1871. The ladinos became the ones who occupied the intermediary positions between the state and the white finca owners on the one hand and the Indian labour force and communities on the other: i.e. the labour contractors, the finca administrators, the merchants, the middle rank army officers as well as the local representatives of the state such as the local *intendentes*, appointed by president Jorge Ubico in the 1930s to control the municipalities. This differentiation cannot be understood solely in class terms: it resulted in '...a new and virulent form of racism in Guatemala, much more powerful than that of the colonial period' (Smith 1990c: 90) and was marked by fear and hatred.

The main reaction of the Guatemalan Indians to all these contradictions caused by the 1871 reform was not to engage in open resistance. The inhabitants of San Pedro Carchá protested at the loss of community lands in 1864-1865 and again in 1878 or 1879 and there was a rebellion on the finca Campur in the 1890s[4], but in general open resistance was remarkably rare mainly because of the vast increase in the repressive capacity of the state (McCreery 1990: 111-113). The Indians' main response was to try to safeguard the relative autonomy of local community life, which remained the primary unit they identified with (Smith 1990a: 263; Smith 1990b: 17-18).

This strategy was enhanced by the fact that the state was unable to develop more effective ways of controlling local community life than brutal repression on the one hand and by the reinforcement of local institutions on the other. In recruiting labour the state had to deal with existing hierarchies within the communities who were to supply the required labour. Moreover in the virtual absence of priests and religious women, the cofradías enjoyed a near monopoly of the organization of religious life. The Indian communities were able to go their own way for decades without church intervention. Already in colonial times the cofradías tended to become indigenized or, in other words, to transform themselves from colonial institutions into expressions of indigenous religion. After 1871 the cofradías became strong promoters and genuine representatives of the latter (Samandú, Siebers, Sierra 1990: 26-27).

Economic and demographic change in the twentieth century

The mixed structure of fincas with considerable numbers of Q'eqchi' permanent labourers and independent Q'eqchi' villages where Q'eqchi'es cultivated small plots of land - the so-called *latifundio-minifundio* system - has basically remained intact since the introduction of the coffee economy. Nevertheless, the Q'eqchi' region has experienced considerable economic changes since then. To begin with, the German finca owners were dispossessed during the second world war when the Guatemalan government joined the ranks of the allied nations. Much of their land was returned to them afterwards but some was distributed to new private owners and after 1968 several dozen dispossessed fincas were transformed into co-operatives.

Another change that has had a more lasting effect on the Q'eqchi'es has been the gradual disappearance of forced labour. Officially, the various laws on forced labour were abolished in 1945 because they were no longer necessary in the country as a whole.[5] Now economic necessity caused by the further expansion of large landownership, especially in the southern part of the country, and population growth left a growing number of Indians no other option than to seek additional income by doing wage labour on the fincas. However, the Q'eqchi' heartland was slow to experience this change. New export crops such as sugar cane and cotton which gave rise to an expansion of fincas in other parts of the country during the 1950s and 1960s, did not penetrate into the region and thus did not encroach upon the lands of the Q'eqchi'es. Here population growth put pressure on the unequally distributed land later than in other parts of the country. In Alta Verapaz, the population increased from a little over 100,000 in 1893 to almost 260,000 in 1964.[6] According to one of the priests who started to work in the area in the 1960s, the municipalities at that time were still forcing the Q'eqchi'es to work for them and on the fincas twelve hours a day, six days a week, and to accept a wage of 0.50 to 1 *quetzal*[7] a day.

Nevertheless the gradual relaxation of extra-economic force did allow the Q'eqchi'es in the villages to grasp new economic opportunities in the 1970s. The introduction of chemical fertilizers and the new export crop cardamom, a spice mainly used in Arab cuisine, allowed these villages to increase both their food and cash crop production in spite of their limited amount of land. Some of these communities were able to earn considerable amounts of money when the price of a *quintal* (45.3 kilos) of cardamom reached 300 quetzales and the quetzal was at par with the US dollar.

Intimately linked to population growth and the relaxation of forced labour practices has been the increasing migration of Q'eqchi'es. Since the 1960s Q'eqchi'es have moved constantly from the heartland to settlement areas in three movements. A first and rather limited one crossed the Chixoy river into the areas of Lancetillo and Playa Grande. A second moved down the Polochic valley and eventually to Río Dulce, Livingston and Belize. A third movement found its way to the Franja Transversal del Norte and eventually to the department of El Petén (see Map 3). In the 1960s and 1970s the lowlands in the Polochic valley and the El Estor area and the northern part of Alta Verapaz were populated, whereas the main influx of Q'eqchi'es in the lowlands of the northern part of Izabal and the southern part of El Petén and Belize took place from the end of the 1970s onwards. Q'eqchi'es built their communities after Guatemalan and Mexican companies[8] had cleared these areas and taken away all their precious hardwoods. Nowadays there is hardly any land available and the first Q'eqchi' communities are appearing in areas further north.

Population growth and the scarcity of land have been important push factors to stimulate Q'eqchi'es to descend from the heartland and move to the lowland settlements, but there is more. The large majority of migrants have especially come from fincas[9]: surplus labour which has been expelled from these fincas, a phenomenon aggravated by the shift of several fincas towards cattle raising with a decrease in labour demand. In addition, a large number of Q'eqchi'es in the settlement areas told me they had left a finca in the heartland because of their deeply felt desire to live as peasants. They wanted to look for a piece of land to which they would have permanent access, on which they can work, with which they could identify themselves, and which could become a source of religious meaning-making for them (see Chapter Four). Mere access to a piece of land in usufruct on the finca did not satisfy this desire. The same desire to reproduce themselves as peasants also explains why urbanization has been limited among the Q'eqchi'es. The largest town in the area, Cobán, has only about 30,000 inhabitants and, in contrast to other ethnic groups, few Q'eqchi'es have migrated towards the capital. It was not only economic and demographic constraints which pushed the Q'eqchi'es towards the settlement areas but economic and cultural aspirations as well.

Individual families or groups of families who migrated usually reached a more or less permanent place only after several years. There, they joined with other Q'eqchi' families to form new communities and met with minorities of other ethnic groups, either because these groups were there already (4000 *Maya-Mopanes* in the town of San Luís Petén, as many *Garífunas* as well as a few hundred Hindu families in the town of Lívingston), or because they had migrated towards these areas as well (Poqomchi'es, Rab'inal Achi'es, K'iche'es, ladinos). In any case, there are very few mixed ethnic communities. Q'eqchi'es prefer to form communities with people of their own kind.

Besides these movements of permanent migration a considerable temporary migration has developed in recent years. Tens of thousands of Q'eqchi'es from the villages in the heartland travel to the settlement areas, especially to the northern part of Alta Verapaz, to work for some weeks for other Q'eqchi'es in their cardamom harvest or to rent a piece of land from other Q'eqchi'es on which to grow their maize and beans. These Q'eqchi'es in the settlement areas usually have access to more land than those of the highlands and are willing to let them use part of their land temporarily.

Land conflicts and violence

Almost everywhere settlement has been characterized by land conflicts. After having formed a community and cleared a piece of land, the Q'eqchi'es have very often been confronted with a *finquero* (finca owner) waving some sort of document that was supposed to prove that the land was his.[10] Army officers in particular, such as the generals Romeo and Benedicto Lucas García - the former was president between 1978 and 1982 and the latter his army chief of staff - have been successful in gaining rights over large tracts of land in the Franja region. Attracted by the possibilities of extensive cattle raising and the discovery of oil, they worked out ambitious plans to develop this region, but the land turned out to be of poor quality and the oil exploitation was not very promising. In the meantime large landownership had established itself with the resulting marginalization of the Q'eqchi' communities.

Land conflicts are a major source of violence in the Q'eqchi' region, even to the present day. In such conflicts the finqueros are usually supported by army or police forces. In May 1978 the army opened fire on a crowd of Q'eqchi' leaders in the town of Panzós after they had been invited by the mayor to discuss land problems. 104 Q'eqchi'es ended up dead in the street. One month later several Q'eqchi' communities invited the army officers to come to their villages for a reconciliation and to avoid further escalation.[11]

Land conflicts are not the only source of massive violence in the region. The appearance of the guerrilla organization *Ejército Guerrillero de los Pobres* has seriously added to the problem causing the army to step up its level of repression and violence. At the national level the counter-insurgency policy of the army was a response to the growing popular protest in the 1970s, the increasing military power of the guerrilla movements and the fear that a revolutionary take-over such as the 1979 revolution in Nicaragua might take place in Guatemala as well. However, in order to explain the massive and brutal violence unleashed by the army between 1978 and 1984[12], other factors have to be taken into account such as the crucial role of racism in Guatemalan society and the inability of the state to control the Indian population other than by violent means (Smith 1990b: 17).

Leftist writers of the 1980s generally subscribed to the interpretation that guerrilla activity was the continuation of "popular struggle", such as the struggle for land waged by the Q'eqchi'es. This view assumes that such popular struggle of peasants for land and labourers for higher wages developed into armed struggle by guerrilla groups at the end of the 1970s.[13] Nevertheless, in the case of the Q'eqchi' region there is very little evidence to support the interpretation that the Q'eqchi'es saw armed struggle as having something to do with the land conflicts in which they were engaged. The guerrilla arrived relatively late in the region - at the end of the 1970s - and the guerrilla had no significant support base among peasant organizations as in other parts of the country because such organizations hardly existed in the region. Before embarking on armed conflict with the army, the guerrilla hardly bothered to explain the objectives of their struggle to the population.[14]

Advocates of this leftist interpretation point to the fact that many thousands of Q'eqchi'es sought refuge in the nearby mountains where the guerrilla had its military strongholds. However, interviews I conducted in 1987 with several of these people after they had left the mountains, as well as sources within the Catholic church, indicated that they had gone to the mountains out of despair to look for safety in areas that are difficult to penetrate. In fact the guerrilla had their strongholds there for that very same reason. In the words of the bishop of Verapaz, Mgr. Gerardo Flores Reyes:

> ...it is well known that, as the *indígenas* of many villages fled to the mountains of Alta Verapaz, this was not so much due to an ideological motive... but to the terror which these communities feared at that time. (Source: AVANCSO 1992: 176)

There are no indications whatsoever that the Q'eqchi' population would have supported or ideologically identified with the guerrilla. Almost all of the Catholic clergy who worked in the region at that time, confirmed this to me. The Q'eqchi'es in the war zones were trapped between two armies.

Nevertheless, there can be no doubt that the army is to blame for an overwhelming majority of cases of violence against the Q'eqchi' population. Bloodshed on a massive scale occurred in the areas of Chisec and Cobán as well as in more isolated parts of Playa Grande, Sayaxché, San Luís Petén, El Estor and Panzós between 1981 and 1983. The army destroyed entire communities, killed part of the population and drove many to flee to the mountains, to neighbouring areas or to Mexico. Based on detailed interviews with respondents who worked in these areas during those years as well as on written sources[15], I estimate at one hundred the total number of Q'eqchi' communities which suffered from massive violence. This number does not include communities in neighbouring Poqomchi' areas of San Cristóbal Verapaz or Santa Cruz Verapaz which suffered very severely as well. Selective killings took place all over the Q'eqchi' region.

Those who at least survived the immediate massacres either fled from or were captured by the army. The thousands who sought refuge in the mountains had to try to survive in extremely difficult circumstances without any support from outside (AVANCSO 1990: 174). Several hundred had to surrender to the army after several years of unbearable hardship, but close to 500 of them came down from the mountains between 1986 and 1988 and were received by the bishop and other Catholic church officials. These officials gave them protection, shelter and food, organized identity papers and set up several integrated development projects for them on land provided by the church.

Those whom the army had captured were first held in prison camps where they received "ideological instruction". Army officers tried to explain the dangers of communism, attempted to convince them of the army's explanation of what had happened to them, and told them to respect the flag and the national anthem. These camps existed for several years. Some of those who had been captured were put to work rebuilding local villages, the so-called "model villages", controlled by army posts. The town of Chisec and ten nearby villages are cases in point. Efforts to transform these villages into a so-called "development pole", including development projects, have failed.

In addition, the adult male population throughout the country was forced to organize themselves "voluntarily" into the so-called "civil self-defence patrols". Every man was required to spend one in every seven to ten days on sentry duty to protect the town or village against guerrilla attacks and, perhaps more importantly, to inform the commander of the nearest army base every few weeks about what happened in the community. In the Q'eqchi' areas struck by violence, these patrols were used by the army to pursue fellow Q'eqchi'es hiding in the mountains.

The period called "*violencia*" has been over since the middle of the 1980s and most of those who had to flee or had been captured by the army have settled down; however the problems are far from over. Many communities were torn apart between those who stayed and those who fled, and the former have sometimes occupied the land of the latter. In addition, these divisions were reinforced by ecclesiastical contradictions. In the war zones the priests were suspected of supporting the guerrilla and had to flee. In these areas pastoral work came to a halt for several years while evangelical churches were invited by the army to come and convert the Q'eqchi'es. There are many cases of evangelical leaders accusing their "religious competitors" of preaching communism with the army reacting violently as a result. Lay leaders of the Catholic church in particular were army targets. As a result of all these incidents there is a general atmosphere of distrust and fear among the Q'eqchi'es in the areas that have suffered from massive violence, and community life and structures in these areas are rather weak.

Catholic restoration

These ecclesiastical contradictions point to the renewed presence of the Catholic church after its disappearance in the wake of the Liberal Reform. Gradually and with occasional setbacks, the church succeeded in normalizing its relations with the state, opening the way for its restoration after the 1930s.

The church was able to achieve this by welcoming an increasing number of foreign priests and religious orders. This increase allowed it to create new administrative divisions. The Diocese of Verapaz, the Apostolic Vicariate of El Petén and the Apostolic Administration of Izabal were erected in 1935, 1951 and 1968 respectively.[16] However, church restoration in the Q'eqchi' region took place rather late, from the 1960s onwards.

One of the main tasks of these new priests and religious women was the instruction and training of lay leaders who were supposed to lead and organize church activities within their local communities. For this purpose the San Benito training centre was set up in Cobán in 1968 for catechists from all over the bishopric of Verapaz. This instruction went beyond a focus on religious issues such as how to lead a celebration of the Word (a Mass-like service without the presence of a priest). The catechists also received training in agricultural methods, how to form a co-operative, the value of community life and the "dignity of every person". This last principle established that everyone, including Q'eqchi'es, ladinos and finqueros, are equal in the eyes of God which aroused much enthusiasm among the Q'eqchi' catechists.

The relatively late recovery of the church in the Q'eqchi' region meant that it took place when the movement of church renewal, linked to the Second Vatican Council and the Bishops' conference of Medellín, was well on the way. As a result the church in the Q'eqchi' region did not regard the Q'eqchi'es as simply objects of conversion which meant that it was able to avoid the fierce conflicts with the cofradías and other indigenous leaders which the Catholic church provoked in other parts of the country.[17] The lay organization *Acción Católica* which played a crucial role in these conflicts, had no stronghold in the Q'eqchi' region. Nevertheless, the fact that young men especially were recruited as catechists constituted a challenge to the authority of elderly couples in the communities, the introduction of new religious practices and meanings did create tensions within the communities and the cofradías lost part of their influence (Cabarrús 1979: 126-128).

Differences within the church included disputes on social and political matters. On the one hand priests, inspired by liberation theology, incorporated a reflection on and judgement of social reality in their pastoral methods and tried to link it to efforts to change this reality. They focused on the demand for higher wages on fincas and villagers' need for more land. On the other hand there were priests who considered these methods as something close to communism. They tried to prevent the Q'eqchi'es from engaging in any political activity. Some priests accused colleagues of supporting subversion while the latter accused the former of justifying army violence.

While the Catholic church restored its presence in the region, it lost its ecclesiastical monopoly. The first evangelical church, the Nazarene Church, established itself in the region at the beginning of this century. It was followed in the 1960s by other churches but they had to wait until the 1970s to convert large numbers of Q'eqchi'es.

Basic aspects of the life-worlds of the present day Q'eqchi'es

Some basic experiences of contemporary Q'eqchi'es have already been outlined, such as the latifundio-minifundio system, the rise of cardamom production, the migration movements, the land conflicts, violence and church influence. In order to complement this picture of the life-worlds of the Q'eqchi'es, I will discuss some other components in the following section. These components include the natural environment, population density, the households, leadership within their communities, identity constructions, external strategies and their approach to politics.

People, households and natural environment[18]

The 600,000 Q'eqchi'es live in a region that covers some 20,000 square kilometres, or about 18 per cent of the national territory. About half of them live in the valleys and on the mountain slopes in the Q'eqchi' heartland (see Map 3), where a moderate temperature prevails, and altitudes range from 600 metres above sea level to 3,015 metres for the highest mountain, the *Qawa' Raxon*. The other half of the Q'eqchi' population live in the tropical lowlands of the settlement areas where temperatures can run as high as 40 degrees Celsius. The soil in these areas provides the Q'eqchi'es with abundant harvests in the first few years of cultivation, but its humus layer is thin and after a few years it rapidly looses its fertility. The highlands have a karst soil and many subterranean rivers. The whole region receives abundant rainfall in the rainy season which lasts from June till January.

Q'eqchi'es live together in local communities which I estimate to number about 1,600. By far the majority of them are independent villages and fincas, but they also include a limited number of co-operatives and local communities in urban neighbourhoods. The largest of the Q'eqchi' communities, numbering up to several thousand inhabitants, can be found in the heartland while in the remote settlement areas communities usually have only a few dozens families. Population density ranges from seven inhabitants per square kilometre in the area of Sayaxché to 406 in the area of San Juan Chamelco. The non-Q'eqchi' population of ladinos, Poqomchi'es, Rab'inal Achi'es, K'iche'es, Maya-Mopanes, and Garífunas numbers about 100,000 persons. Consequently, six out of seven inhabitants of the region are Q'eqchi'es and the total population consists of some 700,000 souls.

The household is the basic unit of social organization in the Q'eqchi' communities. It may consist of a man and a woman with some children and other family members. In the villages where I worked, the average number of persons per household varied from 5.6 to 6.5. To the Q'eqchi'es the decisive criteria to be applied to a household is whether the persons concerned are living in their own house. Couples who live in the house of one of the parents are not considered to be adults nor to make up a household. In one community I studied female headed households make up ten per cent of all households.

A household is often formed when a boy and a girl reach the age of fifteen to eighteen and the general pattern is patrilocal. The girl first joins the household of the boy and then they build their house nearby. Gradually, over several years, they receive land from the boy's parents. In general, those from the same kinship or family line in the same community help each other by contributing labour, crops or money in case of need.

Where possible their houses are scattered. The Q'eqchi'es want to create a separate space including the land they cultivate or leave fallow, the animals they raise and the natural surroundings as part of the economic and symbolic household unit. Moreover, the dispersion of the houses keeps the animals from eating their neighbour's crops and makes it easy to deal with waste. However, as in the old colonial days it is still government policy to encourage the villagers to build their houses in village centres in order to control them more easily. In 1986 the army forced the villagers of Chaabilchoch to build their houses in such a centre.

The Q'eqchi'es build the walls of their houses with sticks but some use planks or even bricks. They thatch the roof but some use corrugated iron sheets as well. Concrete floors are rare. In the centre of the house there is a wall separating the kitchen from the living room. Some households have two separate houses to be used as a kitchen and a living room respectively. In most of the houses there is very little furniture. People sit on a plank resting on some rocks and sleep in their hammocks; food is kept in the attic and clothes hang on a rope. Machetes and pots stand against the wall. Only a few households have chairs, a cupboard and wooden beds. Favourite luxury articles include a marimba or violin, a radio, and pictures or even statues of a saint. All households, except the evangelical ones, have an altar. Almost always, small animals walk in and out of the house.

Local leadership

In every community there are various committees and leaders who make sure that activities of community life are performed. In the last three decades the old leadership of *pasawinq* (couples of elderly men and women) and cofradías, or *chinames* as they are called in the rural communities, has lost its monopoly. It has been complemented by a group of catechists and, in some communities, by evangelical leaders, an auxiliary mayor, a few military commissioners, a Local Development Committee as well as other committees responsible for specific tasks such as the school committee or the cholera emergency committee. In addition, there are several individual leaders such as the local health promoter and the adult education orientator.

Most of these leaders and committees will be discussed in the chapters on religion and the economy. At this stage I will specifically discuss the *alcalde auxiliar* (auxiliary mayor) and the *comisionado militar* (military commissioner). The auxiliary mayor is the personal representative of the mayor in the village. He goes to the municipality every week or fortnight to report to the mayor on the affairs of the community and passes on the mayor's messages to the villagers. He is supposed to look after the community and to solve problems that might arise. He is either chosen by the pasawinq or elected by the whole community and serves for one or two years. In each community there are also one or several of military commissioners whose task is to help the auxiliary mayor, to inform the nearest army commander - sometimes a day's travel - every fortnight about what is going on in the community, and to send young men to do their military service. Contrary to the auxiliary mayor he is not elected by the community but chosen by the army commander.

Concerning these auxiliary mayors and military commissioners, the same thing can be said as was pointed out about the historical role of the cofradías: they are "brokers". On the one hand they embody instruments used by the state to control the communities. In some of the communities the military commissioner was looked at with suspicion when he took his task seriously. On the other hand, these leaders serve the community by representing it before state authorities, keeping the interests of their own communities in mind. In every community the loyalty of these leaders was clearly with their local community. Other community members talked about them in terms of whether they are nice and respectable persons, the same criteria they apply to everyone.

Each committee and leader has its own responsibilities though they are in no way exclusive. In principle, everyone talks about everything and it is not uncommon, for example, for the local development committee to discuss religious matters or the catechists to deal with the prevention of cholera. Moreover, in some communities the most common procedure is for the relevant committee or leaders to present issues that concern the community to the meeting of all adult men in which every man may speak out on any matter. Discussions often take hours before reaching a consensus. In a few of the communities, also some women participated. In other communities the practice of a "general assembly" has been lost. There the leaders and committees take and implement decisions without explicitly seeking a consensus, but they face more difficulty to convince the villagers to execute their decisions.

Local leaders are not able to avoid or solve every internal conflict in the community. I have come across several conflicts between families or hamlets in the same village and even within families and households. There is not much ground for creating a harmonious picture of relations within Q'eqchi' households or local communities.

Identity constructions[19]

Not surprisingly, the two levels of social organization of the community, the household or family and the community as such, appear also as the two main categories to which the Q'eqchi'es feel allegiance. They predominantly identify themselves as a member of these two categories.

Before discussing the identity constructions of the Q'eqchi'es I need to make some comments on the literature on identity constructions in Guatemala, especially the identities of its Indian population. In my view this literature must transcend the various divisions and one-sided positions that have marked a large part of it. Anthropologists have attempted to define Guatemala's Indian groups either in terms of certain cultural traits - dress, language, religion - or in terms of their relations with other groups. Some authors following the former or substantive approach have looked for those cultural characteristics that could be considered typical of a specific ethnic group. Others, in line with Fredrik Barth (Barth 1969), have adopted a relational approach stressing that identities are primarily constructed through stressing differences with other groups in which the cultural traits of one's own group may vary.[20]

Another shortcoming of the literature is represented by the divorce of two circuits of discussion on Indian cultures and identities. On the one hand much is said about these constructions from an outsider's points of view while relatively little attention is paid to how the relevant actors themselves conceive of their identity. These interpretations of Indian cultures and identities include both those who see them as an expression of "super-exploitation" from colonial times onwards and those who stress the continuity from the pre-Columbian past, portraying Indian identities as autochthonous cultures of resistance against internal and external colonialism up to the present day.[21] All these essentialist interpretations, mainly among Guatemalan academics, have in common that they largely neglect what the Indians themselves have to say about their identities. On the other hand there are studies, mainly by foreign scholars, which do take into account the expressions of their respondents on these matters, but due to their foreign status they find it difficult to become actively involved in Guatemalan debates. A more comprehensive approach would have to take into account both the substantive and relational aspects of identity and to pay attention to both characteristics that can be observed from an outsider's point of view and the statements and expressions of the respondents themselves about their identities. Fortunately, in recent years quite some process oriented and constructivist studies expressing such a comprehensive approach[22] and the first collections with articles of both Guatemalan and foreign scholars have appeared.[23]

In studying identity constructions among the Q'eqchi'es, the context-specific and layered character of such constructions became very clear to me. The Q'eqchi'es identify themselves as members of their household, their local community, their church and those who speak Q'eqchi'. Each of these identifications is relevant in a specific context. Within the local community belongingness to a household or specific church community is important and relevant. When they go to the market in the municipal town, the local community of origin is the crucial issue. When they meet a non-Q'eqchi', it is the fact that they belong to the world of Q'eqchi' speakers which matters. Hence, identity constructions have a clearly context-bound character.

However, these identifications are interconnected to some extent and some identifications are more important to them than others because the former identifications are linked to activities and occasions that are more important to them than other practices and contexts. The Q'eqchi'es I had conversations with identified themselves primarily as members of the household and the local community. Moreover, in the following chapters it will be made clear that the household and the local community are also the two principal units which bring the Q'eqchi'es together to perform almost all religious and economic practices. The meanings related to these practices are constitutive of their identities and differentiate them, for example, from non-Q'eqchi'es. Both categories, the household and the local community, not only encompass specific members but also a certain space. The household or family space includes the house(s), the animals and crops, and the lands to which the household or family has access. The community encompasses the buildings, their immediate surroundings and the land and woods belonging to it.

This community identification shows variations, related to the level of economic, social and religious activities that are performed by the community. Moreover in villages that are ecclesiastically divided, the church community partly substitutes for the local community as a source of identification. Especially in the case of minority church groups engaged in tense relations with the rest of the village and who do not participate in social activities organized by the village, allegiance shifts towards the church community.

At a very subordinated level the Q'eqchi'es identify themselves as belonging to their church organization outside of their community and to the Q'eqchi'es as an ethnic group. In the case of the wider church community the Q'eqchi'es feel loyalty to the priest of their parish, to the minister and his central church, to the bishop, the pope. The category Q'eqchi' has both a social and a spatial meaning to them as well. To the Q'eqchi'es, language constitutes the most important criterion to distinguish between Q'eqchi'es and non-Q'eqchi'es. The ability and willingness to speak Q'eqchi' is the most characterizing feature of the Q'eqchi'es. In their eyes another difference between Q'eqchi'es and non-Q'eqchi'es is the fact that they perform *costumbres* (Q'eqchi' religious customs) while the latter do not. These costumbres comprise, among others, the yearly pilgrimages to several of the thirteen central mountains that can be found in the Q'eqchi' heartland. They symbolize allegiance to the Q'eqchi' region as a whole (see Chapter Four). Finally, the typical dress of Q'eqchi' women plays a role in Q'eqchi' identity. Men do not wear any specific items of clothing, but women are proud of their dark skirt and white blouse called *huipil* and of their long black hair.

However in their identity constructions, the wider church community and the Q'eqchi'es as a social and spatial category are very much subordinated to the household and the local community. The Q'eqchi'es have no organizations of their own at the supra-local or inter-local level such as trade unions, and any Q'eqchi' from another community who enters a local community has to face the same challenge as a non-Q'eqchi', that is to gain the confidence of the local community. Relations with the local landscape - household and local community - are clearly more important than those with the Q'eqchi' region as a whole. The pilgrimages to the central mountains constitute the exception to the rule that customary practices are performed either by the household or by the local community. In addition, almost all the church activities are practised at the household or local level and hardly any economic practice is performed by more than one community or by members of various communities together.

In short, in the following chapters it will become clear that there is a considerable level of cultural sharing among the Q'eqchi'es as a group. However, the development of any sort of "imagined community" (Anderson 1978), either an ethnic group, a wider church community or least of all one based on national identity, among most of the Q'eqchi'es is quite limited. The characterization of the Q'eqchi'es as an ethnic group, which assumes that their identification as Q'eqchi'es plays a dominant role in their identity constructions, remains unfounded. Only among some "brokers", especially those who live in towns, is the idea that they belong to a Q'eqchi' or even Maya ethnic group very much alive.

Various units of identification point to various categories of outsiders, but the non-Q'eqchi'es are the most important "others". Relations with them constitute the primary relational aspect of Q'eqchi' identity. They are outsiders in relation to all four units of identification except for the church community. Many of the priests and ministers are non-Q'eqchi'es, but they are perceived primarily as priests or ministers instead of as non-Q'eqchi'es. The importance of language in distinguishing between Q'eqchi'es and non-Q'eqchi'es is reflected in the name which the Q'eqchi'es apply to all non-Q'eqchi'es: *Kastii*, i.e. those who speak *castellano* or Spanish. The fact that the ladinos and whites are included in this category causes no surprise. They are the government officials, the army officers, the large landowners, the finca administrators, the merchants, the development workers and the politicians.

What does cause surprise is the fact that the Q'eqchi'es include Indians from other groups such as K'iche'es and Rab'inal Achi'es in this same category of Kastii. The Q'eqchi'es can only communicate in Spanish with both ladinos and the members of these Indian groups and the fact that only a very few Q'eqchi'es speak Spanish prevents most of them from establishing relations of trust not only with ladinos, but with other Indians as well. The fact that the Q'eqchi'es include both ladinos and non-Q'eqchi' Indians in the same social category questions the assumptions of the Indigenous Movement who use the term "Maya" as a central category referring to the members of all the indigenous groups in Guatemala. At least referring to the Q'eqchi'es there is hardly any basis for talking about "the Mayas"; this term has no meaning to them. Moreover, among all the indigenous population of Guatemala primary identification is focused on the local community (Smith 1990b: 18-19) rather than on the particular ethnic group.

The Q'eqchi'es are very aware of the difference between them and the Kastii, but there is considerable variation among them, both between and within the communities, about the relative degree of trust and mistrust vis-à-vis the Kastii. Answers varied from 'They treat us right' to 'They may want to kill us'. Nevertheless almost all believed that their relations with Kastii are improving mainly because they themselves feel more self-assured towards the Kastii. 'We are awakening', as one respondent said. This holds true especially among the younger generations.

They point to two central sources of this rising self-confidence: access to education and to the Word of God. Only a limited number of Q'eqchi'es have access to education and the effects of education are rather disappointing. However the fact that this number is gradually increasing as is the capacity of the Q'eqchi'es to speak Spanish, makes them feel that their desire to improve their situation is not hopeless. Evangelization is another source of self-confidence. Both Catholics and evangelicals expressed themselves in similar terms: the awareness that in the eyes of God all are equal has considerably improved their self-esteem. One respondent said to me: 'We used to fear Kastii but now, with the attention given to religion, everything has changed. We are brothers'. Another one told me: 'Their [Kastii - hs] seed is different from ours, but in the eyes of God all are the same'.

However this account of their relations with Kastii needs some qualifications. Some Kastii are especially distrusted. Government officials ('gentlemen of authority who speak Spanish and get angry') as well as merchants ('they consider us to be nothing, they go to the other side') are mentioned. The fact that I have not had the opportunity to ask pertinent questions to Q'eqchi'es living on fincas or in areas struck by massive violence probably explains why finca administrators, finca owners and army officers are not frequently mentioned as Kastii whom the Q'eqchi'es distrust.

In short, these special categories of Kastii whom the Q'eqchi'es particularly fear constitute the extreme of negative identification. These *kaxlan wink*, or "foreigners", are most clearly identified as the ladino "others" who merit mistrust. However, it should be emphasized that, although in a far less negative way, the Q'eqchi'es also consider non-Q'eqchi' Indians as "others" who are included in the more general category of those to whom they do not belong, i.e. the Kastii. Moreover, even Q'eqchi'es from another community are not part of those units to whom the Q'eqchi'es primarily identify their belongingness, that is the household and local community.

External strategies and trust

> It is typical of them [the Q'eqchi'es - hs] that, if possible, they try to avoid saying something unpleasant to a stranger. That is why they usually give evasive and appeasing answers, even when they have not the slightest intention to carry out the desired thing (Sapper 1936: 23).

This statement of Karl Sapper at the beginning of this century accurately describes the ways the Q'eqchi'es, even today, continue to deal with those who do not belong to their household and local community. When communicating with such intervening actors the Q'eqchi'es try to establish harmony. They remain polite and are willing to receive anyone. Meanwhile they try to establish whether the actor can be trusted, e.g. whether there is some sort of introduction from a trusted person and whether the intentions of the actor accord with their stated views. When trust is not established or they do not want to carry out the proposal, they will not say so clearly so as to avoid offending the intervening actor. They simply do not co-operate when things have to be done and ensure that the subject does not rise again.

A first key to understanding this way of dealing with intervening actors is that the local community wants to retain its relative autonomy. In the past few decades intervening actors and agencies such as the state have been stepping up their efforts to gain influence within and over local Q'eqchi' communities, but the example of the auxiliary mayor has already made clear that the local communities continue to make use of the limited room for manoeuvre that is left to them. Intervening actors and agencies - including the state - are unable to control the local community effectively.[24]

These intervening actors and agencies are almost exclusively made up of Kastii, or even kaxlan wink, i.e. ladinos. The Q'eqchi'es wish to improve their situation by way of enlarging their access to economic, cultural and other resources without entering into conflict or open competition with them. One of the reasons for avoiding conflict is the fact that they are unable to defend themselves against the Kastii. Talking about Kastii several Q'eqchi'es told me that 'economically and intellectually they are very intelligent, so they can easily do us harm, especially the finca owners'. Another respondent said: 'Many Kastii take advantage of us because we have not studied'.

An important reason for the Q'eqchi'es to want to have access to education is their desire to improve communication with Kastii in order to turn this communication more to their advantage. However, communication problems and lack of trust continue to produce frequent misunderstandings at the interfaces between Q'eqchi'es and Kastii which the latter easily interpret in racist terms.

In order to understand these interfaces we have to take into account that the meaning of the actions taken by both sides is not so much determined by their functionality, but by the social group to which those involved belong. For example, an agricultural extension worker offering some kind of technology to a Q'eqchi' community is primarily viewed by them in terms of whether he or she can be trusted, of the group to which the worker belongs. It is the social background of the worker rather than the usefulness of the technology on offer which determines the meaning the Q'eqchi'es attribute to his or her visit.

Moreover, relations between Q'eqchi'es and Kastii have hardly become institutionalized through functional communication and as a result, the personal factor continues to play a dominant role. An agency is only able to work with a Q'eqchi' community whenever the particular employee who is in charge has managed to create a personal relation of trust with the community. This trust cannot easily be transferred to another employee of the same organization. On the other hand, once a relation of trust has been established, the Q'eqchi'es are sure to be interested in what an intervening actor is offering. Then they decide on whether it is useful to them and whether they accept it.

This emphasis on trust in persons rather than professional expertise has been classified in the preceding chapter as pre-modern. It is certainly related to the fact that only few Q'eqchi'es have had any access to formal education which might have taught them to respect expert knowledge. However, the lack of institutionalized communication as well as the importance of personal trust are in no way limited to Q'eqchi' - Kastii communication, they are quite common to Indian - ladino relations and to ladino society as such. Ladinos very often find the need to confirm their "honour", "friendship", "probity", and "trustworthiness" towards other persons. It is very difficult to have even incidental contacts with ladinos on a functional basis and to avoid being categorized either as "friend" or "enemy". There is little room for a third category of functional communication. Person and function are inseparable.

Moreover, the meaning of communication within ladino society is very much influenced by the places which communicating people occupy in the social hierarchy. One may accumulate prestige by communicating with someone occupying a higher position while the other is creating a clientele. Hierarchical communication moved by the aspirations of the individual to accumulate prestige, honour and wealth, explains much about the functioning of ladino staffed agencies. Official functions, goals and procedures may be quite different from the values that make them actually work.

Politics

Their desire to maintain their local autonomy explains much of the reluctance of the Q'eqchi'es to engage in politics. They want to keep the government away from their life-world as far as possible. Everything related to the government and politics frightens them. They do not consider themselves to belong to any national political entity and do not feel that there might be something to gain from joining a political party or project of whatever colour. The only level of political organization in which the Q'eqchi'es are interested is the municipal level.

This attitude of rejecting any political involvement except for the local level can also be seen in the ways in which the Q'eqchi'es deal with the renewed armed struggle in parts of the Q'eqchi' region during my fieldwork. After the guerrilla movement had been defeated temporarily in 1983 and 1984, the *guerrilleros* reappeared at the beginning of 1991 in the Franja Transversal del Norte. Their actions were primarily destructive in character: they repeatedly blew up the oil pipeline between Rubelsanto and Lívingston, set finca installations on fire and destroyed infrastructure. Rich ladinos or state agencies were certainly not their only targets. I have spoken to several Q'eqchi'es who were lucky enough to possess a dozen or more cows, but the guerrilleros told them to leave the area within one day. In order to save their lives they had to sell their cattle quickly at far below prevailing prices.

Another type of actions consisted of road blockades and village occupations forcing bus travellers and villagers to listen to a political speech or take some leaflets being handed out. The language used in these speeches and these leaflets was usually Spanish while only a small minority of Q'eqchi'es is able to understand Spanish, so their ideological effects must not be overestimated. My own experiences with guerrilleros were confirmed by priests and others: the guerrilleros were unable to speak Q'eqchi'. Moreover, armed guerrilleros have to eat, a need met by forcing merchants and government personnel to pay a "war-tax" and by "asking" Q'eqchi' villagers for food. As a result of the reappearance of the guerrilla movement the army stepped up its repression against innocent people again.

Since the various peace accords that have been concluded between the guerrilleros and the government in the mid 1990s, political violence of this kind has disappeared in the region. The same holds true for the infamous "civil patrols" in which all adult men were forced to spend one day out of every week or ten days patrolling the community commanded by the nearby army officer.

Four local communities in a regional context

In my fieldwork I particularly focused on eight local Q'eqchi' communities, four of which appear in this book. On the basis of the first phase of my research, which has focused on mapping the whole Q'eqchi' region, I have deduced the most important variables that command the main variations among the local communities. These variables include proximity to urban centres versus relative isolation, the level of market integration, the presence of evangelical churches, and the kind of pastoral policy applied by the Catholic church. On the basis of these variables the four villages have been selected because they represent the most common variations based on these variables. The names of the communities as well as those of the leaders have been changed because information on issues such as access to land and conflicts with state institutions are too delicate to be linked to existing names.

Relative isolation

These four communities have been selected among rural communities because these constitute by far the majority of local communities. Yet, isolation versus closeness to urban centres is one of the variables used to choose the four communities. This variable coincides with the intensity of access to external influences and of the role which intervening agencies play in their life-worlds.

At one extreme we find the village of Rubelpec, which is situated in the centre of the Q'eqchi' heartland and belongs to the country district of San Pedro Carchá (see Map 3). The community has existed since time immemorial and its 125 houses are scattered all over its territory. The 125 households make up an estimated 751 inhabitants. I have particularly focused on 71 of these households. The villagers have many contacts with the nearby towns of Carchá and Cobán. Because of its proximity to the offices of government agencies and NGOs, the village is regularly visited by their employees. It has a consumer co-operative, a school with two teachers and a community hall.

At the other extreme there is Xalihá, situated in the isolated area of Chahal. A few hours walk along a small path takes you to the main road. Once a day a bus goes along this road to cover the 165 kilometres to Cobán which usually takes a day. The village does not have a long history as most of the households settled here in the early 1970s. At present[25], the village has 46 Q'eqchi' households in as many scattered houses which accommodate an estimated 258 inhabitants. Of these households, 40 have been included intensively in my fieldwork. The village has a church, a community building and a school with a teacher. Only few agencies reach the community.

As for external influences, Chaabilchoch and Samox occupy an intermediary position between Rubelpec and Xalihá. Chaabilchoch belongs to the area of Raxruhá in the northern part of Alta Verapaz. From Cobán several times a day a bus leaves for the little town of Chajmaïc (five hours) and from there twice a week, on market days, canoes can take you up the river Chajmaïc to Chaabilchoch (two hours). The army have forced the villagers to build their houses in a real centre. Here there is a school with two teachers and several shops. The 78 houses accommodate an estimated 498 persons. Of these households 39 have been specially included in my fieldwork. Most of the present households settled in the village around 1970. Although it is quite close to the war zones it has not suffered from violence.

To look for Samox, one has to go to the southern edge of the Q'eqchi' area where it "clings" to the very steep slopes of the Sierra de las Minas. It belongs to the Telemán area. The villagers often visit the markets in Telemán and La Tinta. It is a three hours walk to these towns and from there, there are regular bus services to El Estor, to Cobán and to the capital. Most of its 42 households settled there between 1975 and 1982. It has 272 permanent inhabitants. There are six Poqomchi' households, but Poqomchi'es and even the few ladinos in Samox are adopting Q'eqchi' language and rituals. The villagers have built a church and a school (no teacher) made of brick and there is a small shop.

Market integration

The same spectrum involving Rubelpec and Xalihá at the two extremes and Samox and Chaabilchoch in between, emerges in relation to the level of market integration. In this respect I have taken into consideration the number of activities oriented towards earning money and their importance to the local economy, the kind of market-oriented activities (agricultural versus non-agricultural) and the level of purchased inputs in production.

Together all these aspects determine the level of market integration, not just the money income per household. For example the community of Rubelpec has a lower money income per household than either Samox or Chaabilchoch, but much more of the economic activities of the villagers of Rubelpec are mediated by the market than those of the latter two villagers. Almost half of the households of Rubelpec have one or more men who are absent from the community for several weeks or even a large part of the year because they work in the cardamom harvest, rent a piece of land or work as travelling merchants mainly in the Franja Transversal del Norte. It has a considerable group of women who regularly work in Cobán and Carchá. Moreover, Rubelpec is one of the few Q'eqchi' communities in which textiles, mainly huipiles, are produced by women who sell them at the markets in nearby towns. Agriculture plays a marginal role in generating income since each household has access to only very little land. This land is mainly used for the production of food crops for which a considerable level of modern inputs such as chemical fertilizers is used.

At the other extreme, the villagers of Xalihá use their land mainly for subsistence production. Their cash crop production, mainly pigs and rice, and other market-oriented activities are limited. The villagers of Chaabilchoch do earn a considerable income per household from their cardamom production. This income from cardamom has enabled several villagers to build two storey brick houses. Every year some fifty day-labourers come to the village to work for several weeks in the cardamom harvest. The hiring of day labourers and the production of cash crops such as cardamom and coffee indicate a considerable level of market integration in Samox as well.

Evangelical churches

Concerning the third and fourth variable, the presence of evangelical churches and the kind of pastoral policy applied by the Catholic church, quite a different panorama emerges. Xalihá has no evangelicals at all and Samox has only one evangelical household who attends services in a neighbouring village.

By contrast, Chaabilchoch and Rubelpec have significant evangelical minorities. In Chaabilchoch there are thirteen evangelical households. One of these joined the *Iglesia Evangélica de Cristo* in a neighbouring village one year ago. The other twelve households belong to the *Iglesia de Dios de la Nueva Jerusalén* which has its own church building in the village. Rubelpec has a church building of the *Asamblea de Dios*. Five local households as well as several others from nearby communities participate in this church. Five other households belong to the large *Iglesia del Nazareno* church in a neighbouring village which has a total of about 125 member households. In addition, several Rubelpec households have a mixed evangelical-Catholic composition and one household belongs to the Baptist church in Carchá.

Catholic pastoral policies

Almost all the other villagers in the four communities participate in the Catholic church. On the one hand, the pastoral policy applied in the parishes to which Xalihá and Samox belong, has been shaped by Dominican priests who continue to stress the positive value of costumbres. They want customary leaders and catechists to work closely together in organizing both Catholic and customary practices. By contrast, Chaabilchoch and Rubelpec belong to parishes run by Salesian priests who promote only Catholic practices and reject customary rituals. They try to maximize the influence of catechists at the expense of chinames and pasawinq. The policies of these two religious orders constitute two opposing poles within the church. No community with a large evangelical majority or an exclusively evangelical population has been selected because such communities constitute only a small minority.

Not only do these four variables appear among the most prominent variables that distinguish the Q'eqchi' communities, they are also the most relevant ones in relation to the themes of religion and economy which will be dealt with in the next chapters. Nevertheless, the selection of these four communities has its limits in terms of representativity related to all Q'eqchi' communities. To begin with, the practical possibility of being able to work in a specific community played an important role in this selection. As a result, fincas have not been studied in detail although they constitute an important part of local Q'eqchi' communities. The research was slowly but steadily made impossible by the plantation owners or administrators. Production co-operatives have not been selected because of their limited number. Secondly, communities in areas that have suffered from massive violence have not been selected either because they present a very special problematic requiring a very special approach. Moreover the anthropologist Richard Wilson has already paid some attention to these communities (See Note on Methodology). However the absence of fieldwork in these two contexts has been partially compensated by considerable relevant information on these same contexts provided by spokespeople with a regional overview. Moreover I was able to interview an important number of Q'eqchi'es who had fled plantations.

In short, despite limitations, these four villages represent very typical Q'eqchi' communities. Together with the data collected at the regional level, the material stemming from these villages reaches a high level of representativity regarding the Q'eqchi' population as a whole.

3

The Religious Field:
Intervening Churches and Local Specialists

'Once we suffered from a terrible drought. We took the cross from the cemetery and went to the riverbank and to the mountain at the other side of the river. There we sacrificed candles and copal pom and asked for rain. All participated and contributed to buy candles and copal pom, even the catechists did. The evangelicals not. The day after it started to rain. This happened one year ago.'

Religion is part of the Q'eqchi'es everyday life. This quote from some of the villagers of Chaabilchoch refers to just one of the many occasions on which the Q'eqchi'es address certain "persons", in this case the mountain and the rain, who in a profane culture would not be considered living beings. In dealing with crucial issues in their daily life most Q'eqchi'es perform rituals that refer to one or more "persons" in the world of gods and spirits.

The word "religion" in relation to the Q'eqchi'es may cause some confusion because they make a distinction between "customs" and "religion". They use the word "customs" related to those practices and meanings that have their origin in their own history whereas they talk about "religion" in the context of church affiliation in the sense of changing from one church - "religion" - to another.

This distinction points to their two main sources of religious meanings and practices. On the one hand there are customs transmitted from elderly men and women to the younger generations. Some of these customs have a Catholic colonial origin, such as the feast of the patron saint. Other customs, such as the rituals celebrated in honour of the mountain, have no Catholic origin at all. Probably the meanings attached to these customs and their forms have changed considerably over time. The Q'eqchi'es themselves are not interested in whether they have a Catholic origin or not. On the other hand there are the religious practices and meanings offered by the various churches and promoted by Catholic and evangelical leaders. In their meaning-making process the Q'eqchi'es make use of representations and practices stemming both from their customs and from churches and in this process I found them to be very creative. Many respondents emphasized that they had left behind some rituals[1] and ideas, while they started to perform other practices and constructed new representations. Q'eqchi' religion is an ongoing process of reshaping and adapting religious practices and meanings.[2]

In this reshaping and constructing the Q'eqchi'es demonstrate a certain level of autonomy, but to a certain extent they are influenced by those who consider themselves to have authority in religious matters. These religious specialists include the cofradías, the chinames and the pasawinq who encourage the community to practise customary rituals. Moreover, there are catechists and local evangelical leaders who proclaim the representations and organize the practices of the churches they belong to. These specialists belong to the local Q'eqchi' communities. In addition there are agencies of an external origin who intervene in these communities in order to influence their religion: the Catholic church and evangelical churches.

In almost all the local communities in the region one or more church buildings catch the eye. The Q'eqchi'es have invested impressive amounts of time and money in building these churches and church meetings make up an important part of social life. The Catholic church and evangelical churches are the intervening agencies that have most successfully established a stronghold in the life-worlds of the Q'eqchi'es. In the previous chapter it was shown that the Q'eqchi'es to a certain extent identify themselves with their church.

Nevertheless, there are strong arguments for conceptualizing churches as intervening agencies[3]. First, churches do not constitute the primary social units of social identification. These units are the household or family and the local community; identification with a church is subordinate to these. Secondly, priests and religious women[4] display all the characteristics of external actors. They originate outside the life-worlds of the Q'eqchi'es. Except for a few priests and religious women all are non-Q'eqchi'es. They live outside the community which they visit only a few times a year. The experiences of one priest who is known for his positive attitude to Q'eqchi' culture are illustrative in this respect. Released from his pastoral duties he spent an entire year in a Q'eqchi' village, living and working on the land alongside the villagers. After this year the villagers told him: 'We are pleased with the fact that at last we see we can really trust a priest. After all these years we feel you appreciate our customs'. It is doubtful whether other priests have reached this level of confidence in the communities. The number of Q'eqchi' ministers is considerably higher, but they are rarely considered to belong to the local communities.

Thirdly, the Q'eqchi'es deal with external religious specialists in much the same way as they treat other intervening actors. They receive them, are very polite, listen to what they have to say and afterwards select those things and meanings they consider to be useful. Finally, the establishment of churches as a real presence in the life-worlds of the Q'eqchi' communities has taken place only in the last few decades, in the case of the Catholic church this presence in several parishes has since then been interrupted because of army repression.

The discussion of Q'eqchi' religion in this chapter will start with an analysis of the religious specialists: various intervening churches and local religious leaders. In the next chapter the main religious practices and the religious discourse of the "ordinary" Q'eqchi'es will be discussed. In Chapter Five this analysis and discussion will be related to the research questions.

The Catholic church

In spite of many setbacks caused by state repression, the Catholic church is the largest in the region. It has a region-wide network of 27 parishes and parish-like units. This number includes the units that in practice function as a parish, the number of official parishes is much lower. I use the word "parish" referring to all those units that function as such in practice. Each of these parishes usually consists of a parish church, one or more priests, sometimes a convent with three or four religious women and a structure of several hundreds catechists working in an average of about 60 local communities per parish. However, not every parish has religious women and there is even one parish that has no priest.

Only four priests and a few religious women work with the non-Q'eqchi' and urban populations. They deal with rather small groups to prepare believers to receive sacraments, with so-called apostolic lay movements such as the *cursillos de cristiandad*, the *legión de María* and *the encuentros matrimoniales*, and with neighbourhood based groups. These groups focus mainly on religious instruction. The priority of all the other priests and religious women is to work with the Q'eqchi'es, particularly those who live in the rural communities. There are forty priests, some eighty religious women and eight lay missionaries engaged in pastoral work with the Q'eqchi' communities. This means there is one priest and two religious women available per forty Q'eqchi' communities and about 2000 Catholic Q'eqchi' households. Their limited number and uneven spread over the region indicate that these "pastoral agents", i.e. priests, religious women and lay missionaries, cannot themselves attend all these communities and households intensively. As a result, they focus mainly on the organization of a structure of catechists and other lay functionaries. In every community there are several catechists who organize church activities, their structures constitute the backbone of the church.

Catechists receive their training in the parish; the parishes of the bishopric of Verapaz send a few of their experienced catechists to courses in the San Benito centre in Cobán. They transmit what they have learned to their fellow catechists in the parish, who pass this knowledge on to their communities. The standard tasks of catechists are the celebration of the Word on Sunday and preparation of the villagers to receive sacraments. The priest administers these sacraments during his visit to the community or centre. Some parishes are organized in centres, which means that the priest visits only a centre community such as Chaabilchoch. Believers from nearby communities come to this centre to meet him. Usually these visits to communities or centres, the administration of sacraments, the saying of Masses and the instruction of catechists are full-time tasks of the priests. In most of the parishes they also organize youth groups, and the religious women work with Q'eqchi' women and girls. In some 150 to 200 communities there is a group of women that gathers every week or month.

Pastoral work in the parishes is supported by the Catholic radio station, Radio *Tezulutlán*. It is one of the few radio stations that transmit exclusively in the Q'eqchi' language. It is on the air several hours a day and has a mixture of entertainment and instructive programmes on religious issues and on issues such as the prevention of illness. The programmes are very popular among Catholics and evangelicals alike in the various communities throughout the Q'eqchi' region. There is another Catholic radio station in Poptún.

Orders and bishoprics

The pastoral agents, the catechists and other groups in the parishes and the radio constitute a structure that is capable of influencing the religious life within the local communities. However, this structure is quite complex and heterogeneous which seriously hampers any effort to develop a common policy towards the Q'eqchi'es. This heterogeneity is typified by the wide range of countries the pastoral agents come from. Apart from the three Q'eqchi' priests only eleven of the priests were born in Guatemala, the remaining other 33 priests who are engaged in pastoral work come from 13 different countries. Among the religious women there is a similar variety of origins, albeit with a larger proportion of Guatemalans and Q'eqchi'es.

The heterogeneity of the church is also manifested in the importance of the various monastic orders. Only six priests are diocesan; the other 38 belong to eight different congregations. In order of number of priests these monastic orders are the Society of Saint Francis de Sales (Salesians), Missionary Sons of the Immaculate Heart of Mary (Claretians), Order of Friars Preachers (Dominicans), Missionaries of the Sacred Heart of Jesus, Congregation of the Immaculate Heart of Mary (Scheutists), Missionaries of the Precious Blood, Order of Saint Benedict, and the Catholic Foreign Mission Society of the Americas (Maryknoll). There are even twelve different female orders involved in pastoral work. The numerically largest of them are the Sisters of the Resurrection, the School Sisters of San Francisco, the Dominican Sisters of the Annunciation, and the Daughters of Charity of Saint Vincent de Paul.

The orders, both male and female, constitute the main organizations which link the parishes. Between parishes staffed by the same congregation there is much communication and co-operation, including the exchange of pastoral agents. Each order has its own vocation, and pastoral policies are discussed and formulated mainly within the congregations. In the words of the bishop of Verapaz: 'Each congregation has its own project, its own religious profile. How to unite them in a common diocesan project? It is difficult to unite Salesians and Dominicans.' Guatemala has a long-standing history of mendicant orders each going their own way and the bishop is still very dependent on these orders to staff the parishes of his bishopric.

Mgr. Gerardo Flores Reyes of the diocese of Verapaz is not the only bishop who works with the Q'eqchi'es. Parts of the Bishopric of El Quiché, of the Apostolic Administration of Izabal and of the Apostolic Vicariate of El Petén also belong to the Q'eqchi' region. The Apostolic Administration and the Apostolic Vicariate are diocesan-like institutions. They are on their way to becoming fully-blown dioceses with all the usual diocesan institutions and stable parishes. Their status is still missionary.

In short, the wide variety of origins of its pastoral agents, the fact that four bishoprics or diocesan-like institutions are involved, the continuing missionary character of two of these institutions, and the dominant role the various religious orders play make it very difficult for the church to work out a common pastoral policy towards the Q'eqchi'es.

Unity and diversity

In spite of these difficulties there are attempts to develop a common pastoral policy. Every two months the clergy and representatives of the catechists of the Q'eqchi' parishes of Verapaz have meetings to discuss topics of pastoral work. In addition, all the clergy and lay representatives of the Bishopric of Verapaz gather for one week every year to talk about general pastoral issues.

The discourses the various pastoral agents preach in their parishes throughout the Q'eqchi' region have at least some characteristics in common. First of all, the life of Christ, the central issues and stories of the Bible, the meanings of the sacraments, the importance of loyalty to the church and its history are explained. Catechists are instructed in how to use the Bible[5], how to preach in public, the basic elements of the Mass, the celebration of the Word and the liturgy. All warn the Q'eqchi'es to be aware of the evangelical churches.

Secondly, the pastoral agents repeatedly emphasize the need to obey the central moral demands they believe God has made on the Q'eqchi'es. The celebration of the Word and preparation for sacraments such as Baptism and Marriage are used as occasions to instruct the Q'eqchi'es in these moral demands. One should worship God and receive the sacraments. Couples should marry, stay loyal to each other, educate their children and, if possible, send them to school. Each should lead a decent family life and perform the tasks he or she is supposed to perform according to the division of labour within the household. All should abstain from quarrelling and stealing, and serve the community and the church.

Thirdly, almost all the priests and religious women are very interested in improving the social reality of the Q'eqchi'es. They consider the existing social reality not to be in accordance with the conditions God wants the Q'eqchi'es to live under. The considerable efforts of the church in education, health care and economy result from this conviction. Its efforts in education are impressive: 215 primary schools (data 1992), seven institutes of secondary education and about 400 adult education groups directly or indirectly set up by the church. In addition, the church is heavily involved in health care projects: 14 health clinics and several health projects with 900 promoters working in about one-quarter of the local communities. In Chapter Six the church's economic projects will be outlined.

The various priests and religious women have these three elements in common. However, next to these elements the differences begin. Differences of opinion frequently arise, and efforts to co-ordinate the activities of the various parishes easily end up in conflict. Basically there are two central pastoral policies, each with its own group of pastoral agents promoting and applying it. The first policy may be called "sacramentalist" and the other "liberating". The former emphasizes the importance of the sacraments and the exclusive role of the priests in administering them, which legitimates a paternalistic role for the clergy in religious and social matters. Those who apply the latter policy want the clergy to play a rather more serving role ceding room for the laity to participate. The concept of liberation has a central place in their discourse.[6]

Sacramentalist pastoral work

The main protagonists of sacramentalist pastoral work are the Salesians. They apply this policy in the parishes of San Pedro Carchá, Campur, Playa Grande, Chisec and Raxruhá. This kind of pastoral policy is practised in the communities of Chaabilchoch and Rubelpec .

Linked to their exclusive right to administer sacraments, the Salesian priests claim to be the only ones who "possess" the pure doctrine and teachings of the Catholic faith. They do not accept the fact that their understanding of this faith is only their interpretation of God's message to man, based on studying the Bible and Catholic doctrine and influenced by their own cultural background which happens to be non-Q'eqchi'. They think they know the real faith; consequently the fundamental logic of their pastoral work is to transmit this faith to the Q'eqchi' laity. Pastoral work is a one-way street from the Salesians to the Q'eqchi'es. The latter are supposed to passively receive and actively apply what they are told.

The religion they promote emphasizes the performance of standard Catholic practices such as the Mass and the celebration of the Word. Rather abstract notions of a "loving God" and "salvation" play a central role in their view. To achieve salvation one must listen to the Word of God, comply with the moral demands God makes on man and stay loyal to the church. The Bible - or more accurately, their interpretation of it - is the only criterion to use in deciding whether a representation or practice is valid; as a result the Salesian understanding of religion has a universalist claim. The moral values of the Salesians are directed to the individual. In addition to the values outlined above the Salesians stress the requirement of abstaining from drinking, contributing to constructing large church buildings, working hard and improving the material well-being of the household. The Salesians consider loyalty to the church to be more important than loyalty to the village. This is symbolized in the fact that in their parishes children receive their First Communion not in their own community but in the central parish church. The main task of the community of believers is to promote the salvation of individual believers.

As a consequence of their paternalistic attitude, they consider their religion to be antagonistic to the main customary rituals and representations. These are associated with getting drunk, adultery and other vices. The Salesians have organized their parishes in such a way that vital conditions for the reproduction of customary religion become disrupted. Knowledge about how to perform customary rituals and related meanings are usually transmitted from the pasawinq to the youngsters in the community. Gradually, these youngsters may achieve the same status and social position within the community as the pasawinq as they grow older and prove to be respectable persons. By selecting young men to become catechists, the Salesians offer them a shorter road to leadership and prestige. They teach them how to read and write in order to give them access to the Bible and other written texts; they give them training and license them to lead official church activities in their communities. In short, these young men can become important leaders in the community, acquire new skills, receive delegated authority from the priest and have exclusive access to a new written source of religious legitimacy, the Bible.

Many young men consider this Salesian offer hard to resist. As a consequence, in many communities the pasawinq have regarded the rise of these catechists as a threat to their social and religious position. The Salesians do not regret this marginalization of customary leaders because 'they have little positive influence on moral behaviour', as one Salesian priest told me euphemistically. He considers customary religion 'to be something of the past'. 'Traditional religions are dangerous', he continued. 'Everything is fear and magic, ignorance and exorcist rituals. All peoples lose these magic ideas. We go for the future'.[7]

In social matters the Salesians are just as paternalistic as on religious topics. In their view the problems the Q'eqchi'es face are caused by lack of education, both religious and social. The Salesian view of social education, like religious education, portrays the Q'eqchi'es as mere receivers of knowledge transmitted to them from outside. The Salesians themselves are able to provide the religious content, but in social matters they co-operate with state agencies. For example, they invite employees of sub-divisions of the ministry of agriculture to come to the villages to teach the Q'eqchi'es new production techniques. In the 129 primary schools and three secondary boarding schools they run as well as in their adult education programmes, they use material produced by the ministry of education. The idea that there might be valuable elements within Q'eqchi' religion and economic strategies is absent. Both in religious and in social matters they believe they have to force a rupture with customary practices and representations and indigenous knowledge.

The Salesians promote a religion that disenchants nature and social relations; these are understood in a secular way. However, these secular views on nature and social reality are linked to religiously based morals intended to motivate the individual believer to improve his or her economic performance: God wants man to work hard and improve his or her economic situation and the way to do so leads through integration in the market economy.

As to the problematic relations between Q'eqchi'es and Kastii, the Salesians have a policy of ignoring most of the cultural content of Q'eqchi' identity, while at the same time supporting the notion of "believers in God" as a unit with which to identify. This category includes both believing Q'eqchi'es and Kastii, thereby reducing the importance of Q'eqchi' identity.

Liberating pastoral work

The Salesians are fiercely criticized by those who follow a clearly opposed pastoral policy. Most of the Dominicans, Scheutists, and Precious Blood Missionaries, some of the diocesan priests and several congregations of religious women have developed a policy of liberating pastoral work. They apply this policy in several parishes including Panzós, Telemán, La Tinta, Tucurú, San Martín Cobán, Chahal and Poptún. They also have considerable influence on diocesan institutions in El Petén and Verapaz, such as the Department of *Pastoral Social*, or Social Pastoral Work, in Cobán. The communities of Xalihá and Samox belong to parishes in which this pastoral policy is pursued.

Liberation theology is the main source of their pastoral orientation, but it has to be stressed that we are dealing here with a very specific blend of pastoral policy which has developed out of the local clergy's experiences within their own social and religious context. This means that the concept of Ecclesiastical Base Communities, for example, a crucial element in liberation theology, has not been taken over in the Q'eqchi' region. There are two reasons for this.[8] First, the church is dealing with pre-existing local Q'eqchi' communities each with their own community life and structures and the church cannot claim these pre-existing communities to be "theirs". The idea is to reinforce the existing local community rather than to replace it with an artificial church community.

Second, the religious women and priests carrying out liberating pastoral work are only too aware of the fact that they are external actors intervening in pre-existing local communities. This awareness makes them reluctant to think in terms of Ecclesiastical Base Communities because that concept embodies a rather romantic notion of equality between community members and the clergy. This relation is problematic and as such an object of discussion.

In the last twenty years the policy of liberating pastoral work has changed considerably. The most important change constitutes a shift of emphasis from socio-economic issues to socio-cultural ones. In the 1970s the central pastoral method was called "See, Judge and Act". This meant that the laity was encouraged first to observe their situation, then to decide whether this situation is right or wrong in the light of what God wants for man, and finally on the basis of this judgement to take action to change this reality. In Chapter Two we saw that the issues focused on were mainly socio-economic, such as the injustice of low wages or unequal land distribution and land conflicts. Now more attention is paid to customary religious practices and representations. The objective of liberating pastoral work is to become rooted in the culture and identity of the Q'eqchi' communities. The clergy who work along these lines no longer want to neglect the role of customary leaders.

The pastoral agents concerned emphasize that they do not have a monopoly on the Catholic message in a pure form; their understanding of it is influenced by their own social and cultural background. In addition, in the various cultures they deal with, such as the Q'eqchi', there are tokens of the presence of Christ to be discovered. Consequently, pastoral work has to focus on reflection by both clergy and laity to discover legitimate values and elements stemming both from official texts such as the Bible and from Q'eqchi' religious practices and representations. Of course there are standard Catholic representations, dogmas and practices, and every priest and religious woman is supposed to promote them. However, in the practice of pastoral work there is considerable room for interpretation. The protagonists of liberating pastoral work try to articulate official Catholic practices and representations with customary ones. They call this the "inculturation of God's Word".

This objective of articulation is most clearly visible in the various efforts at liturgical renewal. Experiments to develop a Q'eqchi' Mass in which various customary rituals and symbols have been integrated into the Mass have taken place in several parishes. The crucial point is that the Sacred Host is made of wheat, but it can take the form of a *tortilla*[9], which of course is much more relevant to the Q'eqchi'es. For example in Poptún the Mass is sometimes celebrated in customary sacred places such as in a cave or on the bank of a river. It includes the offering of maize, meat, candles and *copal pom*.[10] The sacred land is addressed, food and cocoa are served by the pasawinq and customary dances are performed. These are typical ingredients of customary practices (see next chapter).

However, the positive attitude of the priests towards customary rituals and meanings in part entails the reinvention of such practices and meanings. For example, the picture they present of the history of the Maya in catechist training courses and the parallels they draw with the people of Israel is very positive but may not stand the test of historiographical scrutiny (see Wilson 1995: 268-274). While I participated in some of the "Q'eqchi'-ized" Masses several Q'eqchi'es told me that they were unfamiliar with most of the practices that were presented by the priests as having a specific Q'eqchi' origin. Nevertheless, they added that they were very pleased with the intentions of the priests to adapt the Mass to their *na'leb*, their culture. They felt appreciated as Q'eqchi'es.

Liberating pastoral work aims at providing a leading role for pasawinq not only in their communities but in the church as well. In the parish there is a pasawinq council which is consulted on all important aspects of pastoral work.

Representatives of pasawinq from the various communities gather regularly in the parish church to exchange knowledge about customary rituals. They talk about Q'eqchi' history and identity, and encourage one another to continue or renew the performance of customary practices in their communities. In the parish of Chahal the pasawinq council organizes the yearly pilgrimage to the sacred mountain of *Qana' Itzam* near Cahabón to perform the customary ritual of *mayejak*.[11] In several parishes the priest has asked the pasawinq to "purify" customary practices and meanings. The results of their purification remain unclear, but several pasawinq told me that the performance of "customs" includes having a few cups of *b'oj*[12] but not getting drunk. The issue of drinking has become an ideological one because the Salesians - and the evangelical churches - equate customary rituals with getting drunk.

In principle, the pastoral agents who promote liberating pastoral work understand social relations and treat nature in a profane way, but linked to a religiously based moral judgement of social reality. The attention paid to socio-cultural matters does not keep the advocates of liberating pastoral work from taking many initiatives focused on social matters. The parishes, the Bishopric of Verapaz and the Vicariate of El Petén all have their social projects. In particular, the Department of Social Pastoral Work of the diocese of Verapaz is very active in this respect. It has grown out of the emergency efforts to welcome hundreds of displaced people who came down from the mountains after hiding from the army for several years. The Department still spends a major part of its resources on projects dedicated to the communities where these families have settled, but it began to work with other communities affected by violence too, mainly in the San Martín Cobán parish. The Department has also set up a legal assistance subdivision to provide legal assistance to communities with land problems with landlords and with INTA. Chapter Six contains a more extensive discussion of the Departments' projects.

The Department tries to strike a balance between assisting the local communities and avoiding taking responsibility for solving their problems. The Department's aim is to encourage them to solve their problems themselves using their own resources, technologies and skills. Everyone in the local community should participate; they should take the initiative themselves, and any material assistance must be matched by instruction that enables them to run the project themselves. Instruction and training begin with an appreciation of indigenous knowledge, external knowledge is supposed to reinforce their own initiatives and strategies. The Department tries to refrain from creating a dependent attitude. This means that the Department is very restrictive in providing material assistance for free.

This objective has motivated the Department to set up a network of *agentes multiplicadores de pastoral social*. The idea is to invite each local community to select one of its members to become a multiplicador. The multiplicador's task is to motivate the local community to undertake efforts to solve its problems. He receives training from the Department, is supposed to pass this knowledge on to his community and seeks assistance from the Department when his community decides to take action. The network of multiplicadores de pastoral social should not be understood as an effort to create a trade union or a political organization; it is an organization of communities to promote self help and ethnic identity.

The clergy promoting liberating pastoral work encourage the Q'eqchi'es to identify with a Q'eqchi' ethnic group. They draw attention to the customary practices and meanings the Q'eqchi'es have in common, encourage catechists and pasawinq at the parish and diocesan level to discuss these matters, and play an active role in reinventing Q'eqchi' tradition. These activities all encourage the emergence of a supra-local Q'eqchi' identity on the one hand. On the other, the positive attitude towards customary practices and meanings entails a symbolic reinforcement of the identification with the family and local community.

Between two extremes

The concept of sacramentalist pastoral work in its encompassing version described above is put into practice in some five parishes, the encompassing concept of liberating pastoral work in some seven parishes. In most parishes the clergy take a position in between these extremes applying a policy that has elements of both. These clergy do not have an explicit policy of either encouraging or confronting customary practices and the influence of the pasawinq. They just let them go their own way without much interference.

Nevertheless, tensions between the clergy over various pastoral policies often dominate diocesan institutions and programmes. Radio Tezulutlán usually transmits a modestly positive picture of customary religion, while the same station's programmes transmitted from the Salesian *Centro Radial* in Carchá occasionally ridicule customs. The diocesan training programme for catechists representatives was paralysed for some time in 1991. The Dominicans had organized several courses in which a parallel was drawn between the people of Israel and the Mayan people which caused the Salesians to withdraw their catechists for some time.

Evangelical churches

While the Catholic church retains missionary characteristics after a presence of several centuries in the Q'eqchi' region the largest of the evangelical churches, the Iglesia del Nazareno, officially has a mature status. In 1974 the district of Verapaz became the first regular Nazarene district outside the United States. It functions independently in institutional and financial matters (Samandú 1989: 32-33).

Like the Nazarene's church most of the evangelical churches began as initiatives by missionaries from the United States. In their initial years these churches were heavily dependent on resources and guidance from North American centres. Moreover, institutions and foundations linked to the United States government had clear geo-political reasons for supporting the spread of these churches all over Latin America (Dominguez 1994: 12-22; Huntington 1994: 23-33; Stoll 1990). However, most of these churches rapidly reduced much of their external dependence, are staffed by Guatemalans, and their functioning can only be understood by conceiving of them as Guatemalan institutions in the Guatemalan context.

In the following section the various categories of churches, the characteristics of their discourse, the main explanations that are put forward to explain their rapid expansion in the last two decades and their relations with the Catholic church will be outlined. I use the overall term "evangelical" to include all the churches that I present in this outline. I avoid the term protestant because it has a negative connotation in the region. If they are addressed politely they are called '*los hermanos de la capilla*', i.e. the brothers of the evangelical church.

Categories of evangelical churches

The main evangelical churches in the region can be classified into four categories. First, there are the historical churches, which have their origin in the Sixteenth century Reformation in Europe. Their discourse emphasizes the importance of the Bible and of doctrine, but the ministers do not have an exclusive relation with the sacred world in the way Catholic priests do through their monopoly over the administration of sacraments. Nevertheless, the ministers of these churches have received extensive theological and pastoral training. Their relations with the believers and the services are formal and their services are not very participatory (Similox Salazar 1991: 7, 10, 14-15, 20-21, 26). The main representatives of this category of churches in the Q'eqchi' region are the Baptist church and the Mennonite church. These churches hardly ever criticise the Q'eqchi'es for practising customary rituals and accept responsibility for social problems. They run a few primary schools, some small-scale health projects and local clinics and provide agricultural training.

In the Q'eqchi' region the Nazarene's church is the largest within a second category of evangelical churches, the so-called "Holiness" churches. The ministers of the Nazarene church receive a thorough theological training, first in the *Instituto Bíblico Nazareno* in Cobán, and then in the *Instituto Teológico Nazareno* in the capital. They are elected for two years with a 75 per cent vote by the members of the local church. They work together with *mayordomos* who are elected by every fifty believers and are supervised by the district superintendent (Samandú 1989: 32-33).

The ministers of "Holiness" churches emphasize personal conversion and the work of the Holy Spirit. This work becomes apparent in the moral behaviour of individual converts; it is through this behaviour that salvation is to be achieved. Central doctrinal issues are the holiness of Christ, the redemption of sins through Christ's sacrifice, His resurrection and imminent return. Praying, moral behaviour, dedication to God and the Bible, proselytising efforts, church attendance and the need to avoid being contaminated by the world in order to save one's soul from sin are the most important practices. The Nazarenes' services have a rather austere and moderate character and Bible-study meetings are important. Their position on customary rituals is rather negative: these are considered to be contradictory to the Bible's message (Samandú 1989: 35; Similox Salazar 1991: 7, 11, 16, 21-22, 26-27).

The Nazarenes do not want to be contaminated by the world, but they do not portray the world as the devil's arena either. They are not indifferent to social reality. They run some schools and they have set up the *Centro Educativo Kekchí* in Cobán. Their organization, the *Asociación Guatemalteca de Beneficiencia* (AGUABEN) provides medical services and helps communities to build water wells. The Nazarenes have a charity project for children, widows and orphans.

Pentecostal churches constitute the third category of evangelical churches. There are many of these churches in the region, but the largest ones are the *Asamblea de Dios*, the *Iglesia de Dios del Evangelio Completo*, and the

Príncipe de Paz church. The latter is an original Guatemalan initiative. They have much in common with the Nazarene church, including the practices they require the believer to perform, the central importance of the Holy Spirit's work and of the Bible, and literal interpretation of the Bible. However, there are several important differences. The work and gifts of the Holy Spirit are expressed not only in correct moral behaviour, but also in ecstatic and emotional experiences, singing, dancing, speaking in tongues, miracles, appearances, the laying on of hands and spiritual healing in massive meetings. The preaching in their services does not focus on doctrine nor is it intellectual, but rather emotional (Similox Salazar 1991: 23).

Another difference is the strong charismatic character of Pentecostal ministers who stress personal contact with the believers. Pentecostal ministers have had little theological training, nor do they have a monopoly on explaining Bible texts. The individual believer has access to the Bible and his or her direct experiences of the presence of the Holy Spirit need no mediation by a minister. As a result there is little to prevent believers from establishing a separate church. There is a strong tendency towards fragmentation in a countless number of churches.

Pentecostal churches are characterized by the use of simple black-and-white oppositions such as that between the world - the arena of the devil - and the church - the only source of salvation in Christ. In their view it makes no sense to try to improve the situation of the world, the only thing that counts is to seek for salvation in Christ, to follow His demands, and to join His struggle against Satan. After all, at the imminent end of time Christ will return and save the world. They consider social projects and customary rituals to be irrelevant or even pagan. However, Pentecostalism encourages the believer to push for economic advancement because this is conceived of as an expression of the blessing of Christ (Garrard 1986: 194; Martínez and Samandú 1990: 58-61; Similox Salazar 1991: 7-8, 17-19, 23-27).

The neo-Pentecostals constitute the final category of evangelical churches. Their religious discourse and practices have much in common with Pentecostal churches. The most significant difference between them is the fact that the latter concentrate their proselytising efforts on the indigenous and poor ladino people while the neo-Pentecostals focus on the middle and upper classes. They are marked by a strong feeling of being God's chosen people with a special mission (Martínez, Samandú 1990: 48; Similox Salazar 1991: 8, 19-20, 25-26). Another category of churches that have established a foothold within the Q'eqchi' region are considered to be on the margin of the Christian tradition: the Jehovah's Witnesses and the Mormons.

Quantitative growth and its explanations

In the last two decades evangelical churches have experienced impressive growth in terms of their numbers of members, converts and local churches, but not all have had the same success. Reliable numbers referring to this growth in the Q'eqchi' region are not available. The data that are available do not cover the Q'eqchi' region. Nevertheless, in Table 3.1 the number of established local churches in the three departments that include most of the Q'eqchi' region are presented.

Established churches are those that have a minimum membership of about twenty members which in the Q'eqchi' region means more or less twenty families. These churches have a council of elders or deacons, a full-time minister and a church building (Similox Salazar 1991: 60). Many local churches do not meet these criteria and hence have a missionary status; this means that in practice the numbers of local churches are much higher.

Table 3.1: number of evangelical churches in three departments in 1980 and 1987:

Department/evangelical churches	1980	1987
Alta Verapaz	213	537
El Petén	263	420
Izabal	304	451

Source: Opazo Bernales 1990: 37-38, based on figures from the evangelical institute PROCADES.

Assuming that the average membership per church has not fallen dramatically, that the trends are similar in the Q'eqchi' region, and that within that region the trends among the Kastii are similar to those among the Q'eqchi'es a first conclusion is clear: the number of evangelical Q'eqchi'es has risen dramatically between 1980 and 1987. My own estimates based on interviews with evangelical leaders and with priests and religious women in every parish, point to between twenty and thirty per cent of Q'eqchi'es belonging to an evangelical church in 1991/1992. Despite the fact that the largest evangelical church is a "Holiness" one - the Nazarene church - the overwhelming majority of evangelical churches are Pentecostal.

The growth of evangelical churches, especially Pentecostal ones, is a national phenomenon in Guatemala. The earthquake of 1976 is generally marked as the starting point for this rise. Guatemalan authors and spokesmen have put forward several reasons why Guatemalans have resorted to evangelical churches in massive numbers since then.

The first explanation points to the weakness of the main competitor in the religious field: with state support evangelical churches have occupied the space left fallow by the Catholic church. Nationwide, the Catholic church presents a similar picture as in the Q'eqchi' region: it did not establish a stable presence in the daily life of believers in several regions before 1980, and because of the violence at that time it disappeared from many of the conflict-ridden areas of Guatemala. The Catholic church was attacked explicitly by the army in these areas - it even had to close the entire diocese of El Quiché in 1980 - while evangelical churches were encouraged by the army to increase their proselytising work. Almost all of the evangelical churches urged their believers to abstain from involvement in politics, but when general Efraín Ríos Montt - member of the neo-Pentecostal church *El Verbo* - took over the presidency many ministers felt that the struggle against Satan could really take off. In many parts of the country ministers did not hesitate to accuse priests and Catholics of being communist, with the obvious consequences. Not all evangelical churches acted as a 'politically conservative monolith' (Garrard 1986: 208-214), but most of them clearly sided with the army. Conversion to an evangelical church offered a safe haven in a violent context.

Similar ideological arguments have been put forward concerning the relations between the evangelical churches and finca administrators and owners. On the coffee fincas many administrators and owners explicitly try to keep Catholic pastoral agents out, while actively supporting the evangelical churches in their search for converts among the Q'eqchi'es living on their fincas. Evangelical churches teach their members to accept all worldly authority, including finca owners and administrators.

Explanations pointing to the relative advantages of evangelical churches vis-à-vis the Catholic church are complemented by a second category of explanations emphasizing the internal logic of development of the evangelical churches. It is maintained that following several decades of preparation the groundwork had been laid for successful conversion campaigns by 1976. Massive conversions were the logical outcome of Bible translations into indigenous languages, literacy projects to enable converts to read the Bible, and efforts to train and instruct indigenous local church leaders and preachers. Samandú supports this argument with extensive data from the evangelical churches in Guatemala in general and the Iglesia del Nazareno in Alta Verapaz in particular (Samandú 1989: 30-32; Samandú 1990: 81-88).

Garrard is not convinced by this argument. She says that the evangelical churches did not grow faster in communities and among ethnic groups where this groundwork had been laid than in communities where this was not the case. She maintains that radio broadcasting - the evangelical churches have set up several full-time radio channels and regularly buy time on commercial networks - had much more impact on a mainly illiterate population (Garrard 1986: 198). In any case, the evangelical churches were there and prepared to receive massive numbers of new converts when the opportunity to do so arose.

These are explanations for the growth of evangelical, especially Pentecostal churches in the country as a whole. To what extent these explanations apply in the case of the Q'eqchi' region is hard to say, but some remarks can be made. To begin with, the areas that have been struck by massive violence (Cobán, Chisec, Playa Grande, Sayaxché, El Estor) have a considerable evangelical Q'eqchi' population - up to one third of the Q'eqchi'es. Also in areas where fincas dominate, one third of the Q'eqchi' population belongs to an evangelical church. Most of the fincas have several evangelical churches on their territory. There are relatively low percentages of evangelicals in those areas that have not suffered from massive violence and in which there are relatively few and small coffee fincas.

On the one hand these facts suggest that violence and coffee fincas do influence evangelical growth, but on the other hand these percentages of evangelicals are not very much higher than the twenty to thirty per cent, which is the average percentage in the whole Q'eqchi' region. Consequently, other factors must be taken into account. Moreover, simple population growth could account for the absolute growth in the number of evangelicals. For instance, the town of San Juan Chamelco has about 5,000 inhabitants. Almost all of them are Q'eqchi' and more than half the population belongs to an evangelical church. By far the most important one is the Nazarene church. It has been there since the beginning of the century and an important part of the Nazarene community was born into their church. In any case, the crucial question is why so many Q'eqchi'es have converted to an evangelical church. Their motivations for doing so will be discussed in the next chapter.

Customary leaders

Priests, religious women and ministers visit local communities only occasionally. Religious life in both rural and urban communities is mainly organized and led by local religious leaders. These local religious specialists, i.e. those belonging to the local community and playing a leading role in local religious matters are the subject of this section. They include customary leaders, catechists and evangelical leaders. In general customary leaders have few institutional connections outside of their local communities, whereas catechists and local evangelical leaders are supposed to transmit what they have learned from priests, religious women and ministers onto their communities. The customary local leaders that will be dealt with here are the chinames, the cofradías and hermandades, the pasawinq, and the *ilonel* or *tuul.*

Chinames

Chinames are a customary religious institution that was established in the Q'eqchi' region as a result of Catholic colonialism (see Van Oss 1986: 89-92, 109-115), but since then chinames have become an integral element in customary religion in every rural Q'eqchi' community. Only couples, i.e. men and women who have started their own household, can be chinames. Their assistants, or *mertomes*, may be single men. Chinames are always organized in a hierarchical way. The first couple of chinames (*xb'enil*) commands the second (*xkab'il*), the second commands the third (*roxil*), and so on. In general this hierarchy consists of about five couples, sometimes assisted by up to twenty mertomes. In the villages I studied, relations between the chinames were based on co-operation, not on authority. Chinames are almost always dedicated to one or more specific saints, usually the patron saints of the community.

The "office" of chinam rotates. A couple is chinam for one or two years and then they look for substitutes. The new couple are presented to the community which has to approve of them and during the patron saint's feast the "change of chinames" takes place. The leaving xb'enil explain the obligations to the new chinames and the statue of a saint is handed over to the new xb'enil. This may be a statue of the patron saint, but another saint may serve too.

The election of a couple as chinam is a token of the respect they are held in by the community. This respect is accumulated by service to the community and co-operating in community tasks for a considerable number of years. A couple first becomes mertomes and then slowly passes through the levels in the chinames hierarchy. Despite the fact that chinames are expected to contribute substantially to religious feasts, there is no relation at all between the economic performance of a household and which couples are chosen as chinam. In the four communities I studied in detail, those who are chinam or have served as chinam are equally distributed over the various categories of economic stratification.

The tasks the chinames execute are twofold. First, they have their obligations towards the Catholic church. They take care of the cemetery, they keep the church building clean and decorate or repair it, and they build a new one if necessary. They keep the keys to the building, the chinam women put fresh flowers on the altar every few weeks, and the xb'enil man welcomes the priest when he visits. The second task of the chinames is to organize customary rituals that are performed by the community as a whole, especially the feast of the patron saint. They fix a date for the celebrations, visit the households to ask for contributions - Q. 5 to Q. 20 from each household in Samox - and are expected to contribute the lion's share themselves, which can be as high as Q.

250, or a pig in Rubelpec and Xalihá. They ensure that the statues to be carried in the processions are in good shape and organize the music (harp, violin, chirimía, or marimba). The women prepare the meal which the men serve. They ensure that there are enough candles and copal pom, the standard ingredients of all customary rituals, and they receive guests such as social scientists from foreign countries. The role of the chinames in customary rituals is mainly practical. They do not lead these rituals or give talks in public. In other words, they do not have an important discursive role.

This second task of the chinames is the most controversial. In Samox and Xalihá chinames perform these tasks in an all-encompassing way, but in Chaabilchoch they do not perform any customary rituals at the community level at all. In Rubelpec their customary tasks are limited to the patron saint's feast, but in the next chapter it will be shown that this feast has lost much of its importance there. These differences regarding the customary role of chinames coincide with differences in the policy the various parishes apply. In the parishes run by protagonists of liberating pastoral work, the chinames perform both categories of tasks and are regarded as important leaders in all kinds of community affairs.

In the Salesian-staffed parishes the role of chinames is limited to the first task. They are incorporated into the regular parish-promoted activities and are urged by the priests and catechists to relinquish customary practices. In Chaabilchoch the existing line of chinames "of the community", i.e. those responsible for taking care of the church *and* customary activities, was supplanted by a new line of chinames "of the centre" when the parish established its centre buildings in Chaabilchoch. This new line consists of four chinames with eight mertomes; their tasks are limited to the first one.

In Rubelpec several chinames co-operate with the catechists, but it has become increasingly difficult to find new couples willing to become chinames. Some relate this difficulty to the fact that the chinames are expected to contribute a considerable amount of money to the celebration of the patron saint's feast, but it seems more likely that the motivation to become a chinam has diminished considerably because chinames no longer play a prominent role in religious activities in Rubelpec. In Xalihá, where the average income per household is lower than in Rubelpec (see Chapter Seven) and where the contributions expected from chinames are similar, the chinames have no problem in finding new couples to replace them.

The role and importance of the chinames is not only influenced by parish policy; the evangelical churches do not accept the role of chinames at all.

Cofradías and hermandades

Cofradías and hermandades are the urban variants of the chinames. Most of the towns in the Q'eqchi' region have one or more of these hermandades and cofradías, especially the larger towns of Carchá and Cobán. Carchá has two important hermandades - those who wear a *túnica blanca* and those who wear a *túnica morada* - and at least fifteen cofradías. In Cobán there are six or seven hermandades and at least eight cofradías. However, even the small town of Lívingston has seven cofradías. Hermandades and cofradías can have hundreds of members.

Both terms, cofradías and hermandades, are often confused. In general the hermandades take charge of activities during the Holy Week and in some towns at Christmas as well, whereas the cofradías are dedicated to a specific saint and celebrate the feast day of this saint. Their organizational structures are different as well. For example the *Hermandad del Calvario* in Cobán consists of a council made up of representatives of the neighbourhoods to which the hermandad belongs. There is also a committee which organizes the Holy Week processions. The neighbourhoods elect the members of this committee. Like other cofradías, the *Cofradía de San Martín*, based in the same neighbourhoods as the Hermandad del Calvario, is organized on the same principle as the chinames: the hierarchy of xb'enil, xkab'il, roxil, xkaahil, etc. The members of the committee and of the cofradía have to be more than just respectable persons. The president of the committee and the xb'enil of the cofradía need to have a lot of money as well. For example, the former is expected to spend a lot on food that is served to hundreds of people on the Tuesday of Holy Week. So in contrast to the chinames, there is a relation between economic performance and presidency of an urban confraternity.

Cofradías and hermandades constitute arenas in which ethnic and political power relations become visible. The membership of most of them is confined to Q'eqchi'es, but the most prominent have a mixed Q'eqchi' and Kastii membership. The *Hermandad del Señor Sepultado*, a prestigious hermandad which belongs to the cathedral, is led by middle-class Kastii who walk at the head of the processions, while those who carry the heavy structures on which the statues of the saints are borne, are Q'eqchi'es. However, the fact that the Hermandad del Calvario - which is exclusively made up of Q'eqchi'es - decided a few years ago to say their prayers during the processions in Q'eqchi', is considered by many an important symbol of Q'eqchi' emancipation. Before that time this hermandad spoke Q'eqchi' only at internal meetings, in public they prayed in Spanish. These examples reflect the historically ambivalent character of confraternities in Guatemala. In the previous chapter we saw that, on the one hand, they have a Spanish origin and were used to collect tribute in colonial times and to organize forced labour until recently. On the other hand, they have become indigenized and play an important role in customary religion (Cabarrús 1979: 56-57; Falla 1979: 78).

In many parishes priests are not very positive about the cofradías and hermandades. The Salesians take a rather hostile stance towards them. 'People get drunk, these rituals are meaningless and cost a lot of money', one of the Salesians told me. Interestingly, the Salesians have not been able to suppress the confraternities in the town of Carchá, while in the villages they have been much more successful in incorporating the chinames into parish-promoted discipline. In the parish of San Marcos (Cobán), the cofradías have only recently restored relations with the priests. In the San Martín parish (Cobán) the clergy legitimate their activities, but do not give much priority to them.

In general the zest for participating in the confraternities has lessened in recent times. The number of active cofradías is dwindling and the willingness of youngsters to participate has decreased. It has become difficult to find enough people to carry the saints in the processions.

Pasawinq

A couple who have served as chinames and reached a respectable age are regarded as pasawinq, or wise old men and women. Literally, the term pasawinq refers only to men and *pasaixq* is the relevant Q'eqchi' word for elderly women, but the term pasawinq is often used related to the couple. In Xalihá and Samox they are consulted over every important community issue, and several of them take the lead in the performance of customary rituals. Here pasawinq have a rather discursive role: they pray in the name of the whole community at customary rituals and they transmit knowledge on customary rituals to the youth of the community. Pasawinq in both Xalihá and Samox told me that they feel very much supported by the council of pasawinq in their respective parishes.

In both Chaabilchoch and Rubelpec the role of the pasawinq is much more limited. In Chaabilchoch the pasawinq have been marginalized from decisions concerning the church. In Rubelpec there is a group of pasawinq who join the catechists at Saturday to prepare the celebration of the Word the next day; but they do not play an important role in either the preparation or the celebration. In both communities there is a group of pasawinq who do not participate in the celebration of the Word and who want to continue customary practices. They are rather isolated and some of them are accused of being witches. According to some Rubelpec pasawinq the younger generation are not interested in customary practices and meanings any more; there is little transmission of knowledge from the pasawinq to the young people.

The reduced role of pasawinq in Chaabilchoch and Rubelpec is closely related to the policy of the Salesian priests. Their attitude to customary practices is negative but they do not attack them openly. In the words of one of the catechists of Chaabilchoch:

> 'The priests do not say no nor yes. The priests say it is all right to go to Tactic or Esquipulas [customary sacred places - hs] if we have the money to do so; if not we had better not go. Moreover, they say that we have our own place to pray and be heard here in the community.'

In short, the priests say customary practices are superfluous: it is not necessary to perform them when the villagers stick to parish-promoted practices. But by their way of talking about customary religion they create an opposition between customary religion associated with moral vices on the one hand and parish-promoted practices, the Bible and moral behaviour on the other. The real intentions of the Salesians was accurately discerned by one of the pasawinq in Rubelpec: 'Customs have disappeared, because the priests and the bishop are praying that they may disappear'.

In short, as in the case of the chinames the pasawinq retain a predominant role in community and parish life promoting customary practices in Dominican staffed parishes. In Salesian run parishes the pasawinq are either incorporated into parish policy or they are marginalized.

Ilonel and tuul

Sometimes pasawinq are also iloneles; such is the case in Xalihá. Both iloneles and tuules may use their connections with mighty "persons" in the universe either to cure or to inflict damage on someone. An ilonel is a customary healer whereas a tuul is a witch. Each of the five iloneles I interviewed in four communities denied any suggestion that they also work as tuules, but in each of these communities several villagers told me that every ilonel is also a tuul. He - I have not come across any female ilonel - can use his influence for both good and evil purposes.

Every treatment by an ilonel starts with prayers after which the ilonel takes the patient's arm. By feeling his or her pulse and blood circulation, the ilonel is able to diagnose the illness and to determine how much life the patient still has. Life is not considered to be something that exists or does not exist; the amount of life a person has is variable and can be quantified. Having a "shortage" of life means being ill.

The ilonel treats several categories of illness; some such as malaria are universally known; the Q'eqchi'es classify other kinds of diseases in a very specific way. The latter include for example *rilomil tzuul, xiw*, and *awas*. A patient suffering from rilomil tzuul, or 'seen by the mountain', suddenly starts to vomit, faints, is depressed, loses his or her memory, gets a headache and looks black or pale. Soon the person will die. In the case of xiw, 'spirit loss' or 'fright', the spirit leaves the person's body. All of a sudden the person starts to shake and sweat, he or she falls backwards, goes insane and will die in a few days. Awas is the expression and result of an offense against someone or something in the neighbourhood. Everything and every "person" has its specific rules which Q'eqchi'es must respect. For example, if Q'eqchi'es do not observe all the specific ritual rules they are supposed to obey when they plant their maize, this maize may adopt very strange forms and illnesses.

A nice example of awas is expressed in the following story which one of the iloneles told me. Once a few merchants came to his village to buy cardamom. The villagers told the merchants they were willing to sell, but they should return later. The merchants wanted to do so after some time, but the villagers did not want to sell because the prices were too low. They sent a boy to the merchants to tell them that the cardamom was not ready yet. Despite this, the merchants came to the village, became angry, started to make trouble and finally left. Two weeks later the boy became seriously ill with stomach problems. The ilonel examined him and concluded he was bewitched. He prayed to God to improve the boy's life and gave him an extract of herbs to drink. The boy vomited and threw up cardamom shells. This story shows that illness can be a physical expression of a social problem: disturbed relations with someone or something imbued with a spirit in the patient's vicinity. It can only be cured by turning to God to restore the patient's amount of life.

The main role the ilonel plays is to restore the disturbed relations with the "ones" who are able to provide life. For every illness there is a special prayer, which he repeats several times in the presence of the patient. Each prayer is dedicated to a special important "person" in the universe, which can be a saint or a mountain or God. This repertoire of prayers is complemented by a repertoire of herbs. For each disease there is a specific herb. The patient is supposed to make tea from this herb and drink or bath in it. The idea of adding to the life of someone is very apparent in the fact that iloneles are often called in when a woman is pregnant but unable to give sufficient life to the embryo. Sometimes the ilonel also gives meat and tortillas to the patient to eat or to place on special parts of his or her body to feed the illness. Such feeding may convince the illness to leave the patient.

Not every community has an ilonel but iloneles in some communities, such as the ones in Xalihá, are famous enough to draw patients from far away places to visit them to be cured. Some train classes of young boys to become iloneles whereas others have a conflictual position in the community. This conflict may be due to the very negative attitude of ministers and Salesian priests towards them, but also to the fact that they are suspected of being tuul as well which induces fear in other community members.

In short, the iloneles' role in the life of local communities is rather variable and coincides with the importance of other customary leaders. In some places they are among the prominent leaders of the community, but in other communities their role has been downgraded along with that of other customary leaders.

Catechists

The presence of customary leaders dates back to colonial times or even earlier; catechists have a much more recent origin. They have been introduced in the context of the Catholic restoration since the 1960s. At present there is a group of catechists organizing church life in every community. Unlike customary leaders the catechists are appointed for life on an individual basis. The rotating principle is not applied to them nor do they work as couples. In general there are between five and fifteen male catechists in every community. Only in those communities where a women's group meets regularly there are a few female catechists, but their role in standard Catholic practices is limited. Moreover, in practice the priests or their fellow catechists are the ones who choose and appoint them, not the community as a whole. As a result, the community has fewer formal means of controlling the catechists than it has of influencing chinames; an increasing role for catechists means a reinforcement of the public role of men. An appointment as catechist by the priest is a shortcut to local leadership. On the other hand, without the implicit approval of the community a catechist can do nothing.

The catechists told me that among their principal motivations to take on the role was their desire to feel appreciated by the community. They want to play an active role in their community and enjoy the opportunities for going to the parish or even Cobán to participate in courses. Moreover, several of them told me that they felt a vocation at the moment they decided to become a catechist, that they were called by God. Four catechists in Rubelpec and Chaabilchoch said that before becoming catechists they used to drink a lot and their lives were a mess. Becoming a catechist meant making a change in their personal life, stopping drinking, behaving in a proper way, and restoring their family relations.

In all communities catechists perform *grosso modo* the same activities. They lead the celebration of the Word, advise parents on the significance of the baptism of babies, and instruct young people on the value of the First Communion. They advise young couples on family life, help widows to do their work, pray for community members who are ill and help them in maintaining their households.

In addition to these standard activities the catechists play various roles. In the Salesian-run parishes there is a strictly defined hierarchical organization with the priest at the top. One catechist is made responsible for each standard activity. So-called instructors occupy a higher place in the hierarchy than "ordinary" catechists. They lead and train catechists from several communities, see to it that the latter perform their tasks in their communities, give sermons in the celebration of the Word and pass on the meanings and contents the priest has imported to them.

The so-called *ministros* occupy a even higher position. There is one ministro in every local community. They take Holy Communion from the parish to the communities where they administer it to the believers on Sunday. They obtain their training directly from the priest and solve problems in close co-operation with him. The ministros decide when instructors have any doubts as to Bible interpretation, inform the priest about what is going on in the villages, choose the persons to become catechists and keep an eye on them. Their control function is underlined by the fact that they work in a community other than their own most of the time. In this way their double loyalty problem - to the priest and to the community they belong to - is solved. The women who lead the women's groups are trained by the religious women, but they are supposed to conform to the guidelines laid down by the ministros.

In practice this hierarchical system in the Salesian-run parishes influences the way the church intervenes in the communities and how it is viewed by the Q'eqchi'es. To begin with, there is no place for deviant opinions in church meetings. Moreover, in Rubelpec being a Catholic means being a "collaborator of the catechists". The villagers associate Catholicism with the work the catechists do. This association should be viewed in the light of the fact that there are evangelical churches in the village as well; it is a means of social and religious identification. Nevertheless, it indicates that in Rubelpec "ordinary" believers do not believe they have much influence in deciding what is legitimately Catholic; they are inclined to leave that decision to the catechists who depend directly on what the priest tells them. It goes without saying that this hierarchical conception of Catholicism reflects a strong power position on the part of the clergy, and to a lesser extent on the part of the catechists. In addition, these local leaders have access to the benefits of the Salesians' social projects, such as literacy, health care and education projects.

In other parishes responsibilities and relations among the lay leaders are not so clearly formalized and circumscribed as in the Salesian-run parishes. In these parishes there is hardly any differentiation among the catechists. Those who receive instruction and have contact with the priest may vary and there is more room for their own initiatives. In their contacts with the communities the priests do not emphasize their authority as much. In both Samox and Xalihá differences between catechists and other community members are not very clear-cut. Here the villagers talk about Catholic activities as community matters which are not monopolized by the catechists. The catechists clearly play a leading role, but the things they do are open to discussion.

Those priests who practise liberating pastoral work try to avoid concentration of power and influence in the hands of catechists. For instance, agentes multiplicadores de pastoral social, health promoters and literacy orientators are explicitly recruited among non-catechists. This limitation on the catechists' influence creates room for the community in general and pasawinq and chinames in particular to take initiatives.

In practice, the catechists have resisted this positive attitude towards customary religion and the role of pasawinq. The majority of these catechists had been trained before this new positive attitude towards customary religion developed in the 1980s. Before that time catechists were told that customary rituals were either irrelevant or blasphemous and relations between catechists and customary leaders were tense.[13] For example, in the late 1970s the parish of Telemán was led by a priest who urged catechists to break away from the authority of the chinames and pasawinq. He used the new translation of the New Testament into Q'eqchi' to prove that customary rituals had no place in the Bible. Chinames from various communities banded together and threatened to kill him.

Since the new positive attitude towards customary religion developed many catechists have found it hard to follow this change in pastoral policy. Now there is a further structure legitimized by the parish, the pasawinq council, which has eroded their exclusive parish-promoted authority. In the parish of Poptún the pasawinq are even encouraged by the priest to take over tasks that used to form part of the catechists' standard repertoire such as deciding on who should receive First Communion, giving talks and advising young couples who are going to be married. As a result, the priests' effort to restore the authority of the pasawinq is sometimes resisted by their catechists. On the other hand, especially in the town of Cobán there are catechists who sometimes take a more radical stance in favour of customary practices and meanings than the clergy themselves do, but it is the clergy's explicit policy there to stimulate the catechists to take their own initiatives.[14] Nowadays, in parishes run by priests who apply the concept of liberating pastoral work relations between chinames, pasawinq and catechists have relaxed. In both Samox and Xalihá they co-operate closely with each other in both parish-promoted and customary rituals and invite each other to become one another's *compadres*[15].

The catechists are generally able to make the "ordinary believers" participate in their activities, but in the areas that suffered from massive violence the catechists have a difficult job in this respect. In these areas they are confronted with the destruction of community structures and sometimes the pasawinq reject the role of catechists.

Evangelical leaders

In more than half the local Q'eqchi' communities local evangelical leaders have become part and parcel of religious life. In the communities I studied none of the evangelical churches had a permanent minister. The church in Chaabilchoch is visited by a minister every two weeks and once in a while ministers from other towns visit the church. In the absence of a regular minister two or three members of the church lead the services. The Asamblea de Dios church in Rubelpec welcomes a minister every few weeks and a so-called "worker" every week. The Nazarene church in the neighbouring community is visited by a minister every Sunday, but their meetings and services on Wednesday, Friday and Saturday are led by lay leaders. None of these local leaders has received any training. The only "condition" is that they should be able to read Bible texts and explain them, but no one supervises them on the correctness of their explanations.

The answers the respondents of these churches gave to my question referring to the influence of external and local leaders on their local churches suggest that this influence is in fact very limited. Referring to ministers and lay leaders from elsewhere a member of the Nazarene church said: 'There is no need for anyone to come from far away to lead our services'. A member of the Chaabilchoch Iglesia de la Nueva Jeruzalén stressed that: 'There is no guide who leads us. Each individual member tries to follow the Word of God and we just organize ourselves in the church'. The members of this church stressed that it does not make much difference to their meetings whether a minister is present or not. It is said that there is more emphasis on Bible study when he is there, but the respondents do not consider this to be a major difference. Only one respondent, a member of the Asamblea de Dios in Rubelpec, told me: 'Without those who come from Carchá we cannot do much', but he added that they have several weekly meetings in their church at which they do not need any leader at all. I did not come across similar expressions of autonomy vis-à-vis external and local religious specialists among Catholics.

Competing religious specialists

As we saw above, the relations between religious specialists are quite variable. Before the first half of the 1980s the catechists were trained to play a leading role in their communities at the cost of the influence of chinames and pasawinq. Nowadays, in the parishes where the concept of liberating pastoral work is applied the catechists, chinames and pasawinq work closely together, but in parishes in which a sacramentalist pastoral policy is applied, there is much more continuity with the situation prior to the 1980s. There the pasawinq and chinames are either incorporated into regular parish-promoted practices or they are marginalized. In parishes in which neither a clearly liberating nor an overtly sacramentalist policy is pursued, there are few conflicts between customary leaders and catechists; they all go their own way in promoting their activities without interfering with one another.

In the evangelicals' view, the Catholic faith and customary leaders and practices go together. Relations between evangelical leaders on the one hand and catechists and customary leaders on the other are usually delicate. The Catholic church and the evangelical churches regard each other as clear religious competitors. Relations used to be openly conflictual, especially in the years of massive violence. Since then tensions have relaxed and the times when ministers denounced priests and priests accused evangelical leaders of being collaborators in bloodshed are over. In general, ministers and priests ignore each other, but do their utmost to keep believers from passing over to a competitor.

There are examples of both open conflict and co-operation. The one evangelical household in the community of Samox has a hard time. The man tries not to offend the Catholics, he even helped to build the Catholic church, but his fellow villagers do not appreciate him. The local development committee only gave him half the land he is officially entitled to and his fellow villagers refuse to help him plant his maize. By contrast, in a neighbouring village the minority of Nazarenos were just building a new church. They knew I had good connections with the Catholic church. Once they stopped me and asked whether the bishop would be willing to send them corrugated iron sheets for the roof of their church. Apparently, ecclesiastical divisions were not very fundamental to their way of thinking.

In general, relations between catechists and evangelical leaders are peaceful, but strong potential for conflict remains. In both Rubelpec and Chaabilchoch Catholics and evangelicals started recently to plant their maize in mixed groups of Catholics and evangelicals (see next chapter). Nevertheless, the evangelicals criticize the Catholics for their drinking, dancing and moral deficiencies and for worshipping saints. In addition, leaders of the various churches are very wary of efforts to convert each other's believers. In Chaabilchoch the evangelicals offered to help the Catholics to build their church if they would help them to construct theirs. The Catholics turned down the invitation.

The case of one of the school teachers in Rubelpec is instructive. According to one of the Catholics a new school teacher started to work in the village two years ago. She turned out to be evangelical and - again according to this Catholic - began to preach to the children. The parents went to the municipality and some civil servant wrote a letter to the ministry of education. The ministry in turn urged the teacher to leave, which is what she did.

The competition between the various churches can partly be explained simply in terms of interests. In terms of discourses there is quite some coincidence between, for example, the Salesians and the evangelic churches. The delegitimization of customary practices and representations, the Bible-centred character of their discourse, and the central idea that salvation can be achieved by observing individual moral standards and by loyalty to the church catch the eye. The struggle against the consumption of alcohol, the erosion of the social and religious role of pasawinq, the stimulus to improve economic performance, and the promotion of the church as the central focus of identity also come to the fore. Of course, there are important differences such as the role of the sacraments, the central authority of the priests, and the role played by social projects in Salesian policy; but the similarities are striking. The clearest contrast to Pentecostalism within the religious field is represented by liberating pastoral work.

4

The Religious Field:
Practices and Meanings of the Q'eqchi'es

The influence exercised by religious specialists on the Q'eqchi'es is an indispensable part of Q'eqchi' religion, but the core of this study focuses on the religion of the "ordinary" Q'eqchi'es themselves. This religion is the subject of this chapter. It is based on interviews with respondents who have a regional overview and on the fieldwork I did in various local communities. Of course, on the basis of this material I can only discuss the most important religious practices and representations, allowing for their common denominators as well as their main variations. It is impossible to go into the details of the rich diversity of rituals and meanings of every individual Q'eqchi' and Q'eqchi' community.

This chapter begins with an emphasis on practices. The most salient religious practices performed by the Q'eqchi'es and the meanings related to these practices will be analyzed in the first section. In the next section these meanings will be brought together to detect the common denominators as well as the main variations within the religious discourse of the Q'eqchi'es. These religious practices will be presented according to their source: those that have their origin in customary religion, those promoted by the parish at present, and those that are stimulated by the evangelical churches. These categories are not unequivocal nor are they mutually exclusive. Practices which may be promoted in one parish may not be stimulated in another. Many customary practices are actually promoted by parishes which apply a liberating concept of pastoral work. Moreover, most of the Q'eqchi'es use practices and meanings from these three sources as "inputs" into their meaning-making process. Within this process, these meanings and practices do not stay the same and one of the questions to be raised in this chapter is precisely to what extent "ordinary" religious meaning-makers combine and redefine inputs from different sources. However to do so these sources must first be distinguished.

Customary practices

The first category of practices that will be outlined are customary ones. The most eye-catching ones of these practices are: the feast of the patron saint, the *mayejak*, the planting rituals, the *b'antioxink* and the *wa'tesink re li kab'l*.

The feast of the patron saint

The patron saint's feast has its origin in Catholic colonialism but it no longer belongs to standard practices promoted by the Catholic church. Only priests who apply the concept of liberating pastoral work show a positive interest in its observance. Usually a community has one or several saints after which it is named. Since these saints have their own days on the calendar, one or several days are celebrated each year to honour them. In an urban context there is usually one patron saint for the whole town plus one for every neighbourhood.

One of the most elaborate celebrations of this feast I have come across took place in Xalihá on January 13 and 14, 1992. The priest arrived on the afternoon of the 13th and was received by the xb'enil man. In the meantime other chinam men slaughtered a few pigs while the chinam women were busy preparing the food for the evening. After a few hours all the villagers came together in the church and the priest celebrated a Mass. After that the emphasis shifted towards customary religion and the pasawinq men took the lead. All the villagers gathered in front of the church on a little meadow lit by the moon. The pasawinq put four large candles in a square and a large piece of copal pom in the centre, which were lit. Several villagers explained to me that the four candles represented the four corners of the universe while the copal pom stood for the villagers offering their sacrifice to everyone within it.

The ritual that followed is called *yo'lek*, which literally means to keep vigil. It started when the pasawinq began to say the Lord's Prayer and Hail Mary. After that all joined in, repeated these several times out loud and began saying their particular prayers out loud in an unco-ordinated way. They expressed their worries, such as the fear of poor crops for example, and mentioned all the important "persons" in their universe. After a while only one of the leading pasawinq, *Qawa' Bex*, stayed on and addressed the universe in name of the community. He mentioned the names of God, Santa María, the sun, the moon, the rain, the wind, the thirteen central mountains in the Q'eqchi' region, the surrounding mountains and villages, the saints, the Lord of Esquipulas (their patron saint), several other saints, the men and the women, the pasawinq and pasaixq of the community, the children, the houses, the crops, the trees, the animals, the priests, the religious women, Cahabón (the place of origin of many of the villagers), the bishop, the pope and the ancestors. He addressed these "persons" repeatedly in a random sequence.

By way of addressing these "persons" the villagers intended to create a harmonious relationship with them. After mentioning their names, the pasawinq indicated the good things that everyone in the universe was doing. He asked for forgiveness for cutting down some trees, for a good harvest and protection against all sorts of problems and appealed to those in the universe to keep the animals from eating too much of their crops. Qawa' Bex was talking about vital and practical aspects of the life of the villagers. The yo'lek was wound up with some Lord's Prayers and Hail Marys after which all gathered in a building next to the church where there was food, chatting and laughing. All joined in and danced to marimba music, men and women in separate parts of the building. Meanwhile, for those who wanted to go on in a contemplative manner there was harp and violin music in the church.

In the early morning, a procession left the church headed by the pasawinq carrying a cross and some candles; it ended up in the house of Qawa' Bex. There he thanked everyone for joining in, again mentioned the main "persons" dwelling in the universe and stressed the importance of all the customary rituals which he considered as gifts from God. The next day another procession carried the cross from Qawa' Bex's house back to the church. During the Mass that followed a few couples were married and the so-called "change of chinames" took place. The departing chinames handed over the image of Santa María to the new ones, the women chinames placed incense, food and flowers on the altar and the men buried a little meat and cocoa in the ground, burned candles and copal pom and a short yo'lek took place on the meadow. So much for this particular feast in Xalihá.

In Samox there are two saints' days, one coinciding with Christmas and dedicated to San José and Santa María, and another held on the Friday before Palm Sunday and during the Holy Week, celebrated in honour of *Jesús Nazareno*. Both feasts have their own line of chinames and are performed using the same ingredients as the feast of Xalihá. In addition, some of the pasawinq go to a nearby mountain to sacrifice candles, copal pom and meat to this mountain as well as to have a yo'lek.

The community of Xalihá is dedicated to the Black Christ of Esquipulas. Christ is supposed to have appeared with a black skin at Esquipulas, now a famous place of pilgrimage in the Guatemalan department of Chiquimula. In 1953 church leaders and conservative politicians organized a tour of his statue to every corner in the country in order to reinforce faith and to mobilize the people against the supposedly communist regime of Jácobo Arbenz Guzmán. The villagers are unaware of all this. They know that "their saint" is an important one so he is an excellent saint to serve as their patron saint. They hardly refer to Christ: to them, the *Señor de Esquipulas* is just another saint.

The Señor de Esquipulas is a clear example of the villagers attaching meanings to a symbol, which are different from its "official" version. To them their saint stands for the unity and well-being of the community. The community cannot live without him. In the words of some respondents:

'The saint helps us unite the community. We do not want to think about what might happen to us if we did not celebrate his feast... Not celebrating his feast is as if there were no people in the community.'

The patron saint symbolizing the unity of the community is a common phenomenon among the Q'eqchi'es, not only among the villagers of Xalihá.

In both Xalihá and Samox, almost all the villagers participate in these feasts. In Rubelpec the feast has changed considerably in recent years. It used to last several days with much music and dancing, and many villagers told me it would end in fighting and drunkenness. In recent years the priest has been celebrating a Mass on San Esteban's day, the first of November, and afterwards all but the chinames go home; the chinames have a meal together. There is a procession from the house of the departing xb'eniles to the house of the new ones carrying the statues of several saints. The chinames pray before the saints. Some of them told me that they ask the saints for protection, thereby expressing their faith in the personal power of the saints. However, they went on to say that the saints should be seen as images only and that they are actually praying to God. Apparently, they felt the need to defend themselves against evangelicals criticising them for seeing saints as gods, and certainly the priest would not be very pleased to see them praying to saints.

San Esteban's feast in Rubelpec does not have the same significance as the patron saints' feasts in Xalihá and Samox. It is not complemented by customary practices such as the yo'lek or the mayejak and almost all but the chinames and mertomes participate only in the Mass. The evangelicals do not bother about San Esteban at all. The patron saint of Chaabilchoch, Santa

María, has her day on the tenth of May, but it does not arouse much enthusiasm among the villagers, here nothing special is done.

The fate of the patron saint's feast in Rubelpec and Chaabilchoch illustrates what has happened to this feast in most of the communities in the parishes run by the Salesians. It used to be celebrated for several days, but now and the Mass has taken its place. The common meal continues, but the rest has disappeared. The only place in the Carchá area where the patron saints' feast has remained outside the clergy's control is the town itself.

Mayejak

The idea of the patron saint has its origin in Catholic colonialism whereas the central "persons" that are addressed in other customary rituals have an indigenous source. These rituals mainly focus on the mountain and the valley where the community is situated, which provide the community with their crops, their animals, their health, i.e. with the essential things they need to survive. In order to secure these things they have to address this *Tzuultaq'a* (*Tzuul* means "mountain" and *taq'a* means "valley" in the Q'eqchi' language) through a variety of rituals, one of which is called *mayejak*.

Literally the word 'mayejak' means 'to sacrifice', but it refers in particular to a ritual performed by the community just before the land is cleared. This usually takes place in March and April, at the start of the main maize cycle. The pasawinq may decide to perform more mayejaks, for instance when a flood or a drought threatens the crops. These "intermediary" mayejaks follow the same sequence as the most important one in March or April and which in Xalihá and Samox is celebrated in a very comprehensive way. In February the chinames and pasawinq decide on the dates when the rituals will be performed and start to collect money from each household to buy the necessary copal pom, candles, turkeys, cocoa, fireworks and food. In Samox prayers are said during the nine days preceding the mayejak.

In Samox the 1992 mayejak started with a celebration of the Word in the afternoon. The things that were to be sacrificed such as the copal pom, the candles, the cocoa, the meat and the tortillas, were placed on the altar. The chinam women circled the church building three times while they sang and played the guitar and the tambor. In the evening the male chinames placed candles in a cross, then burned copal pom and all the villagers lit a candle. Then the first chinam turned towards the north and started praying; the second chinam joined in the prayer and turned south, the third chinam did the same while turning east and the fourth turned westwards. After that, one of the pasawinq continued to pray out loud in the name of the community.

The chinames told me that the four winds referred to the entire universe and to the land related to the Tzuultaq'a. The pasawinq addressed all those who are important in the universe in much the same way as the yo'lek in Xalihá: those present, visitors, the animals and crops belonging to the villagers, the houses, nearby villages, the priests, the religious women, the bishop, the pope, God, Christ, several saints, the sun, the moon, the wind, the rain, and the important mountains. As to the Tzuultaq'a, he first addressed some important and more distant mountains such as *San Pablo Xucaneb'* and *Qawa' Kojaj* (see Map 2) and then the nearby mountains. The pasawinq thanked all these "persons", especially God and the mountains, for all the good things they provided to the villagers in the preceding year. Then he asked for a good harvest for this year, that their crops and animals may grow well, and that insects and worms will not eat all the crops. He asked for protection and that the visitors and neighbouring villages may live in peace. It would seem that all these things depend on God and the mountains.

The meeting was concluded by a meal served to everyone and prepared by the chinam women. After this ceremony some eight male pasawinq gathered the things that were on the altar and, in groups of two, walked to nearby mountains to the north, the south, the west and the east. A similar ceremony was performed on each of these mountains and the pom, candles, cocoa and turkey meat were sacrificed to the mountain. They "sowed" these things; they put the turkey and cocoa in the ground, thus into the skin of the Tzuultaq'a. At the same time representatives of the community, both men and women, joined those from other communities in Telemán and went to some of the central mountains such as San Pablo Xucaneb' and *Chi Ixim* in Tactic to perform the same sacrifice ceremony. On their return they were received by the other community members. So much for this specific mayejak in Samox.

In Xalihá the mayejak has the same three basic elements: the meeting of the whole community, some pasawinq go to nearby Tzuultaq'as and other pasawink go to some of the central mountains. Only in recent years have the villagers started to come together to say farewell and to wait for the pasawinq who go to a nearby or central Tzuultaq'as. In the past, the pasawinq practised the mayejak without the villagers getting together. Two pasawinq visit a special cave in the nearby mountain of *Santa María Semococh* to perform their mayejak. They have to leave outside all objects made of materials that do not have their origin in their own life-world such as combs, hats and mirrors. Meanwhile Qawa' Bex joins the pasawinq from other communities for the pilgrimage to the mountains *Qana' Itzam* and *Qawa' Siyab'* near Cahabón.

This pilgrimage is a way of confirming their roots in the Cahabón area from which they migrated a few decades ago. The same holds true of the pasawinq from the settlement areas of El Petén and Izabal who go to the central mountains of Calvary Cobán, Kojaj, San Pablo Xucaneb', or Chi Ixim. It restates their relations with their places of origin. In the settlement areas the pasawinq do not visit nearby mountains because there are none in these areas. Instead, they visit caves which represent the sacred landscape to them.

At the mayejak rituals in Xalihá and Samox, the pasawinq address God and various other "persons" such as the sun, the rain, the wind and the moon. Qawa' Bex told me that when he visits the mountain Qana' Itzam, a sudden wind sometimes rises: 'It is God announcing that He is also there and asking for attention'. However, the pasawinq primarily address the Tzuultaq'a. In the words of one of the Xalihá villagers: 'The mayejak is directed towards the mountain while the celebration of the Word is especially addressed to God'. In Xalihá and Samox it is the community, represented by the pasawinq, which presents itself to the Tzuultaq'a.

Similar community style mayejak rituals used to be performed in Chaabilchoch and Rubelpec, but significant changes have taken place in these communities. In recent years there is a group of some eight men in Chaabilchoch who go to the mountains in Tactic, Cobán and Cojaj once every few years to do their mayejak. Nevertheless the other villagers no longer contribute to cover the expenses, the same group does not visit nearby mountains, and there is no meeting attended by everyone nor a yo'lek in the village. Here the mayejak has become a matter of individual initiative. The others do not feel represented by those who go to Cojaj and Cobán, most of them do not even know that there is a group going there at all. An old lady told me that she is one of the few villagers who go to a nearby mountain to burn candles but others criticize and even accuse her of being a witch. Needless to say that knowing the present state of the mayejak, I was very surprised to hear that all except the evangelicals had gathered the year before during a period of drought to perform a mayejak ritual along the river to ask for rain.[1] The drought was sufficient reason to at least temporarily reactivate the mayejak.

In Rubelpec the mayejak had a similar fate. Several respondents associated the loss of the community mayejak to evangelization, the Word of God and the influence of the priest. One of them told me: 'The pasawinq used to tell us that we have to ask the mountains to bless the harvest, but with evangelization all this has changed. There is only one living God'. Nevertheless, there are some practices in Rubelpec that substitute for the community mayejak. First of all in April, most of the Catholics go in pairs to visit several of the central mountains such as Calvary Cobán and Tactic. There, they perform the same practices as the pasawinq of other communities and ask for the same things. Secondly before they clear the land, the Catholics pray individually, burn copal pom and candles and put a cross on the land. They ask for the usual things: for permission to cultivate the land, for protection against accidents and snake-bites, for a good harvest, health, food, and enough rain and sun. The evangelicals do the same except for the copal pom, the candles and the cross.

In short, in Rubelpec there is some level of continuity with the past. Almost all the villagers feel the need to pay ritual attention to the clearing of the land. They perform elements of a mayejak and ask for the same things as in a mayejak. Moreover two thirds of the respondents address both the Tzuultaq'a and God on these occasions while only one third of them only address God. For most of the respondents the Tzuultaq'a remains an important "person" who refers to customary meanings. The evangelicals only address God but pay ritual attention to these moments, and they ask of Him the same things which pasawinq would request from the Tzuultaq'a. The main difference with a mayejak ritual is that almost all of the villagers ignore the nearby mountains - the only Tzuultaq'as they address are the central ones - and that they perform these practices individually. In the words of one of the villagers: 'We cannot do this as a group because not all of us agree to do so.'

Another practice which substitutes for the mayejak in Rubelpec is the fact that Catholics offer money and part of their crops to the health clinic of the religious women in Tzunutz or to the church in Carchá at Christmas and after the Holy Week. The members of the Asamblea de Dios do the same to their church. All give thanks to God and ask for more good harvests. This might be a continuation of all sorts of contributions which the Indian communities were supposed to make to the Catholic church since colonial times (see Van Oss 1986: 79-108) and of the tithes which the evangelicals are supposed to pay to their churches, but the fact that they use the term mayejak for their gifts points to a practice which is substituting for the customary mayejak.

Referring to the mayejak the same picture emerges as regarding the patron saint's feast: in most places these rituals are performed in a comprehensive way, such as in Xalihá and Samox. In Lancetillo a revival of mayejak rituals is even taking place. The places where the mayejak has lost much of its communitarian character are mainly situated in the Salesian-run parishes and in the areas that suffered most from violence due to the destruction of community structures, the death of many pasawinq and the atmosphere of suspicion within communities. However, the example of Rubelpec shows that both Catholics and evangelicals may work out substitution practices that show a significant level of continuity, both in practice and meanings, with the community mayejak. Even catechists assist in these practices.

Planting rituals

Once the land has been cleared and prepared, the maize can be planted. To this moment in the maize cycle almost every Q'eqchi' pays ritual attention. Planting rituals are performed at the household level, which coincides with the fact that most of the land in the communities has been allocated to individual households. The maize is planted at the end of the dry season, just before the first rain falls in June.

Planting rituals show a remarkable uniformity all over the Q'eqchi' region. They start with a preparation period of several weeks. The men of the community decide among themselves whose maize is going to be planted on which day. During this preparation period the man of the household selects the seed to be planted and the couple abstains from sexual intercourse for several days or weeks. The Q'eqchi'es consider the planting of maize as something similar to sexual intercourse. Planting means inserting one's seed in the earth, which is considered to be female. Consequently only men are allowed to plant, and having sex during the preparation period would mean adultery. Both sexual intercourse and planting precede the creation of life and refer to fertility. The women heads of household can do all kinds of agricultural labour except the planting. They call in a son, a brother or a neighbour to do it.

The night before the actual planting takes place the man slaughters a turkey, part of which is to serve as food, while the rest is to be sacrificed. Chickens are not accepted as a sacrifice because they do not originally belong to the natural surroundings of the villagers, but the Q'eqchi'es are practical when there is no turkey available and slaughter a chicken. The man puts the seed on the altar of the house and burns candles and copal pom. Most Q'eqchi'es put cocoa and blood from the turkey or part of its meat on the seed. Some get together at this night and even organize some music, but usually the man of the household keeps vigil and prays on his own.

In the early morning, the man goes to his land. He puts candles in a square and burns copal pom in the centre as a sacrifice. He prays and plants the first seeds. Most of the respondents put a cross on the land and bury a piece of meat, turkey soup, cocoa or the water they used to wash the turkey. After that, the man returns to his house where about fifteen relatives, compadres, friends and neighbours are waiting. They pray together; the man takes the group to the plot of land and together they proceed with the planting. They stand in a row, each carrying a stick and a bag of seeds. The row moves slowly forward, the men use the sticks to make holes and put some seeds in every hole. Once the planting is over, they return to the house where, assisted by neighbouring women, the woman is waiting for them to serve lunch. The next day, the man joins the group which is going to plant the land of another household.

In Xalihá and Samox almost all the villagers consider the planting rituals to be indispensable for a good harvest. The meanings they attach to the planting rituals are similar to those of the mayejak. The villagers address several "persons" including God, the Tzuultaq'a, the sun, the moon, the rain, the wind and the saints. The local mountains as well as some of the thirteen central Tzuultaq'as receive special attention. The copal pom and candles which they burn and the cocoa and meat they put in the ground are sacrificed to them. The villagers request permission to cultivate the land, ask for protection against illness, accidents and snake-bites, plead for an abundant crop and ask the animals not to eat too much of the crop. The man who addresses the Tzuultaq'a during his prayers the night before the planting and on his land in the early morning, represents the community much as the pasawinq represent the community during the mayejak. This idea of representation is also reflected in the group-wise planting of maize.

Most Q'eqchi'es attach a very special symbolic importance to maize. They consider maize to be their 'seed of life', imbued with a spirit stemming from the Tzuultaq'a. In the words of one of them: 'Maize is alive, it is people'. As a result, during the planting rituals it is not only the Tzuultaq'a as the source of maize who will be addressed but also the maize itself. The attention which the man devotes to the seed and the blood, the cocoa and meat he puts on the seed the night before the planting, are ways of reactivating the life or spirit of the maize to make it grow well. The joyful atmosphere during the group-wise planting serves the same purpose. The cross which many villagers place on the land symbolizes the spirit of maize: 'The god of the good harvest', as a Xalihá villager said. Some also relate the cross to Christ's death while to others the cross symbolizes the universe and their land. We have here a good example of a symbol having both customary and official Catholic meanings.

Also in the eyes of a large majority of the Catholics of Chaabilchoch and Rubelpec, their food and daily subsistence depend heavily on the performance of these rituals. This majority perform more or less the same rituals as the villagers of Samox and Xalihá. However, among them a variety of views exists about specific elements of these rituals and the meanings attached to them. In Chaabilchoch and Rubelpec only half of the Catholic respondents put blood on the seed and place a cross on the land. Those who do so attribute to these practices the same meanings as the villagers of Xalihá and Samox. Others just ask God to bless the seed when they keep vigil, reject the practice of putting blood on the seed and place a cross on the land only because Christ died on a cross. In Rubelpec everyone believes that maize has a spirit. Here there is discord about the sacrifice of meat as well. Half of the Catholic respondents in Chaabilchoch and Rubelpec reject this practice while others said explicitly that they do offer this sacrifice.

These differences are closely linked to the question of to whom the villagers address themselves when they pray during these rituals. In Chaabilchoch and Rubelpec a large majority address both God and the Tzuultaq'a, but a considerable minority pray only to God. Only a few actually know the names of nearby Tzuultaq'as; the mountains they pray to are the central Tzuultaq'as. All mention the rain, the wind, the sun and the moon in their prayers, but some address them as "persons" while others only ask God and the Tzuultaq'a to send them enough rain, sun and wind for their crops to grow well.

All the evangelicals in both villages pay ritual attention to the planting of their maize. They hold a service attended by all their fellow church members in their house or in the local church the night before the planting. If the service is held in the house, they put their seed on the table (they do not have an altar), keep vigil and pray, and some burn candles. No one puts meat or blood on the seed or burns copal pom. The morning after, the man goes to his land, prays and plants the first few seeds. He does not offer a sacrifice nor does he put a cross on the land. He then returns home where a mixed group of Catholics and evangelicals is waiting for him. They pray, plant the maize and have a meal.

In short, concerning both Catholics and evangelicals in Chaabilchoch and Rubelpec, there is a considerable level of continuity in relation to the planting rituals in Samox and Xalihá. Almost all of the participants pay ritual attention to this moment and ask for the same practical things needed for their survival. Most of the Catholic respondents perform the known customary practices with only a few elements causing disagreement. The evangelicals perform some customary practices, but the controversial elements which refer to the Tzuultaq'a and to the spirit of maize are left out. In its place they have an official practice promoted by the church - a service - and they pray only to God, but they ask God for the same practical things. The fact that even in Rubelpec almost everyone considers the planting rituals of crucial importance is all the more remarkable because agriculture is far less important to the local economy than in the other communities (see Chapter Seven).

The main discontinuity lies in the much more prominent role which God plays in the prayers of the villagers of Rubelpec and Chaabilchoch compared to those of the villagers of Samox and Xalihá. The evangelicals leave out the Tzuultaq'a altogether. In Chaabilchoch and Rubelpec God has taken over most of the relevant meanings of the planting rituals that are attached to the Tzuultaq'a in Xalihá and Samox. Nevertheless a large majority of respondents go on to address the Tzuultaq'a as well, albeit only the central thirteen ones.

Planting rituals are mainly performed when planting maize, but the planting of other subsistence crops such as beans also receives ritual attention. In contrast, the planting of cash crops such as cardamom and coffee does not receive any ritual attention. The only doubtful case I have come across refers to rice planting in Xalihá. The villagers did not agree about whether rituals should be performed at the rice planting, which may be related to the fact that rice is both a food and a cash crop and was taken up as a crop recently.

Such disagreement does not exist regarding the planting of maize, that is on their own land. Disagreement does arise as to whether these rituals should be performed when maize is planted on rented land. On such land the villagers of Samox perform planting rituals and plant their maize group-wise whereas the villagers of Chaabilchoch do the same individually without any ritual.

B'antioxink

The ultimate goal of the maize cycle is the harvest. In three of the villages almost all of the respondents pay ritual attention to this occasion. Chaabilchoch is the exception: twenty per cent of the households do not do anything special during their maize harvest while the others only do so when the harvest is a good one.

These rituals are called b'antioxink, or thanksgiving. Those who perform these rituals place a few of the new cobs of maize on the altar of the house, pray and invite friends and neighbours to have a meal with them. The Catholics burn copal pom and candles and, together with the maize, they take the cross to the house to symbolize the transfer of the spirit of maize to the house. Some of the villagers of Rubelpec visit some of the central mountains as well. The evangelicals of Rubelpec come together in the church and in the house of the household whose crops are going to be harvested. They bring the first cobs to the church and pray. In the house they pray again and have a meal.

Most of the respondents in the four villages address their prayers to God and the Tzuultaq'a and give thanks for the harvest and protection. For some of the villagers of Chaabilchoch God has replaced the Tzuultaq'a as the one who provides them with maize. According to them maize is given directly by God with no mediation by the Tzuultaq'a, and the church - not a mountain - is the place to offer sacrifice. Five respondents express this idea by bringing a bag of maize to the church as a token of their gratitude towards God. In the words of one of them: 'It is like a loan from a bank: when we return this loan the bank is satisfied'. He compared the church and God to a bank that lends them life, and after the harvest they have to return this loan of life to God.

Wa'tesink re li kab'l

The performance of customary practices is not limited to the agrarian cycle; finishing the construction of a house is another occasion which requires such rituals. At least, all but a few households in most of the villages I studied think that way. The exception is again Chaabilchoch, where one third of the respondents does not consider this moment to have any special importance.

The relevant customary ritual is called wa'tesink re li kab'l, or 'feeding the house'. The ceremony is led by the man of the household or a male pasawinq. He slaughters an animal, puts burning candles and copal pom in the four corners of the house and at the centre, he puts the animal's blood and cocoa on the walls or doors in the shape of a cross. He places b'oj and tortillas in the corners, presents food to the saint on the altar and some 'sow' meat at the centre or in the corners; some throw the water used to wash the animal on the roof and all of them pray. As in the case of the mayejak and planting rituals, the animal has to be a turkey as "alien" animals such as chickens should not be used. The ceremony closes with a meal afterwards.

The villagers of Samox and Xalihá perform the wa'tesink re li kab'l rituals in this way. In these communities all but a few villagers address both God and the Tzuultaq'a as well as the spirit of the house. This spirit emanates from the life that was inherent in the materials which went into building the house: the wood, straw etc. These trees and plants should perhaps not have been cut because the Tzuultaq'a might have had another purpose for them. In the words of one villager: 'We have to give food to the materials and throw a bit of blood on the walls to make sure that the spirit of the mountain cools down, because we cut down some trees.' Another respondent told me: 'After cutting a tree or a branch it will cry for three days so we have to feed it'. Just like the spirit of the maize, the spirit of the house stems from the Tzuultaq'a, and just as the villagers feed the maize seed by putting blood or cocoa on it before the planting, they feed the spirit of the house before entering the house.

When addressing the Tzuultaq'a and the spirit of the house, the villagers ask them for protection from illness, accidents, bad spirits and harm. They ask for their well-being, for peace in the house, that their children may grow well and that the house may not move from its place. The villagers of Xalihá and Samox believe that illness, problems and harm are like persons or 'strange men' who can 'enter the house', so they ask the spirit of the house to not let them in. In their eyes these rituals are a very serious matter. They stressed that if they are not performed then the spirit of the house and the Tzuultaq'a may become angry and cause someone to suddenly become very ill.

In Rubelpec almost all pay attention to the moment when they enter a new house, but not all perform the same practices. Eighty per cent of the households perform customary practices similar to those of Samox and Xalihá. All address God, a few the Tzuultaq'a as well, and eighty per cent of the respondents actually believe that the house has a spirit that has to be addressed. This spirit stems from the life which is inherent in the building materials. However in contrast to the villagers of Samox and Xalihá, the respondents in Rubelpec do not think that these materials originate in the Tzuultaq'a but that they stem directly from God. One of the evangelicals added the idea of Satan substituting for bad spirits:

'The wood and the trees that we cut down, no one knows how many years they had. God gave life to all these trees. We have to come together and pray to assure that evil may not enter the house. If we do not, Satan will harm someone, an animal will die, or even a person.'

Apart from those practising customary rituals there is a group of fifteen respondents in Rubelpec who invite friends, neighbours and relatives to come together to pray and have a meal. The evangelicals as well as some Catholic households do so substituting for customary rituals. The members of the Asamblea de Dios do not address the Tzuultaq'a and they do not believe that the house has a spirit. One of them said: 'Because of Christ there is no need for crosses of blood any more'.

Compared to wa'tesink re li kab'l rituals in Xalihá and Samox, continuity in Rubelpec is expressed by the fact that almost all pay ritual attention to this moment and ask for the same things as in Xalihá and Samox. Discontinuity is apparent in the practices which substitute for customary rituals and in the fact that those who believe in the spirit of the house relate that spirit to God rather than the Tzuultaq'a.

As in the case of the b'antioxink rituals, there are important differences among the households in Chaabilchoch. Here one third of the respondents practice customary rituals, another third including the evangelicals perform the same substitution rituals as the minority in Rubelpec while the rest do nothing to mark this occasion. Moreover, almost none of them believe that the house has a spirit. The respondents in Chaabilchoch address their prayers primarily to God and only some of them mention the Tzuultaq'a as well, though subordinated to God. The requests remain the same, though. This relative weakness of wa'tesink re li kab'l rituals in Chaabilchoch may be related to the fact that many of the houses are made of materials, such as bricks and corrugated iron, that do not grow "on the Tzuultaq'a". However, in Samox important parts of the houses are made of the same materials and the villagers there consider customary wa'tesink re li kab'l rituals to be very important. Thus, these materials do not entirely determine the fate of these rituals.

Parish-promoted practices

Customary practices do not constitute an unequivocal category, the same holds true regarding practices promoted by the parishes since they differ from one parish to another depending on the kind of pastoral work that is applied. The practices that all parishes have in common will be discussed in this section: the Mass and the celebration of the Word, the administration of sacraments and the preparation of those who are to receive them, women's groups, as well as Christmas rituals, the Holy Week, All Saints' Day and All Souls' Day.

The Mass and the celebration of the Word

One of the special occasions in the religious life of every community is the visit of the priest a few times a year. During these visits he celebrates one or two Masses, marries young couples, baptizes new babies, gives the First Communion to young children and if necessary administers the extreme unction to some of the villagers. In villages that have been appointed as parish centres such as Chaabilchoch, members of surrounding communities participate in the meetings with the priest as well. Despite the new experiments in creating a special Q'eqchi' Mass, the Masses roughly follow a classical scheme. The women and small children usually sit on one side of the church while the men and boys from the age of eight or nine onwards sit on the other side. The catechists and sometimes the pasawinq are seated at the front and the focus is on the priest. Only in communities belonging to parishes where a liberating pastoral policy is applied, the priest refers to customary practices and meanings in addition to standard Catholic themes.

One such Masses I attended in Xalihá in 1992 illustrates this. The building was decorated with fringed strips of plastic. Flowers, candles, tortillas and small bottles of b'oj were placed on the altar. The pasawinq started by saying the rosary and burning copal pom and candles. The Mass allowed for little active participation on the part of the villagers except for the many Q'eqchi' songs and the time left over for individual prayers after the Communion. The villagers used this time to pray aloud in a very dedicated way, talking about their family, children, animals and crops, the land they cultivate, their sorrows and their worries. They mentioned God, the saints, Esquipulas, Christ, the prophets, Santa María, and asked them to provide for the well-being of their family, crops, animals and community in much the same way as in a yo'lek. I was impressed by the apparently deeply felt need to address all these "persons". Their prayers touched on their daily problems and anxieties.

This practical characteristic of religion in Xalihá was also expressed when the priest asked God to make sure that worms and insects would not eat the villagers' crops. The villagers used to have many problems with these creatures but then they organized a special Mass and they disappeared. Now the animals had returned and God had to be asked once again to do something about it. There were lots of small bottles with worms and insects on the altar and these were blessed by the priest. Afterwards the animals were returned to the fields, supposedly still alive and instructed by God not to eat too much. The idea was to ask God to help solve this problem without denying the worms and insects a fair share of the crops. The priest went along with these customary practices and meanings. So much for this particular Mass in Xalihá.

In general the celebration of the Word follows the same pattern as the Mass, only some of the catechists - and in Samox and Xalihá some pasawinq as well - take over the leading role of the priest and there is no consecration. The celebration of the Word has replaced the former customary "change of the flowers" feast on Sunday before the Catholic restoration. The pasawinq led the prayers in latin and addressed everyone about the values of community life. All would place flowers before the statue of the saint. There was marimba and harp music, food was served and several elderly respondents told me that many would get drunk every Sunday. Nowadays, in the celebration of the Word the catechists stress standard Catholic contents and meanings.

The celebration of the Word is the occasion for a majority of the Catholics to meet every Sunday. In Rubelpec and Chaabilchoch there are several households that refuse to attend these celebrations and in Rubelpec, many adult men rarely attend the celebration because their work takes them elsewhere. In Xalihá and Rubelpec a few households sometimes go to nearby towns on Sunday. In Xalihá, a problem arose because the newly formed football club planned to have its matches on Sunday morning. Whether this indicates a dwindling interest in the celebration on the part of young men or whether the attraction of the game is simply impossible to resist, is hard to say.

The sacraments

The priests administer the sacraments, but it is the catechists who instruct the parents of babies who are to be baptized, the children who are to receive their First Communion and the young couples who are going to be married. During courses that last several days, they teach them the values of parenthood, of membership in the church and of marriage. The catechists' discourse indicates that the existing division of labour between men and women, the need to lead a decent life, responsibility towards each other, towards their children, towards the church and the local community are linked to God's will.

Before the child is actually baptized the parents choose the *padrinos* (the godparents of the child) who take the child to the priest to be baptized. After the ceremony the family invites the grandparents, compadres, uncles and aunts to celebrate the occasion, to eat meat and drink *atol*[2]. In the past the villagers of Xalihá would carry the child to the mountain and stay there for three days but now Catholic practice has replaced this customary ritual.

Marriage procedures are quite complex among the Q'eqchi'es. To start with, marriages arranged by parents have been quite common among the Q'eqchi'es. Nowadays the father of the young man has to visit the girl's parents up to six times to ask for the hand of their daughter. After the final approval is given, several months are spent preparing the celebration. After the Mass, friends and relatives gather together, and the girl is accompanied to the house of the groom's parents. There they all have a meal and the parents and padrinos give advice to the couple. In Rubelpec three days after the wedding the couple goes to the Calvary to pray for happiness.

We have here an example of customary practices which do not appear to be controversial because they confirm family life and thus coincide with official parish goals. The same holds true for funeral rituals. After someone has died, friends, relatives and neighbours keep vigil for one or two nights and beans and tortillas are served to those present. The *petate*[3] he or she used, some white cloth and his or her broken thurible are placed in his coffin. The day after, they pray and bury the dead with lots of flowers. During nine days a novena is observed to make sure the deceased is received by God.

In the villages that I studied, most of the Catholics had received the sacraments and participated in the preparation courses. Nevertheless in Xalihá, some complained about the catechists telling them how to behave: 'They [the catechists - hs] are no better persons than we are, so what gives them the right to tell us these things'. In Rubelpec and Samox there is a considerable minority of households headed by an unmarried couple, 17 out of 42 households in Samox. In Rubelpec several Catholics have not been baptized. In short, while the priests in these four villages are successfully urging the villagers to accept most of the sacraments, their influence has its limits.

Women's groups

In three of the four communities, there are active women's groups. Only in Xalihá was there none, and the religious women of Chahal complained that in their parish, the male population does not allow their daughters and women to meet without men being present, let alone to go to the parish to follow courses.

Both in Samox and in Chaabilchoch there is a group of forty women who meet a few times a month under the guidance of two female catechists. In Rubelpec there are separate groups for older women, young married women and for girls, each group having between thirty and forty members. These groups sing and pray, listen to Biblical explanations and moral guidelines, visit the sick, help them and pray for them. The catechists teach the women practical skills such as weaving, embroidery and pottery. There is no room for criticizing existing gender patterns in these groups.

The elderly women in Rubelpec call themselves 'The Daughters of Santa María' and Santa María plays an important role in their prayers. Santa María is an important "asset" for the Catholic church in defining its profile vis-à-vis evangelical churches. However, the women express clear customary features in their ways of addressing Santa María: she is asked to protect their families and animals and to provide food, drink, maize and good harvests. Moreover, they sacrifice copal pom and candles to her. We have here a nice example of a Catholic symbol being reinterpreted in a customary way.

In the parish of Carchá a network of women's groups has emerged which is beyond the control of the priests. They are supported by lay leaders who apply a liberating pastoral policy. These groups have both Catholic and evangelical members and, besides learning practical skills, they discuss national problems and aspects of social reality. One of their initiatives was to send a delegation of women to the capital to see how people in the popular neighbourhoods live. After returning home they told the groups what they had seen and concluded that it was better to stay where they are and to not migrate to the city. Comparing this example with the restrictions found in Chahal and Xalihá, it becomes clear that among Q'eqchi'es there is considerable variation in the freedom women have to move from one place to the other.

Christmas

Of course, the observance of Christmas is strongly promoted by the priests, but in all four communities its celebration starts with the customary practice of the *posadas*. This means that during the nine days preceding Christmas, a statue of a saint is carried in procession from one house to another, staying one day in every house. There, the people gather to pray and say the rosary and dinner is served at midnight. On Christmas Day a celebration of the Word is held. These are standard elements of the celebration of Christmas.

However there are substantial differences between the communities. In Rubelpec and Chaabilchoch, the central meaning of the celebration is to commemorate the birth of Christ. In Chaabilchoch an image of Christ is carried in procession and He is in the mind of the villagers. In Rubelpec the villagers thank God for the year that is coming to an end and ask for a good new year. By contrast, in Samox and Xalihá saints such as Santa María and San José, instead of the birth of Christ, are the focal point of the celebration of Christmas. In Samox both saints are carried in procession as Christmas serves rather as a patron saints' feast dedicated to these two saints and as an opportunity to perform mayejak.

In Xalihá, Christmas is not even celebrated by the community. Some go to San Agustín Chahal to participate in the celebrations there. In Semococh, one of the four hamlets which make up the village of Xalihá, Christmas is celebrated at the hamlet level: only the residents of Semococh participate. A few years ago they bought an image of San José which is kept in one of the houses rather than in the village church. Since San José is there, the posadas are observed. This new role of San José reflects the tensions between the hamlets. The fact that the residents of Semococh bought their own saint may indicate that they are constructing their own patron saint's symbol, which is the most visible mark of a distinct community. Rumours about the construction of another church in Semococh should be seen in the same light.

In short, in the two communities that belong to Salesian-run parishes the Biblical meaning of the birth of Christ dominates the celebration of Christmas. In the other two, where the policy of liberating pastoral work is applied, Christmas is rather focused on customary meanings (the saints, patron saints' feasts, mayejak). The customary practices included in the celebration of Christmas in Rubelpec and Chaabilchoch do not cause any problem with the priests as long as their meanings remain Bible-oriented.

Holy Week

Holy Week is another such moment in the religious calendar which the priests want the Q'eqchi'es to pay attention to, though its observance incites the Q'eqchi'es to perform customary practices. This is the case in Samox, Chaabilchoch and Rubelpec. In Xalihá by contrast, most of the villagers pay little attention to Holy Week. Some of them go to San Agustín Chahal to participate in the processions and Masses there. In Samox, Rubelpec and Chaabilchoch celebrations of the Word or Masses are held on several days during this week, processions take place and the villagers have meals together to which neighbouring communities are invited. In Rubelpec some go to San Pedro Carchá to join the processions. In Chaabilchoch the statue of Christ is carried from the graveyard to the church stopping at several houses, the feet of twelve men are washed in public and the priest hears confessions. In Chaabilchoch and Rubelpec the Bible-oriented meaning of the death of Christ predominates in these activities. In Samox this meaning is complemented by customary ones: after the celebration of the Word the pasawinq perform their mayejak on a nearby mountain. Christ's resurrection does not receive much attention in any of the villages.

In the towns of Cobán and Carchá the Holy Week celebrations are impressive. In Carchá the hermandades of the túnicas blancas and the túnicas moradas organize activities such as processions, the Way of the Cross and the feet washing on various days of the Holy Week, but the priests do not approve of these activities. In Cobán the hermandades are more appreciated by the priests but their activities do not constitute a priority for them. Here the Hermandad del Calvario organizes a Way of the Cross six Fridays before Easter, starting at the church on the Calvary mountain and ending at the house of the president of the hermandad. The procession stops to pray at 14 houses that have put up an altar with an image of Christ, two cups of water, candles, flowers and copal pom in front of their house. Only Q'eqchi'es participate: men carry an image of Christ and women a statue of Santa María. On both sides of the street, women and girls stand in line and hold candles and all of them listen to the rather depressing music coming out of an amplified speaker.

On the Monday of Holy Week, the hermandad organizes a similar Way of the Cross. At the houses where the procession stops, the members of the hermandad receive food and in many cases, the woman of the house becomes particularly emotional, crying and talking about her problems and worries. On Tuesday the people of the neighbourhood of San Vicente are invited to have a meal at the house of the president. On Wednesday there is another procession and on Maundy Thursday it is the children's turn to have theirs. On Good Friday all join in the procession of the Hermandad del Señor Sepultado.

On the Monday of Holy Week, the bishop leads his own Way of the Cross leaving the cathedral and going around the central square. At the fourteen stops he calls on everyone to pray for those who have been in the news recently because they suffer from injustice. During the Way of the Cross in 1991 he mentioned those who have to endure human rights violations, the refugees in Mexico, widows, and the communities involved in land conflicts. He was not afraid to denounce those responsible for these sufferings.

The day of the deceased

All Saints' Day and All Souls' Day are further examples of parish-promoted feasts which give rise to customary rituals. In Samox and Xalihá the ceremonies of the first and second of November include three ingredients. First, a celebration of the Word is held. Secondly, the villagers visit the graves of their deceased relatives, place flowers on the graves and say the rosary. Finally, the villagers adorn the altar of their house, put flowers, fruit, cocoa and food in front of it, burn copal pom and candles and pray. They invite neighbours, relatives and friends to pass by and have food.

Almost all the Catholics in Rubelpec and most them in Chaabilchoch do the same on those days. In Chaabilchoch a considerable minority of Catholics pay no attention to this occasion. The same holds true for a majority of evangelicals in Chaabilchoch and Rubelpec but several evangelicals actually do perform customary rituals on these days. Here the observance of All Saints' Day and All Souls' Day does not coincide with ecclesiastical categories.

Almost all those who practice these rituals agree that these days are meant to commemorate those who have passed away. However, some stress the idea that the deceased return to the house and eat some of the food that has been put in front of the altar. In the words of one of the respondents: 'The deceased pass by like the wind. They say that the deceased come to have a look at what they left behind. If we do not put anything in front of the altar they return sadly.' Another respondent told me: 'Once a relative did not perform this custom. Then his deceased grandmother came, she cried and asked him why he had not put the things on his altar and waited for her.' Some even emphasized that the deceased will cause harm or illness to those who do not wait for them. As to whether the deceased actually return and whether they can cause harm there are clear differences of opinion in all the communities.

In short, although the observance of All Saints' Day and All Souls' Day is parish-promoted, almost all the Catholics, and even some evangelicals, perform customary rituals. Especially in Xalihá and Samox the villagers attribute customary meanings to these rituals alongside official meanings.

Evangelical practices

The example of evangelicals performing customary practices at parish-promoted occasions shows that Q'eqchi' religious categories are far from exclusive. In order to complete the analysis of their religious practices the standard practices and their related meanings as promoted by evangelical churches still need to be discussed. This discussion is based primarily on interviews with evangelical respondents in Samox, Chaabilchoch and Rubelpec. The practices that will be presented are the evangelical services and campaigns, prayer healing meetings, conversion and the tithes. For practical reasons initiation rituals such as baptism, marriage and the funeral practices as well as the celebrations of Christmas and Holy Week will not be discussed. This is not because these practices would not be important to the Q'eqchi'es, but because such a discussion would not bring up meanings which do not appear in the analysis of other practices.

Services and campaigns

The services of the churches on which I have information - the Asamblea de Dios church in Rubelpec, the Nazarene church in a neighbouring village, the Baptist church in Carchá, the Iglesia de Dios de la Nueva Jerusalén in Chaabilchoch and the Nazarene church close to Samox - have similar standard elements: the believers read and comment on Bible texts, pray and sing. The emphasis is on addressing God, listening to what they think God wants them to do, and learning how to lead a decent life. Bible explanations determine which issues are raised and their moral consequences.

A woman in Rubelpec, who participates in both the Baptist church in Carchá and the Asamblea de Dios church in Rubelpec, told me that the services in both churches are almost the same. Her statement suggests that the differences that are stressed in the literature (see Chapter Three) concerning the various types of evangelical churches should not be overestimated. I have statements on a historical church (Baptist church), "Holiness" churches (Nazarene churches), and Pentecostal ones (Asamblea de Dios, Iglesia de Dios de la Nueva Jerusalén), and their members come up with precisely the same answers to my question about what they do in the most important element of their practices: the services.

Moreover, the statements of several respondents who have experiences of participating in various churches, including the Catholic one, suggest that ecclesiastical differences do not account for much: 'All the churches belong to God and the Word of God is the same'. The only difference between the evangelical churches and the Catholic one they pointed to was the role of saints. Either the differences in practices and discourse between the churches are not very substantial, or the villagers are not very interested in these differences and hardly notice them.

The evangelical churches hold an impressive number of services, between twice to four times a week including the Bible study meetings. The members of these churches told me that they attend all these services and meetings, which means that the evangelicals probably spend much more time in their church meetings than the Catholics. Moreover fellow believers from other villages regularly come along to these services and vice versa. The church offers an intensive community life and significant possibilities for socialization to its members, which transcend the limits of the village.

The attraction of evangelical churches is especially demonstrated when they organize special campaigns once in a while. Then they have meetings involving hundreds of fellow believers from several villages and missionaries and ministers from other places come to visit. They preach the Word of God, some are baptized and they all have a meal together. The evangelicals invite all the villagers, Catholics and evangelicals alike, to take part in order 'to win over the soul of everyone'. In general, though, the proselytizing efforts of the evangelicals are not very aggressive.

Prayer healing

This is not to say that religious competition is not important. A prominent asset in this competition is prayer healing. During the services the evangelicals pray for sick villagers, both Catholics and evangelicals, and they often visit patients after the service. They help them with household tasks or work on their land and sometimes even collect money for them.

The main reason for their visits is to pray for the patient and they all firmly believe in the healing power of their prayers. One of the Rubelpec evangelicals gave me the example of his son who suffers from cancer. The members of the Asamblea de Dios came to his house to pray and now he no longer feels any pain. Prayer healing visits are part of the standard practices of all the evangelical churches but in the case of the Nazarenes, not everyone participates. The proselytizing character of prayer healing meetings is shown by the fact that in both Chaabilchoch and Rubelpec, the Catholics have taken over the practice and are criticized by evangelical leaders for this reason.

Conversion

What is at stake in the competition among churches is winning over Q'eqchi'es and converting them. In the previous chapter the conversion of Q'eqchi'es to an evangelical church and some explanations of this conversion, including the influence of the army and the finqueros, were discussed. However the crucial question still needs to be answered: why have so many Q'eqchi'es turned to an evangelical church in the last few decades?

One of the explanations that have been put forward in the literature on this question in Guatemala as well as by respondents in the region points to the fact that many of the new converts live in conditions of constant poverty and marginalization. These conditions are often aggravated by alcoholism, disease, social isolation and violence which destroy family life and exhaust their capacity to cope with their problems. In such a situation, existing symbolic frames of reference may no longer be adequate as a way of making sense of their lives. Pentecostalism especially seems able to provide a meaningful alternative: it says that Guatemalans are tempted by the devil who is putting them to the test. The Bible is "proven" to have predicted all their suffering and things get worse until Christ returns to renew all things and put an end to anguish and misery. Within this perspective, the dark world and the hardships they suffer begin to make sense and there is hope for the near future.

Moreover the individual can do something about the situation by turning to Christ, accepting God's grace and the work of the Holy Spirit. He or she should put his or her life in order, stop drinking and lead an industrious family life. Pentecostal churches offer spiritual healing in case of illness and by turning to an evangelical church one opens up the possibility for reconciliation with those who threaten violence. In addition, Pentecostal churches offer opportunities for re-socialization to those who have lost their family or local community, as well as an opportunity for individual salvation. In short, this explanation maintains that Pentecostalism offers a symbolic frame of reference which allows people to make sense out of their difficult situation and to solve at least some of the immediate problems which tend to aggravate it (see Garrard 1986: 201, 207; Martínez, Samandú 1990: 58-61).

By contrast, other authors hold that evangelism meets the symbolic needs of precisely those who have a higher income and are experiencing upward social mobility. The austere evangelical morality, the positive attitude towards education, literacy, sobriety and thrift stimulate believers to improve their economic position, while success is interpreted as a sign of God's spiritual grace (Annis 1987: 75-106; Garrard 1986: 194). Moreover, evangelical churches have the same advantages as those offered by the Salesians to their younger catechists: one does not need to wait for years before a position of respect and status is achieved within the local community or spend a great deal of money on social obligations attached to the position of cofrade or chinam.[4]

In the end, these two explanations are not necessarily contradictory. Someone may turn to evangelism as a way of making sense of a difficult situation while feeling stimulated by the church to do the utmost to improve his or her economic position. Nevertheless, it is still an open question to what extent conversion to an evangelical church means a complete rupture with previous life and culture. Garrard states that those evangelical churches that have reached the highest level of "indigenization" are those that have been most successful in winning converts. She points to Guatemalans taking over the leadership of their church, thus curtailing the influence of North American missionaries, and to those churches that were founded by Guatemalans. Garrard claims that a minimum degree of continuity eases the transition to an evangelical church (Garrard 1986: 202-204, 216).

In the case of the Q'eqchi'es, there is much to be said in support of these explanations. Many of them certainly live in a situation of poverty and marginalization aggravated by illness, alcoholism, social isolation and violence and evangelical churches offer a remedy for most of these aggravations. They offer curative services and help patients cope with their economic problems. Several evangelicals indicated that they consider prayer healing meetings to be a very attractive aspect of their church.

Conversion can also serve as a way of dealing with alcoholism. Of the twenty evangelicals I interviewed, eight told me that their conversion was directly related to their desire to stop drinking and to start living an organized life. 'I wanted to make a change', several evangelicals told me after explaining that they used to drink a lot, that they had many quarrels and problems within their household and spent their money on alcoholic beverages. Evangelical churches urged them to stop drinking, offered them a strict set of moral values to hold on to and welcomed them in their community. One respondent in Rubelpec said: 'God invited me to leave all the bad things behind'. The evangelicals consider the moral behaviour, the discipline and devotion of their fellow church members to be very attractive. They think they take their religion more seriously in relation to their personal behaviour than Catholics.

Other reasons mentioned by evangelical respondents to explain their conversion include the need to re-socialize and personal feuds with leading Catholics. In Rubelpec three evangelicals indicated that some sort of conflict with Catholics had caused them to leave the Catholic church. One was involved in a land dispute with leading Catholics in the place where he used to live. Several priests indicated that it was precisely those who were on the margins of community life who converted to an evangelical church.

The important role played by personal conflicts and social isolation in converting to an evangelical church and the fact that those on the margins of the community were most likely to become converts, undermine the argument of many Catholics that the evangelical churches were dividing the communities. It would appear that there was no such thing as a united local community before evangelical churches managed to gain converts. If there is a process on the way which is leading towards more internal stratification and differences (see Chapter Seven), then the introduction of evangelical churches seems much more a part of this process than a major cause of it.

The fourth aggravating factor, violence, is also relevant to explanations of Q'eqchi' conversions to an evangelical church. In the previous chapter we showed that such a conversion was seen as a way of saving one's life in the conflict-ridden areas of the Q'eqchi' region. In short, my data confirm the explanations of the growth of evangelical churches which point to the fact that these churches deal with specific factors which aggravate an already difficult situation: illness, alcoholism, social isolation and violence.

However, this confirmation only refers to the practical, social and moral aspects of these explanations. There is hardly any indication that the alternative meaningful framework allowing evangelical churches to provide a new sense to their lives played a significant role in the conversion of my respondents. Apart from a religiously based morality and God's capacity to cure diseases, my respondents mentioned no specific religious meaning that attracted them to the evangelical church. Moreover, several catechists expressed the same motivation for becoming catechists as the evangelicals for their conversion: to stop drinking and pull their life together.[5] Apparently an evangelical conversion and the decision to become a catechist can work out the same way: making a break or change in one's personal life. Apart from the dispute about saints, the villagers are not very interested in specific religious meanings which differentiate one church from another. One evangelical told me about the Catholic church: 'The only problem about them is their drinking, all the rest is all right'. The very limited role of meaningful differences between the Catholic church and evangelical churches within the conversion process points to an important level of symbolic continuity. This limited level of discursive consequences linked to the practical, moral and social benefits of evangelical churches outlined above may largely explain the success of conversion efforts by these churches.

The tithes

Activities such as campaigns and the maintenance of the church building cost the evangelicals a considerable amount of money. To raise this money every household is supposed to contribute ten per cent of earnings. This may seem to be a considerable amount of money, but whether the evangelicals actually do contribute that amount is hard to say. One of the members of the Asamblea de Dios told me that he spent about five to ten quetzales each month which comes to 60 to 120 quetzales a year. However, his gross income (GP, see Chapter Seven) in 1992 is Q. 6464.24 so his contribution does not even come close to ten per cent. The Nazarenes told me they contribute about ten centavos every week. In practice contributions do not seem to amount to considerable sums.

Religious discourse: the customary principle

The foregoing section has shown that Q'eqchi' religion is by no means homogeneous or uniform. Every practice has its own variations among the communities and even between the various households of the same community. However it is precisely these variations which make it possible to draw some general lines and capture some common trends.

In the previous sections the emphasis was on particular religious practices and the meanings associated with each one of them. In the next sections the various religious meanings will be discussed. They have become intelligible to me by clustering them into two main principles which "organize" the discourse of the Q'eqchi'es. One of these may be called "the customary principle", and the other "the Bible-oriented principle". The organization of these meanings into these principles allows for both consistency and coherence, and for contradictions and tensions to become explicit.

This differentiation into two principles is primarily based on the main distinctions made by the Q'eqchi'es themselves. In the previous sections on Catholics becoming catechists or converting to an evangelical church, it has been shown that the Q'eqchi'es have little interest in differences of meanings between the various churches. By contrast, we have seen several examples of Q'eqchi'es treating as opposites customary meanings and practices on the one hand, and meanings and practices that point to a contemporary Biblical origin on the other. Especially in Chaabilchoch and Rubelpec several villagers make it a point of opposing customary meanings and practices to the Word of God and to good moral behaviour. In the words of one of them: 'We changed our lives, we come together with the Word of God, that is why the mayejak has no importance any more.' In short, if the Q'eqchi'es themselves differentiate at all among religious meanings, then the main difference they make is between customary religion and contemporary Bible-oriented religion, be it evangelical or Catholic. This differentiation is the main reason for distinguishing between a customary and a Bible-oriented principle.

This Bible-oriented principle and church-promoted religion are not the same thing. The former points to the Q'eqchi'es own discourses whereas the latter is about what the churches want the Q'eqchi'es to think, which need not coincide. The first principle that will be discussed is the customary one. First, the customary universe will be mapped and then the ways in which the Q'eqchi'es deal with the "persons" in this universe will be outlined. Finally, the relevance for social reality of the main "person" in this universe, the Tzuultaq'a, will be discussed.

The customary universe

Q'eqchi'es want to be able to cultivate a piece of land. This fundamental desire holds true even in the case of those who live in towns, who cultivate a piece of land on the outskirts of the town. Moreover, those who have to live on a finca usually have access to a piece of land to grow their maize and beans.

Living in the mountainous landscape of the Q'eqchi' heartland, the Q'eqchi'es feel heavily dependent on the mountain and the valley, i.e. the Tzuultaq'a,[6] on whom they are literally located. The mountain gives them all the essential things they need to live. The maize and beans as well as the wood to make fire and to build their houses grow out of the mountain's skin. Water comes down the mountain's slopes. The mountain feeds their animals and grows medicinal herbs to cure diseases and so on. To be sure, at the beginning God created everything and in the end God is the source of all life, but in practical daily life, it is the Tzuultaq'a on whom the Q'eqchi'es depend for their survival. The Tzuultaq'a is the prominent "person" in customary religion.

These maize, beans, turkeys, trees, water, medicinal herbs and so on are considered to be imbued with life originating in the Tzuultaq'a. In the eyes of the Q'eqchi'es there is a vital unit consisting of the mountain, the valley, the land they cultivate, the animals they hold, the plants they grow, the sun, the rain, the wind, the moon and the saints among others. Life is the central "substance" within this unit and is inherent in all these elements in contrast to the things that have their origin outside this unit. The origin of "things" and animals is important. The pasawinq have to leave all "alien" objects behind before entering a sacred place to perform their mayejak and the Q'eqchi'es are not supposed to use "alien" animals such as chickens as a sacrifice to the Tzuultaq'a or to 'feed the house'. Moreover, they should not sell their maize, i.e. alienate maize from the unit, 'because the maize will cry', as a widow from Xalihá indicated as the reason why she sells hardly any maize. The yo'lek clearly expresses the elements that belong to this unit and are imbued with life.

The clearest examples of "things" imbued with a spirit stemming from the Tzuultaq'a are maize and the house. The idea of spirits originating in the Tzuultaq'a is expressed also when the Q'eqchi'es ask the Tzuultaq'a not to allow insects or birds to eat too much of their crops. In addition, the Tzuultaq'a can send snakes to bite and punish them. The Tzuultaq'a can also send invisible spirits to either help the Q'eqchi'es or cause them harm. In the latter case, the spirit is called *ma'us*. A ma'us incites someone to have a bad thought or behave in a reprehensible way which results in illness or accidents.

On the question of whether there are separate good and bad spirits, or whether the same spirit can be both benevolent and malignant depending on the occasion, Q'eqchi'es are not very clear. Consequently, the distinction made by Carlson and Eachus between *xdiosil* and *xwiinkul* referring to spirits does not make much sense.[7] They consider the former to be benevolent and sacred while the latter are malevolent and profane. Should the Q'eqchi'es not treat them right, then a xdiosil just becomes sad while a xwiinkul becomes angry and punishes the Q'eqchi'es. Indeed, the spirit of maize - a xdiosil - simply fails to grow well whereas the spirit of the house - a xwiinkul - actively inflicts illness or provokes an accident when Q'eqchi'es fail to perform the necessary rituals. Nevertheless spirits of both categories depend on the Tzuultaq'a; they have to be treated in very specific ways and the consequences of not treating the spirits of maize or a house properly - a bad harvest, illness or accidents - are both negative. In both cases relations with the Tzuultaq'a and the spirit concerned have to be restored.

Saints and ancestors have been incorporated into the customary universe in much the same way. In the case of the women's group Daughters of Santa María in Rubelpec, it has become clear that the women consider Santa María to be capable of providing them with the same things which the pasawinq request from the Tzuultaq'a: food, drink, maize and good harvests. Saints play a central role in both the community and the household. The patron saint promotes the unity of the community and urges the villagers to celebrate his or her feast. In much the same way, every house has its saint placed on the altar of the house and frequently requiring attention. Ancestors have to be treated well and can cause harm if one does not do so. The customary All Saints' Day and All Souls' Day rituals include the idea of giving them food to keep them satisfied in much the same way as food is given to the seed before the planting of maize or to the spirit of the house at the wa'tesink re li kab'l rituals.

The Tzuultaq'a remains the central customary "person" expressing many sides. The Tzuultaq'a can be male or female and has a Spanish and a Q'eqchi' name. For example, one of the central Tzuultaq'as is called Santa María Itzam and is female while another important mountain, San Pablo Xucaneb', is regarded as male. The Tzuultaq'a is a mountain, but he or she can be encountered in special places such as a cave, a river or the top of the mountain. Moreover, every mountain has its own name and thus every mountain is a distinctive "person". However the idea of a single Tzuultaq'a encompassing the whole Q'eqchi' region is alive as well. This distinction between a single all-encompassing Tzuultaq'a and a particular Tzuultaq'a next to other Tzuultaq'as is demonstrated by the fact that at a mayejak pasawinq go to both the particular local mountains and to several of the central thirteen Tzuultaq'as. These thirteen are sacred places where the single general Tzuultaq'a is to be addressed. Q'eqchi'es often express themselves in both singular and plural terms when talking about the Tzuultaq'a as is exemplified by the following quote from a pasawinq in Samox: 'The mountains are one person with various names. If we address only one of them the others become jealous. We have to pay attention to all the mountains we know.' The most famous of these thirteen are San Pablo Xucaneb' south of Chamelco, Qana' Itzam and Qawa' Siyab' between Cahabón and Lanquín, Qawa' Kojaj north of San Pedro Carchá, the Calvary mountain in Cobán, Qawa' Raxon Tzunqin south of the Polochic river and Chi Ixim in Tactic (see Map 2).[8]

A Tzuultaq'as symbolize power: the control of the land and of all who dwell upon it. In this sense several respondents in Xalihá compared the Tzuultaq'a with a patrón, i.e. a landlord. It has to be stressed, though, that when the respondents used this metaphor, it was limited to these specific meanings. The comparison between a landlord and the Tzuultaq'a should not be pushed too far as Wilson (Wilson 1993: 127; Wilson 1995: 57-58) seems to be doing. He holds that the image which the Q'eqchi'es developed of the Tzuultaq'a after the introduction of the coffee plantations adopted characteristics of German landlords: 'Since both are authority figures and owners of the land, the *personas* of the mountain spirits and plantation landlords are merged to a degree'. However, almost none of my respondents consider the Tzuultaq'a to be arbitrary, bad tempered or cruel, characteristics usually attributed to German landowners. According to my respondents he or she is very trustworthy and there is no need to fear the Tzuultaq'a.

Of course the Tzuultaq'a is relevant in the rural context. In the customary universe of town dwellers, saints, spirits and ancestors occupy a special place and the Tzuultaq'a has not the same prominence. They pray to saints and ancestors and ask them for the things they need. Bad spirits are counteracted by praying to God, not so much to the Tzuultaq'a.

The Q'eqchi'es dealing with customary "persons"

Customary religion involves few abstract notions, it is about crucial and practical aspects of daily life: a good harvest, the lives of their animals, protection from illness and accidents and against disasters such as drought, plagues and heavy rainfall as well as from conflicts within the household and the local community etc. The Q'eqchi'es try to secure these things by entering into an almost tangible and practical "contract" with the important "persons" in their universe, the Tzuultaq'a in particular.

The part of the contract which the Q'eqchi'es are supposed to observe consists of three elements. First, they show their respect towards the Tzuultaq'a and other "persons" by addressing them and mentioning their names. Secondly, they sacrifice part of what they have received from the Tzuultaq'a such as maize and a turkey as well as precious things such as candles and copal pom. Thirdly, they thank the Tzuultaq'a and the others for what they have received and ask for the things they will need again in the future.

These three elements belong to the standard procedure of almost all the customary rituals. In the eyes of the Q'eqchi'es, this contract is strictly reciprocal: if they comply with their obligations, the Tzuultaq'a will reward them with abundance and protection. Several pasawinq in Samox and Xalihá related the quantity and quality of their harvests directly to the seriousness with which the villagers perform their customary rituals. This reciprocal character also means that when the Q'eqchi'es do not perform the necessary rituals, the Tzuultaq'a and the other "persons" will punish them severely. They do so, for instance, by telling snakes to bite them, causing illness or accidents, ordering the rain, the wind or the sun to destroy their harvest, sending animals to eat their crops, issuing a spirit to cause them harm etc. Diseases such as 'seen by the mountain' (*rilomil tzuul*) and 'spirit loss' (*xiw*) are directly attributable to the Tzuultaq'a becoming angry. However, the Tzuultaq'a does not strike at once; he or she first issues a warning. Several respondents said that the Tzuultaq'a does so by appearing in a dream in the shape of an old man or woman, looking sad or angry. The Tzuultaq'a can also appear in a dream just to help them. One of the respondents in Samox told me that he dreamt of a certain plant. The day after, he looked for this plant, found it and gave it to a sick woman in the village. After using the plant she recovered quickly.

Customary rituals are performed both by the individual households and by the community as a whole, but the balance tips towards the communitarian side. The patron saint's feast is the symbol of the community. The community mayejak requires the participation of all its members. Even in the case of rituals performed at the household level such as the 'house feeding' rituals, friends, relatives and other villagers are invited to take part and have a meal together. This shared meal is the clearest expression of the notion that life is reproduced in a communitarian way. In the planting rituals this communitarian character is emphasized by group-wise planting and by the man of the household representing the community when performing these rituals. The Tzuultaq'a has to be addressed in a united and communitarian way.[9]

The Tzuultaq'a and the spirit of a house or maize are not the only "persons" who must be dealt with in very specific ways. There are rules governing the way of handling every "object" that has a spirit. Cabarrús and Carlson and Eachus give many examples of these rules (Cabarrús 1979: 50; Carlson, Eachus 1978: 52-62), but whether the Q'eqchi'es actually take all of them seriously remains open to question.

The Tzuultaq'a and social reality

Even when only some of these rules are known to most of the Q'eqchi'es, they would not find it easy to observe all the rules they know. Salesian priests emphasize that customary religion is marked by fear and submission to nature. Carlson and Eachus write that the 'beings' in the universe of the Q'eqchi'es are very sensitive and easily offended (Carlson, Eachus 1978: 41). Of course the Q'eqchi'es depend heavily on natural forces which they are unable to control so a certain sense of fear and uncertainty may be expected. The individual prayers after the Communion during the Mass, the prayers said by individual Q'eqchi'es at the start of a yo'lek as well as the emotional utterances during the processions of the Hermandad del Calvario in Cobán, all these express the difficulties they have to face in reproducing their existence.

Be that as it may, it is precisely customary religion which presents excellent ways of allowing the Q'eqchi'es not only to express their anxieties but also to make sense of uncertainty brought about by the dependency on nature. Nature is conceived in terms of "persons" and through customary rituals, the Q'eqchi'es enter into a perfect reciprocal contract with them. The image which the Q'eqchi'es have constructed of the Tzuultaq'a allows them to "solve" their dependency on nature in a symbolic way: they convert nature into something that depends on them rather than the other way around. Even when they perform the necessary rituals, disasters, bad harvests and diseases can be interpreted as a punishment handed out by the Tzuultaq'a because their dedication or devotion may have been insufficient.[10] The reaction of the Tzuultaq'a depends on whether the Q'eqchi'es comply with their contract with him or her. The Q'eqchi'es appear as the active actors and nature as the reactive counterpart that can be trusted. Despite the fact that the community mayejak in Chaabilchoch had been lost for years, the drought which threatened the crops of the villagers in 1991 caused a temporary revival of the community mayejak. This example clearly illustrates the capacity of customary religion to make sense of problems thrown up by nature.

Customary religion is intimately related to the natural surroundings of the Q'eqchi'es and thus to their agricultural activities. Mayejak, planting rituals and b'antioxink practices are related to the cultivation of maize. Customary practices and meanings are especially relevant to crops and animals that are produced and consumed within the household, i.e. that belong to the direct relations between the Q'eqchi'es and the Tzuultaq'a. Customary religion is not relevant to activities oriented towards the market or cash crops which do not instil in the Q'eqchi'es the need to perform customary rituals.

Religious discourse: The Bible-oriented principle

The second religious principle which "organizes" this discourse and may be called Bible-oriented because it focuses on God and His Word. It portrays God as the only relevant and omnipotent "person" in the universe. God has created nature, but nature is neither personified nor imbued with life in the way that man is. This life has been granted to man and, in the end, it will return to God. In the meantime man has to comply with His demands. God wants man to pray frequently to Him and believe in Him, to listen to His Word, to love and worship Him, to be loyal to the church and to obey His moral demands.

Catholics and evangelicals mention exactly the same things when asked what God wants them to do, and the moral demands coincide perfectly with the official discourses of the various churches on the one hand and with the customary requirement of unity in their presentation to the Tzuultaq'a on the other. Nevertheless, the emphasis of God's demands is different. These are much more rooted in individual responsibility. It is primarily the individual who addresses God and He calls on the Q'eqchi'es to comply individually with His demands. God is able to do good things to individuals who have changed their lives. The main function of the church community is to stimulate the individual to look after his or her relations with God.

About what God will do when an individual obeys His wishes my respondents are unanimous: God will show Himself to be benevolent and will provide them with 'the good things'. However, these 'good things' are not so much related to specific things such as when the Q'eqchi'es address the Tzuultaq'a and ask for a good harvest or protection. God provides them with abstract matters such as 'the blessings of God', their general well-being and destiny. Whether God would actually punish them in case the Q'eqchi'es did not obey Him is not clear. Sometimes He actually does so. Some respondents told me the story of a minister who fell in love with a fifteen years old girl and changed his way of life. He went to a neighbouring town to get drunk and there he died. This was a concrete proof of the wrath of God. On the other hand God may decide not to punish them: either He does so only after death or at the end of times, or He forgives them 'because He loves both the believer and the drunkard'. What are the conditions which will lead Him to forgive or to punish remains unclear. One of the evangelicals said on this issue: 'God will have His reasons although we do not understand them'. As a consequence of this uncertainty as to God's punishment when they fail to comply with His demands, relations with God are not strictly reciprocal.

The idea of reciprocal relations is also undermined by the view that they very often commit a sin without being aware of it and are later punished by God: 'We often do not remember that we fail in the eyes of God. We do not know anything, we are sinners'. As a result of the important role which moral behaviour plays in relations with God, the concept of "sin" and the need to "obey" and to ask for "forgiveness" are closely linked to God. Add to this the unpredictable character of God's wrath and punishment, and the need to fear God becomes obvious.[11] The respondents in Xalihá who compared the Tzuultaq'a with a large landowner used the same metaphor to refer to God, but in this case they emphasized His much more authoritarian character: 'God is like a *patrón*. If we do not work for Him He gets angry. He can punish us because of our sins. He watches our sins'.

An apparent difference between Catholic and evangelical respondents is the fact that evangelicals stress that dream appearances are important to them. This shows a remarkable continuity with the role of dream appearances in customary religion. However in the case of the evangelicals, only God, Christ or the Holy Spirit appear in their dreams. Almost all the evangelicals gave account of stories of such dream appearances.

In short, relations with God have a rather individual, moral, abstract and not strictly reciprocal character. In this respect relations with God differ considerably from the tangible "contract" with the Tzuultaq'a. The tangible character of relations with the Tzuultaq'a and the relatively abstract and not strictly reciprocal nature of relations with God coincide with the fact that the Tzuultaq'a and most of the customary "persons" have both a physical and a spiritual appearance. By contrast, the Bible-oriented principle makes a strict distinction between visible persons and the only invisible One.[12] Cabarrús quotes a Q'eqchi' who makes a distinction between God being far away or 'in the clouds' and the Tzuultaq'a, the 'god of the tangible'.[13]

God and social reality

The tangible character of the Tzuultaq'a and the rather abstract features of God are related to important differences in the ways in which the two principles are linked to social reality and nature. The customary principle is directly related to nature and the agricultural cycle of subsistence crops. The Bible-oriented principle has no such direct link to any specific economic activity and is mainly relevant to the life-cycle of individual Q'eqchi'es, as expressed in the baptism and marriage rituals. In addition, because of the not strictly reciprocal relations with God the Bible-oriented principle does not have the same capacity to symbolically "solve" problems of uncertainty and dependence on nature as the customary principle.

Nevertheless, His rather abstract character does not keep God from playing a crucial role in practical matters. As has been pointed out He encourages them to leave behind alcoholism, protects them from violence, cures them in case of illness and offers them opportunities for socialization. Moreover, God's capacity to improve the general well-being of the Q'eqchi'es is especially important to those who spend a lot of time and depend economically on non-agricultural activities to which the Tzuultaq'a is irrelevant. This relevance of the Bible-oriented principle partly explains the predominant role of God in the community of Rubelpec, where an estimated 42 households have someone who earns a living as a merchant and where an estimated 69 households have a member who works as wage labourer elsewhere for some time every year. The importance of these non-agricultural or market-oriented agricultural activities suggests that in the case of Rubelpec, problems of uncertainty are more likely to be "solved" symbolically in relation to God.

The relevance of the Bible-oriented principle to economic life does not stop here. It has been shown above that God encourages the Q'eqchi'es to put their life in order and to lead an industrious life. In the Salesian-run parishes, Q'eqchi' respondents told me that God urges them to work hard and to improve their economic performance. In the case of the evangelicals, this idea is even more pronounced. In the words of one of them: 'We pray both to God and Jesus Christ. If someone does his *k'anjel* well he will receive the blessings of God. Good k'anjel brings about the favours of God.' Interestingly, he used the word k'anjel which in Q'eqchi' has the general meaning of "effort": both an effort in terms of moral behaviour and in terms of work and economic activity. Enjoying economic success can be interpreted as a token of the blessing of God and working hard results in obtaining God's favours. Here we have a clear religious stimulus to improving one's economic performance and there is no objection to doing so through market integration.

The Bible-oriented principle not only encourages the evangelicals to improve their economic conditions but evangelicals from various communities said that they are also supposed to support the state. They said that once a week, they pray for the president, the army and for those who are responsible for the municipal government. An evangelical respondent said: 'It is all right to obey the law of God and the law of the constitution and the decrees of the municipality. We have to pray to God so that the violence may stop.' However this ideological statement should not be interpreted as explicit political support for specific parties or political actors; rather, it expresses the wish that these potentially dangerous actors and institutions will just leave them alone. Moreover Bible-oriented religion can easily become associated with an image of God as a promoter of social justice and human rights, which has quite opposite ideological connotations. Ideological consistency is not the Q'eqchi'es' primary concern.

The customary principle dominating in Xalihá and Samox

On the one hand, these two principles which organize the religious discourse of the Q'eqchi'es not only put emphasis on different issues, they contradict each other in several aspects. For example is nature, in the end, to be conceived of as personalized or not? Is God the only transcendent "person" or is the universe inhabited by several "persons" that have a spiritual character such as the sun, the moon, the Tzuultaq'a, the saints and so on? Is religion mainly a matter for individuals or for the local community? On the other hand, almost all of the communities and individual households I studied expressed the central meanings of both principles.

The clue to this paradox is to be found in three basic aspects of the way Q'eqchi'es deal with their religion. First, although respondents did make a distinction between customary meanings and Bible-oriented ones, most of them were not very interested in coherence and consistency or to eliminate contradictions. When faced with questions pointing to inconsistencies, they often responded by saying: '*Chi junil*' ('It is all the same'). In speaking about these matters, they forged a unity in their discourse by mentioning all the important "persons" in their universe and expressing the various meanings attached to these "persons" in much the same way as a pasawinq addresses all these "persons" at a yo'lek. The desire to create a harmony of all these "persons" and to allow them a place in the universe is their principal explicit way of creating unity of discourse. The fact that aspects of related meanings may be inconsistent does not bother them very much.

Secondly, the Q'eqchi'es may sometimes express the central meanings of the two principles, but never at the same moment or occasion. The lack of a single universal or permanently valid discourse raises the possibility that each particular moment or occasion determines the principle which will be relevant and thus expressed through religious practices at that time or occasion. Practices have an occasion-specific character and meanings are mainly related to these practices at these specific occasions or moments.

Moreover, in some communities one principle predominates while in another community the other principle has gained momentum. The third way in which the Q'eqchi'es "reconcile" the two principles in their discourse is by modifying the subordinate principle in order to make it as compatible as possible with the dominant one; however its basic meanings remain valid. In Xalihá and Samox, the customary principle predominates whereas in Chaabilchoch and Rubelpec it is the Bible-oriented one which governs the religious discourse. However in each village, the dominant principle does not rule out the other principle, it simply induces the villagers to modify the other.

In Samox and Xalihá both principles are relevant because almost all of the Bible-oriented and customary practices outlined above are performed and the villagers expressed the relevant meanings related to these practices. In both communities only a few villagers do not participate actively in both categories of practices. There is remarkably little variation between the various households in these villages in terms of religious practices and meanings. This holds true for catechists as well as for chinames and pasawinq.

In Samox, there is even a revival of customary practices going on. The pasawinq of Samox emphasized that they have not always performed customary rituals. They said that 'in the old days', the villagers would plant just a little maize and that the Tzuultaq'a rewarded them with generous harvests. At the beginning of the 1980s they began to neglect customary rituals, they did not celebrate their mayejak any more and the harvest has been diminishing ever since. The priest at that time 'brought us the New Testament and told us that doing the mayejak makes no sense'. Then, some six years ago, the village was hit by a serious drought and the crops were lost. Some young men took the initiative to go to the mountains nearby to do their mayejak and it started to rain. After that the cardamom and coffee harvests began to be affected by disease. One pasawinq told me:

'Perhaps because of a neglect on our part, because we lost the devotion to sacrifice. The harvest was very poor, that is why the pasawinq started to come together in Telemán. The reason for the problems with the bad harvest exists within ourselves.'

Moreover the new Dominican priests 'took up the mayejak again'. From that time on, the villagers have been performing their mayejak regularly. In short, the revival of customary rituals and meanings in the last five years is related, first of all, to the capacity of customary religion to make sense of a problematic situation related to nature. Secondly, the changing pastoral policy of the parish has been a crucial factor as well: five years ago it stimulated the pasawinq to start their meetings again and to revive customary religion.

The strong position of customary religion in both communities is partly responsible for the fact that many religious practices and meanings have an articulated character: they combine parish-promoted practices and Bible-oriented meanings with customary practices and meanings. For example when the procession entered the house of Qawa' Bex at the feast of the patron saint in Xalihá, he emphasized that the customs have their origin in God, and the yo'lek as it is practised there is preceded by several Lord's Prayers and Hail Marys. Christmas and the Holy Week in Samox are complemented by mayejak rituals during which the Tzuultaq'a is addressed. Of course, the articulated character of many practices in these communities is made possible thanks to an explicit approval granted by the priests.

The customary principle dominates the religious discourse in these two communities as evidenced by the fact that several parish-promoted practices receive customary meanings. For example at the Christmas and the Holy Week rituals in Samox, saints such as Santa María, San José and Jesus Nazareno take centre stage instead of the official remembrance of the birth, resurrection or even the death of Christ. The importance of customary rituals and meanings at the All Saints' Day and All Souls' Day in both communities show the same dominance of the customary principle.

God, the Tzuultaq'a and other "persons"

Both God - the central "person" of the Bible-oriented principle - and the Tzuultaq'a, the sun, the rain, the moon, the wind, the saints, the ancestors, the spirits etc. - the central "persons" of the customary principle - are present in the universe of the villagers of Xalihá and Samox. However, the very fact itself that God is not alone in this universe, something which contradicts the Bible-oriented principle, points to the customary principle dominating the villagers' view of God, the Tzuultaq'a and other "persons". On the relations between God and the Tzuultaq'a, one of the Xalihá villagers told me: 'God has created everything including the mountains. He looks after the mountains as if they were His animals, and the mountains take care of us.'

The Tzuultaq'a appears as an intermediary between God and themselves. To be sure, God is the greatest and is the creator of everything, but in daily life the villagers deal primarily with the Tzuultaq'a. One respondent stressed the importance of the Tzuultaq'a by saying: 'We are children of the mountain'. Still another went as far as to say that 'the Word of God is there to enrich our ways of addressing the Tzuultaq'a'. The Tzuultaq'a even appears as the one who commands the rain, the wind, the moon, the sun and other "persons". The practical character of their relations with the Tzuultaq'a is reflected by the fact that to the villagers of Samox and Xalihá, the nearby mountains on which they actually live, are more important to them than the central or more distant ones.

The dominance of the customary principle is also expressed in the image of God which these villagers have constructed. They attach the usual Bible-oriented meanings to God, but in line with a customary logic, the villagers also ask Him for practical things such as a good harvest, protection from illness and disease, animals growing well and so on. Moreover the villagers' relations with God are as reciprocal as their "contract" with the Tzuultaq'a and it is primarily the community and not so much the individual who enters into contact with God. However the villagers try to secure these necessary things mainly in their "contract" with the Tzuultaq'a, their relations with God having a secondary importance in this respect.

The relations between the villagers and the Tzuultaq'a are almost the same in Samox and Xalihá. An important difference is that at the mayejak ceremonies, the pasawinq of Samox not only ask for a good harvest of food crops, they also explicitly ask for a good harvest of cardamom and coffee, their two main cash crops, and they demand 'that they may earn their pennies'. In the words of some of the respondents: 'Both cardamom and maize serve us, the Tzuultaq'a approves of both. Maize is for food, cardamom is for earning money to buy our clothes. To the Tzuultaq'a it is the same, but maize is celebrated more.' Another villager from Samox told me that the Tzuultaq'a advised him to work as a merchant and that the Tzuultaq'a helps him to do so. In short, the villagers of Samox have constructed an image of the Tzuultaq'a which is relevant and favourable to a good performance in both subsistence and cash crop production. Not surprisingly, the villagers of Samox are much more integrated into the market economy than their fellow Q'eqchi'es of Xalihá (see Chapter Seven).

However this does not mean that the Tzuultaq'a is indifferent to these categories of crops and products. First, he or she does not accept as sacrifice things that do not originate in the local environment. All the things that are to be sacrificed - cocoa, turkey meat, copal pom and candles - do have their origin in the local environment. A chicken or a turkey that has been bought is not accepted as sacrifice in Samox. Secondly, maize and other food crops continue to be special to the villagers of Samox. Planting and b'antioxink rituals are performed only at the time of planting maize, not when planting coffee and cardamom. Moreover, the villagers of Samox do not think that cash crops are imbued with a spirit.

The Bible-oriented principle dominating in Chaabilchoch and Rubelpec

In contrast to Xalihá and Samox customary religion exists only marginally in Rubelpec and Chaabilchoch, at least so I thought on my first visits to these communities. Several times, I tried to raise the issue of customary rituals at a meeting of catechists and other Catholics in Chaabilchoch but this only provoked laughter. This was obviously not something that could be discussed and their reactions suggested that almost no customary rituals were practised.

Because of this experience I was very surprised to find that in private, even catechists were willing to admit that they perform quite a few customary practices and that they believe in many customary meanings. It was the Chaabilchoch ministro himself who told me in private[14]:

'My parents used to pray mentioning the mountains of Qawa' Xucaneb', Qana' Itzam and Qawa' Kojaj. Before planting their maize my parents would go to the mountains. In those days the land gave good harvests, now much less. Now the land is not very fertile any more *because we do not go to the mountains any more.*'[15]

The fact that they no longer go to the mountains appears as one of the explanations of why the land provides poorer crops: a logic that touches the heart of customary religion. Actually in Chaabilchoch, two catechists join the group which performs the mayejak in Cobán, Cojaj and Tactic, one of them even directed this mayejak in 1992. The catechists I interviewed in Chaabilchoch perform customary planting, b'antioxink and All Saints' Day and All Souls' Day rituals; almost all of them believe that the mountains are alive and address them during their planting rituals. Only wa'tesink re li kab'l rituals receive little attention by catechists in Chaabilchoch. In Rubelpec a similar picture emerges: almost all the catechists perform the customary rituals, as outlined in the previous section, except for the individual mayejak visits to some of the central Tzuultaq'as. In Rubelpec only the ministro and the two instructors I interviewed do not perform most of the customary rituals, but they continue their planting and b'antioxink rituals.

The contradiction between public and private statements suggests that in Chaabilchoch and Rubelpec, there is a difference between, on the one hand, a public level dominated by the church and the catechists leading parish-promoted practices and, on the other hand, a private or household level on which even catechists may practice customary rituals and express customary meanings. They are able to combine these two levels as long as the priest does not attack customary practices openly and as long as customary practices do not interfere with the meanings and practices they promote as catechists.

The public level

In Chaabilchoch and Rubelpec the public level is almost exclusively dominated by parish-promoted and evangelical practices and Bible-oriented meanings. Religious meetings in which a considerable part of the local community participates consist of either the evangelical services and campaigns or the celebrations of the Word and the Masses. All except a small minority participate in these practices. The related meanings are Bible-oriented.

This does not mean that customary practices do not now nor have ever had a place on the public level. In Chaabilchoch the patron saint's feast just lingers on but in Rubelpec, the chinames at least pay attention to San Esteban's day but without other community members participating. The mayejak is only performed by individual households in Rubelpec; in Chaabilchoch only a small group visits the central mountains without community support.

In Chaabilchoch the mayejak used to be celebrated in a comprehensive way by the whole community, but now the youngsters and the evangelicals reject it. Some respondents related the loss of the community mayejak to the fact that the pasawinq who used to direct it have died and that the others 'do not know the mountains'. This personal relationship of some pasawinq with the mountains which enables them to talk about the mountains and to know their names, is important to the mayejak rituals. Another crucial factor in this respect is the negative influence of the priest. Public church-promoted practices may be complemented by customary aspects such as the posadas and processions at Christmas and the Holy Week as long as these aspects do not contradict basic Bible-oriented meanings.

The private level

While the most important customary practices may have been lost at the public level in Chaabilchoch and Rubelpec, the private or household level presents a very different picture. The occasions on which customary rituals focusing on the households are performed, i.e. the clearing of the land, the planting and harvesting of maize and the inauguration of a new house, receive ritual attention on the part of almost all the villagers. Most of the respondents perform customary practices at these moments. Only in Chaabilchoch is there is a minority of villagers who do not pay attention to the harvesting of maize or the inauguration of a new house. Moreover everyone except this minority asks for the things that are relevant to that occasion such as a good harvest, protection from accidents and snake-bites and permission to cultivate the land. The fact that these occasions apparently require ritual attention and that they ask for essential things which they need to survive shows that essential aspects of the customary principle are maintained in Chaabilchoch and Rubelpec. This holds true in the case of both Catholics and evangelicals.

However, as to what the villagers actually do on these occasions or whom they address, there is a wide variety among the households. This variety shows the relatively individualized nature of religion in both communities. As to the practices they perform, the variety goes from comprehensive customary rituals to customary rituals which leave out some of the most controversial elements, to substitution practices, and finally to only some prayers on these occasions. Concerning those whom the villagers address, some pray only to God while others include the Tzuultaq'a as well. Some of the villagers mention only some of the central Tzuultaq'as while others refer to some of the nearby mountains as well. Some address the sun, the moon, the wind and the rain personally while others ask God and/or the Tzuultaq'a to provide them with enough sunshine, air and water to let their crops grow well. Some are convinced that the seed of maize and the house are imbued with an important spirit while others explicitly reject this idea.

A considerable number of respondents do not perform customary rituals in a comprehensive way and not all are convinced of the importance of the Tzuultaq'a, of the spirits of maize and the house, and of the need to address the sun, the moon, the wind and the rain; this constitutes a departure from the customary principle. Customary practices and meanings that are left behind are replaced by Bible-oriented ones, which indicates that the Bible-oriented principle is not only dominant at the public level but it also exerts its influence on customary rituals at the private or household level.

These differences in terms of practices and "persons" to be addressed do not coincide with ecclesiastical distinctions. On the one hand there are a few evangelicals who perform customary rituals and who consider the Tzuultaq'a to be alive and the house to be imbued with a spirit. On the other hand there is a small group of Catholics in both communities who perform hardly any customary practices and who reject crucial customary meanings. Nevertheless, in general Catholics who wish to pay ritual attention to these occasions perform customary practices, though some leave out the most controversial aspects, and the majority of them address the Tzuultaq'a next to God. In general, the evangelicals in both communities perform substitution practices on these occasions and almost all of them address God exclusively.

My concept of substitution practices is in line with what is referred to in the literature as one of the strategies for evangelical churches to deal with indigenous cultures (Garrard 1986: 202-204; Samandú 1990: 94-101). Based on his fieldwork with the Nazarene's church in Alta Verapaz, Samandú distinguishes three such strategies: eradication, agreement[16] and substitution. According to Samandú, those aspects of indigenous cultures that contradict essential elements of the official discourse of these churches are fiercely attacked. Referring to the Q'eqchi'es, he mentions all that is related to the saints, the sacrifice of animals, the use of alcoholic beverages and important aspects of agricultural rituals. Those aspects that do not pose any problem to the evangelical doctrines are accepted, such as the use of native languages, traditional dress and medicinal herbs. Finally, some aspects of indigenous cultures are replaced by similar elements of official evangelical discourse. Referring to these aspects Samandú gives the examples of the substitution of bad spirits by demons, prayer healing taking the place of traditional healing methods and the importance of revelation in both indigenous and evangelical discourses (Samandú 1990: 94-105; Samandú 1989: 38-44).

Indeed, I found an important level of continuity between customary healing methods and prayer healing practices in Pentecostal churches. One of the evangelical respondents in Chaabilchoch told me:

> 'When a child becomes ill all of a sudden, some people say that the child is seen by the mountain [rilomil tzuul - hs], they burn copal pom and do all sorts of things. But we do not believe this. It may be a sin or one of the parents may have done something wrong. It can be cured only by praying to God for the health of the patient.'

In his words, the classification of the illness in terms of rilomil tzuul and the practices designed to cure it are substituted by interpreting the illness as a moral problem which has to be dealt with by praying to God. In any case, disturbed relations with a central "person" in the universe, in this case God substituting for the Tzuultaq'a, remain at the heart of the illness and contacting this "person" constitutes the central act of curing the disease.

Samandú tries to qualify the frequently heard view that evangelical churches are launching a frontal attack on indigenous cultures. Nevertheless, he includes important aspects of agricultural rituals and everything having to do with saints in the category of eradication: these aspects touch the heart of the customary principle. In this way Samandú continues to underline a rupture with indigenous cultures. I would like to go a step further. My analysis of the evangelicals in Chaabilchoch and Rubelpec points to much greater continuity. Indeed, the saints are a delicate matter and evangelicals take the Catholics to task for believing in saints, but they themselves often talk about the saints in personal terms as well. The dispute between Catholics and evangelicals is not so much whether the saints have any influence at all on the harvests, but rather whether this influence is positive or negative.

In addition, everything that is related to agricultural rituals is not simply rejected by the evangelicals in Chaabilchoch and Rubelpec. The phenomenon of substitution practices is applied by almost all the evangelicals on these occasions. Substitution practices can be defined in the following way: they pay ritual attention to the same occasions as those recognized by customary rituals and ask for the same essential things needed for survival on these occasions. They substitute official church-promoted practices for customary rituals and modify the "persons" who are addressed in a Bible-oriented direction.

It has been shown above that the evangelicals frequently perform substitution practices instead of customary rituals. For example instead of comprehensive maize planting rituals, the members of the Asamblea de Dios in Rubelpec have a service in their church the night before the planting. The evangelicals have a service instead of customary practices when they inaugurate a new house. On both occasions most of the evangelicals stress that they pray to God instead of the Tzuultaq'a or the spirit of the house, but they ask God the same things which others would ask from the Tzuultaq'a and the spirits of maize and of the house.

There are many similar cases of substitution practices which suggest that there is not only discontinuity concerning customary practices but an important degree of continuity as well. The things which the evangelicals reject most explicitly and which they associate with customary religion, i.e. drinking, dancing, music and quarrelling, make sense from their perspective of making a rupture with the past and putting their life in order, but these things do not touch the heart of customary religion. In short, my findings indicate much more continuity than Samandú suggests. This difference may be related to the fact that he writes mainly about the strategies of evangelical churches and leaders while my findings focus on what "ordinary" evangelical church members do and think. A considerable difference in this respect between church leaders and "ordinary" evangelicals may of course be expected.

Evangelicals have no monopoly on substitution practices. The substitution of the 'change of flowers' meeting on Sundays by the celebration of the Word and the sacrifice of products and crops to the church in Carchá by Catholics of Rubelpec replacing their mayejak are similar phenomena. Substitution practices are clear expressions of the continuity and modification of customary religion within the context of a dominant Bible-oriented principle.

God, the Tzuultaq'a and other "persons"

The dominance of the Bible-oriented principle in Chaabilchoch and Rubelpec is related to the fact that God plays the central role in the religious discourse of the villagers. When talking with them about their religion, they mainly refer to God and, only reluctantly if at all, to the Tzuultaq'a.

They express the Bible-oriented meanings of their relations with God - rather abstract, individualistic, moral and not strictly reciprocal. In addition, God is the main "person" they address during customary or substitution practices and they ask Him the things they need to live. God has taken over specific characteristics that are attributed to the Tzuultaq'a in Samox and Xalihá. According to several villagers, God is the source of their maize harvest. Almost all of those who said that the house has a spirit continued to say that this spirit stems from the trees and bushes they use to build their houses, and that God instead of the Tzuultaq'a is the origin of the life of these plants. Moreover almost all the villagers said that they believed in spirits that can cause them harm, but they turn to God to protect themselves against them.

In both villages the Tzuultaq'a is subordinated to God. Some villagers do not even address him or her during customary rituals. On the question of whether the villagers believe the Tzuultaq'a is alive, there is difference of opinion. Most Catholics think he or she is while a most of evangelicals hold the mountains to be just "things". However one evangelical in Chaabilchoch confirmed the customary view that the mountain is sacred because he is the origin of their food and is created by God, but he makes an interesting reorganization of existing customary "persons" such as the Tzuultaq'a, the wind and the rain, saying that 'the mountain is alive because he has clouds around him. With these clouds he worships God just like a bird who sings in praise of God. Man should do the same.' So man, the birds and the mountain are put on a par: they are alive and have the same obligations towards God. In short, in Samox and Xalihá the most important religious relation is between the community and the Tzuultaq'a seen as an intermediary between them and God. In Chaabilchoch and Rubelpec, the importance of the Tzuultaq'a - if he or she has any - consists of his or her role in worshipping God, next to man. Here the most important religious relation is between man and God.

The relations between the villagers of Chaabilchoch and Rubelpec and the Tzuultaq'a have an individual character, but all the other traits of these relations are customary: they are practical, tangible and strict reciprocal. In the words of one of the villagers of Rubelpec: 'The mountain is good to you when you are good, the mountain is bad when you are bad'. The villagers do differentiate among the mountains. The central mountains are more important to them than the nearby ones. In Chaabilchoch almost everyone knows some of these thirteen and talks about them with respect. They call these mountains the 'old mountains' because they know their names. The nearby mountains are unknown to most of them because these mountains are 'new'. Apparently, they have not developed a relationship with the nearby mountains in the two decades since the community has existed, but took the relationship with some of the thirteen with them from their places of origin when they settled there.

The same phenomenon can be observed in Rubelpec but the community was probably founded centuries ago. Here the relative importance of the thirteen can be explained by the fact that they live quite close to some of the thirteen, such as the Calvary in Cobán and the mountain Kojaj, so the distinction between the thirteen and the local Tzuultaq'as becomes blurred. Moreover many villagers work outside the village at least part of the year so their relations with the central Tzuultaq'as, who represent the landscape in all the places they go to within the Q'eqchi' region, is much more relevant.

Q'eqchi' religion in historical perspective

Until this stage I have referred to the present state of affairs of Q'eqchi' religion, but what can be said about it in terms of process and change? On the one hand, the example of the fate of the mayejak in Chaabilchoch illustrates the general impression that Bible-oriented religion is on the offensive in this village and Rubelpec. On the other hand, the revival of customary rituals in Samox points to the opposite conclusion regarding this community and Xaliha. However, this general picture becomes seriously blurred when we take into account that in Chaabilchoch and Rubelpec there is a considerable degree of continuity of customary meanings, especially at the private or household level. Indeed, many respondents in both villages told me that there is a loss of customs, but most of them refer particularly to negative things such as getting drunk or quarrelling which do not touch the heart of customary religion.

Also in Xaliha several pasawink complained about a supposed loss of customs for which they blame the school. However when asked which customs have been lost, the pasawink told me they did not know. Moreover, we may ask whether these complaints represent an actual situation or whether they reflect the responsibility which they feel for the continuity of customary religion. In any case, my interviews do not confirm the general idea that the youth may be losing interest in customs. They do not perform fewer customary practices nor do they express fewer customary meanings than older villagers.

5

Q'eqchi' Religion and Modernization

After discussing the religious practices and meanings of "ordinary" Q'eqchi'es in the previous chapter the question whether these meanings and practices can be classified as pre-modern, early modern or contemporary modern will be tackled first in this chapter. Second, the character and the power of the specialists' influence on the religion of ordinary Q'eqchi'es will be evaluated on the basis of the material presented in Chapter Three.

Q'eqchi' religious meanings and practices in a modernizing framework?

The important religious meanings and practices that belong to the customary principle show clear pre-modern characteristics. This principle views nature in a personalized way; it exposes the dependence of the Q'eqchi'es on this enchanted nature, and is oriented towards the manipulation of natural powers. The Q'eqchi'es assume an active role in their relations with these powers which thus become predictable rather than arbitrary. Relations with them are practical and tangible. Customary religion underscores the importance of subsistence agriculture and basic economic elements are also viewed in a personalized way: e.g. the image of land as the skin of the Tzuultaq'a and maize and houses which are imbued with a spirit. Religious rituals are indispensable to ensure a good harvest and other things crucial for survival.

Moreover, customary religion marks the ways the Q'eqchi'es map their life-worlds and identify themselves. It provides ritual and symbolic substance for the Q'eqchi'es' primary identification with their household and local community which are symbolized as two vital units. The first consists of the household, the house, their land, the plants, crops and animals on this land and the specific saint and ancestors related to the household. A second unit includes the community, the mountain, the valley, the land the community cultivates, their animals and crops, the sun, the rain, the wind, the moon and the saints among others. Life is the central "substance" within both units and is inherent in all these elements unlike things that have an external origin. In addition, customary religion underscores a secondary level of identification: the Q'eqchi'es as a group. I refer to the thirteen mountains representing the general Tzuultaq'a which encompasses the whole Q'eqchi' region and is addressed by Q'eqchi'es from different communities at their mayejak.

However, the importance of the community is paramount in customary religion as is reflected in the patron saint's feast, in the community mayejak and in the communal meal as a standard ingredient of all customary rituals. Giving food reaffirms good relations with other members of the community as well as with other "persons" such as the Tzuultaq'a (mayejak), the house (wa'tesink re li kab'l) and the spirit of maize (putting food on its seed).

In short, the personalization of nature; the importance of religion in the Q'eqchi'es construction of identity and in their ways of conceiving of social relations; the emphasis on subsistence agriculture and on rural life; the personalization of important aspects within this subsistence agriculture, and its practical, immediate, communitarian and tangible character clearly give customary religion a pre-modern character. Only the trustworthy and predictable as opposed to the arbitrary character of personified nature contrasts with the pre-modern religious traits as outlined in the first chapter.

By contrast, the Bible-oriented principle displays modern traits. Nature is created by God, but in itself it has no personal character. It is disenchanted and can be used in an instrumental way. Bible-oriented religion is not related to any specific economic activity, but it encourages the Q'eqchi'es to maximize their economic performance by means of market integration. Bible-oriented religion does not conceive of social reality in such direct religious terms as customary religion. Nevertheless, it has important consequences for social relations and constructions of identity. Bible-oriented religion may help the Q'eqchi'es to embark on an ordered life, it emphasizes moral standards of behaviour and social relations are understood in moral terms which are linked to God's will. It underscores the importance of the church community rather than the local community, which does not exclude the fact that Bible-oriented religion focuses mainly on the individual and on his or her relations with God. These relations are not clearly reciprocal and God has a rather abstract character. God has to be feared related to the concept of sin.

In short, the profane ways in which nature and social reality are portrayed, linked to the encouragement of economic improvement and *Selbstzwang*, the moralization of social relations as well as the principle of equality of all human beings and the importance of the church community are all modern characteristics of Bible-oriented religion. The same holds true for its emphasis on the individual's relations with God and the importance of a written text as the ultimate religious authority. Only the image of a fearful God contrasts with the characteristics of modern religion as outlined in the first chapter.

Religious creolization

The ways the Q'eqchi'es deal with both principles, articulating modern and pre-modern meanings and practices, clearly have a creolizing and associative character.[1] To begin with, this character is expressed in the very fact that the Q'eqchi'es use both principles in their religious meaning-making and that they perform practices that express meanings belonging to both principles. Next, while the Q'eqchi'es associate specific occasions with specific practices and specific practices with specific meanings they are generally not bothered very much about whether particular meanings from both principles can be interrelated in a consistent or rational way. This points to a primarily associative rather than rational method of dealing with religious meanings. To be sure, there is clearly a degree of convergence between customary and Bible-oriented religion, such as the coincidence of the customary obligation of the whole community to maintain unity vis-à-vis the Tzuultaq'a and moral requirements of Bible-oriented religion. However, where there is difference of meanings the Q'eqchi'es evade questions pointing to such inconsistency.

Nevertheless, the basic associative character of their religious creolization does not exclude the fact that they do try to secure some level of synchrony in cases of difference. The distinction made by the villagers of Rubelpec and Chaabilchoch between the household level and the public level allows them to publicly adhere to the dominant Bible-oriented principle while maintaining a considerable level of customary meanings and practices on the private level. Moreover, meanings and practices of the subordinate principle are adapted to the dominant one, which leads to varying relations between the "persons" in the universe, notably between God and Tzuultaq'a. Substitution practices present the best example of the articulation of difference with continuity. Other examples are presented by such central elements of both principles as the cross and the mountains. The cross refers not only to the death and resurrection of Christ, but also to the customary universe and the spirit of maize. Most Tzuultaq'as have both a Catholic Spanish and a Q'eqchi' name.

In the process of adopting both customary and church-promoted practices the Q'eqchi'es adapt the meanings attached to these practices to respond to their practical and symbolic needs. For example, the villagers of Samox made use of the capacity of customary religion to symbolically "solve" problems in relation to nature by making the Tzuultaq'a relevant to the cultivation of their coffee and cardamom when these crops became affected by disease. Q'eqchi' religion is very alive in responding to particular needs, which is expressed in a large number of practices articulated in creative ways even in villages that have been founded only recently - such as Xalihá, Chaabilchoch and Samox. In terms of customary religion, migration may create problems because the link with the sacred landscape of the places the migrants left becomes disrupted. An identification with local Tzuultaq'as in the new places of settlement is difficult in the beginning because 'we do not know their names' or 'because these mountains are new' as some villagers of these communities told me. This fact underscores the relative importance in the settlement areas of pilgrimages to some of the central thirteen Tzuultaq'as, but after some years identification with the local landscape may come about.

The religious blend the Q'eqchi'es make out of elements adapted and adopted from both customary and Bible-oriented religion points to the creolizing character of this blend. However, creolization is of all times which means that the Q'eqchi'es' creolizing way of dealing with pre-modern and modern aspects of their religion is not just a contemporary modern response to relativization (see Chapter One). Its associative features can be traced back to originally modern popular or lay religion and even pre-modern religion. Hence a further classification of Q'eqchi' religion into pre-modern, and originally or contemporary modern terms has to take other elements into account: its reflexive or non-reflexive nature, the level of privatization of religious decision-making, the level of fragmentation or its shattered character and the influence of religious specialists or the field character of Q'eqchi' religion.

This creative articulation points to the fact that there is no real difference between customary and Bible-oriented religion in implicit or explicit terms. Customary rituals are not just practised out of habit or because the pasawink tell their fellow community members to perform them while meanings remain implicit. Nor are the practices offered by the churches adopted "consciously" by the Q'eqchi'es who are completely aware of all the explicit meanings attached to them. To some degree customary practices are objects of discussion and active meaning making whereas to some extent churches are able to use their authority to make the Q'eqchi'es perform the practices they want them to perform. Both customary practices and Bible-oriented practices have implicit and explicit aspects or dimensions.

Religious meaning-making takes place in the context of a plural supply of practices and meanings which encourages some level of privatization of religious decision-making. It encourages some people to emphasize customary meanings while others stress Bible-oriented representations. This level of privatization of religious decision-making is reflected in the variety of religious practices and meanings within the community and in the number of households that can be regarded as mixed in ecclesiastical terms. In Chaabilchoch and Rubelpec variation of religious practices and meanings is relatively large and in Rubelpec a minority of households even have members belonging to different churches. However, in every community the household remains the dominant unit in deciding on church membership and almost all my respondents adhered to the central meanings of both religious principles. In Xalihá and Samox religious variation hardly exists at all.

Not only is the degree of privatization of religious decision-making limited, the same holds true as regards fragmentation or the shattered character of religion. Of course, the Q'eqchi'es show relatively little interest in resolving inconsistencies and there are considerable contradictions between meanings from both principles. However these considerations are insufficient to characterize Q'eqchi' religion as a mismatched conglomerate of indeterminate beliefs of contemporary modern religion (see the first chapter). The Q'eqchi'es have their ways of ordering their representations and practices.

Regarding the question of whether Q'eqchi' religion can be classified in terms of a religious field, several considerations have to be taken into account. First, concerning the level of separation between economics and religion, this level will be discussed in Chapter Seven and Chapter Eight and the conclusion will be reached that there is a limited but real level of autonomy between these aspects of Q'eqchi' reality. Second, there is a separate category of religious specialists who try to influence the religious practices and meanings of the "ordinary" Q'eqchi'es. Consequently, the criteria which would enable us to speak about a religious field have largely been met.

In short, the low level of privatization and individualization of religious decision-making, the low level of fragmentation of religious discourse, the fact that there is at least a minimum level of religious reflexivity and the fact that the concept of religious field can be fruitfully applied; all these arguments allow me to conclude that Q'eqchi' religious creolization is inscribed in an originally modern context of popular or lay religion in relation to official religion propagated by religious specialists.[2]

The influence of religious specialists

In performing religious practices and constructing religious meanings, "ordinary" Q'eqchi'es are influenced by intervening churches and local leaders. This section advances three central arguments which would lead us to classify the influence of Catholic pastoral agents and ministers as modern. First, the presence itself of bishops, priests, religious women, and ministers, their claim to authority on religious matters and their attempts to influence the religion of the "ordinary" Q'eqchi' believers are all early modern traits.

However, there are considerable differences among them as regards the claim to authority. Sacramentalist priests make the strongest claim. They consider themselves as having exclusive access to pure doctrine and the exclusive right to decide on which religious practices and representations are valid. Competing specialists are either incorporated or marginalized. The authority claim of pastoral agents practising liberating pastoral work is not exclusive. They seek co-operation with customary leaders and emphasize the need for reflection by both clergy and laity to discover the legitimate representations and practices stemming from both official texts and existing religious practices and representations. Nevertheless, pastoral agents from both tendencies reserve for themselves the right to perform standard Catholic practices and to decide on the meanings of these practices.

The exclusive right to administer the sacraments and the emphasis on the role of the priest in mediating between believers and the sacred world is absent in evangelical churches. Believers have direct access to the works of the Holy Spirit and their own religious responsibilities are emphasized. Nevertheless, even among evangelical churches claims to authority vary. In "historical" churches and in the Nazarene's church the authority of the minister is based partly on his theological training whereas in Pentecostal churches this training is much more limited. In the latter, the minister does not have a monopoly over interpretation of Bible texts. Direct sacred experiences of the believers are emphasized and the minister has to establish his authority through his personal relations with the believers.

A second argument to characterize the influence of intervening churches as modern is provided by the fact that the religious contents which they promote have a clearly modern character as well. They all preach a rational, systematic and moralizing religious discourse which claims an eternal and universal validity. They all portray God in a rather abstract way, emphasize the Bible and focus on the individual's moral responsibility. However, the discourse they proclaim is in no way static or constant. There is no such thing as church-promoted or customary religion in its "pure" form. Some elements may constitute an important part of religious discourse and policy at one time to be criticised at another. An example of this change is the importance given to the cofradías in colonial times and to apostolic movements such as the *cursillos de cristiandad* and the *legión de María* until recently, whereas they are presently rejected or neglected in contemporary sacramentalist and liberating pastoral policy respectively.

Moreover, the religious discourse proclaimed by the churches is not systematic and directive enough to prevent differences of opinion arising not only on pastoral policy but also on central discursive and theological issues. In daily practice such differences may be as important as aspects of the discourse which they share. Pastoral agents working along the lines of liberating pastoral work complement these early modern aspects with pre-modern customary elements. The growing importance of these elements is reflected in the change of emphasis in liberating pastoral work from "consciousness raising" focusing on a "just" variant of economic, social and political modernity in the 1970s, to encouraging Q'eqchi' identity today. They encourage the Q'eqchi'es to perform (pre-modern) customary practices and to reproduce customary meanings which are incorporated into standard Catholic practices.

Sacramentalist pastoral work tries to exercise a much more unambiguously modern influence. The priests' claim to exclusive authority means that they try to "dispossess" the Q'eqchi'es as regards religious meaning-making. The Salesians portray God as a "loving God" and the Provider of salvation who makes moral demands on the individual believer. Their religious discourse is universal and needs no "inculturation" into local cultures. In their eyes loyalty to the church has a higher priority than loyalty to the local community. They conceive of nature and social relations instrumentally, and in their social projects emphasize modern elements such as market integration and scientifically developed technology. Some Salesian priests told me: 'We promote a rational interpretation of the world', and 'God wants man to dominate nature and not the other way around as in the case of those bad customs which make them fatalistic'. However, the Salesian modernizing variant has a paternalistic character both in religious and social matters, which hampers a more participatory or democratic variant of modernization.

Most evangelical churches share almost all the modern characteristics of the Salesians discourse, but also in this respect there are important differences among evangelical churches. The rational and systematic character of religious discourse is much more pronounced in the case of the "historical" churches than in the Pentecostal churches, with the Nazarene's church in between. In Pentecostal churches coherent theology and doctrine have to give way to individual and direct religious experiences. This opens up the possibility of a more fragmented religion which emphasizes private religious decisions. The continuous process of splitting up of churches with groups of individual believers starting their own church, may represent or enhance private religious decision-making. The latter is an indicator of a more contemporary modern form of religion.

Moreover, the tensions that have come to the fore in recent decades, first between priests and catechists on the one hand and customary leaders on the other and later between Catholic and evangelical leaders, demonstrate that it has not been easy for religious specialists to come to terms with increasing, contemporary modern pluralization and relativization. Some leaders accept a high degree of merging of discourse and flexibility while others stick to a defensive attitude towards others trying to promote their idea of a pure and absolute official discourse. In both cases, however, they end up with a more or less articulate and assembled discourse.

A third argument which would lead us to classify the influence of churches as modern is provided by their attempts to intervene in social matters. Both sacramentalist and liberating pastoral work are strongly committed to dealing with problems that are created in fields other than the religious one. Catholic pastoral agents consider poverty, insufficient access to education and health care - and in the case of liberating pastoral work the violation of Human Rights - to be incompatible with God's will; and this obliges them to set up an impressive number of projects and activities. In addition, both pastoral agents who apply a sacramentalist pastoral policy and evangelical leaders promote religiously based morals which encourage the individual to improve his or her economic performance and to work hard.

Next, church leaders try to influence the Q'eqchi'es' identity constructions. Liberating pastoral work encourages them to identify with their local community and tries to reinforce their identification with the Q'eqchi'es as a supra-local social category. Both sacramentalist pastoral work and most of the evangelical churches encourage the Q'eqchi'es to be proud of themselves but delegitimize specific cultural and religious contents which may underscore

Q'eqchi' identity. Salesians and evangelicals promote the identification as "believers in God" as a contribution to a wider Guatemalan national identity.

Finally, especially during the period of massive violence, every group of religious specialists exercised its ideological influence: liberating pastoral work questioned power relations both at the local and national levels, while Salesians and most of the evangelical churches tried to keep "their" believers from engaging in political activity. In the first chapter all these types of social intervention were classified as modern. The influence of intervening churches can generally be classified as modern.

In addition, there are local religious leaders who are typical "brokers": most of them play an intermediary role between a church and their local community while they symbolize the legitimacy of creolizing customary and Bible-oriented meanings and practices. In the case of catechists and evangelical lay leaders, priests and ministers teach them to promote Bible-oriented meanings and practices as their primary task. However, these lay leaders belong to the local community and use its relative autonomy to modify external practices and meanings and to incorporate them selectively. Either only in private (in Chaabilchoch and Rubelpec) or also in public (in Xalihá and Samox), most catechists and local evangelical leaders perform customary or substitution practices and adhere to crucial customary meanings. The fact that they do so legitimatizes other community members to creolize (modern) Bible-oriented with (pre-modern) customary representations and rituals.

It was pointed out that until a few decades ago customary leaders such as chinames and pasawinq played an important role in publicly promoting both customary religion and representations and activities related to the church. Nowadays, they are unable to do so in the evangelical churches and in Salesian-run churches they are either marginalized or incorporated into church activities with the proviso that they abstain from promoting customary practices in public. However, even in the latter case the chinames and pasawinq continue customary religion in private. In churches run by priests who work along the lines of liberating pastoral work chinames and pasawinq retain their capacity to articulate the promotion of customary religion, even in public, with the promotion of Bible-oriented practices and meanings.

In short, only pasawinq who have been marginalized from both the evangelical and the Salesian-run Catholic church are not in a position to promote the articulation of customary with Bible-oriented religion. Except for these particular pasawinq all local religious leaders have a primary responsibility to promote either customary or Bible-oriented religion, but in their daily lives they exemplify the legitimacy of articulating pre-modern and modern religion. In this way their "broker" character becomes apparent.

Religious power

The predominantly originally modern influence of churches and the mixed pre-modern and originally modern impact of local leaders tells us something about the kinds of influence the specialists exercise. Their capacity to do so is another question.

There are a number of facts that indicate a considerable degree of power on the part of priests, religious women and ministers. A first indicator is the importance of the Bible-oriented principle in Q'eqchi' religion. The standard meanings and practices which the Catholic and evangelical churches promote largely coincide with the Bible-oriented principle within the religion of the Q'eqchi'es. In all four villages that have been presented here, the villagers perform almost all the practices that are promoted by the various churches. Exceptions are the small minority of villagers in Chaabilchoch, Samox and Rubelpec who do not participate in any church and the minority of couples in Rubelpec and Samox who are not married. In Xalihá the villagers do not pay much attention to Christmas or Holy Week.

In addition, priests of both pastoral tendencies are able *grosso modo* to achieve their objectives of either integrating catechists and customary leaders into the performance of both parish-promoted and customary practices, or incorporating the chinames into parish policy and marginalizing the pasawinq who want to go on performing customary practices at the community level. The Salesian priests are even able to make the performance of customary practices at the community level very difficult; the activities organized by cofradías and hermandades in the town of Carchá being the main exceptions. The importance of the customary principle in Samox and Xalihá is at least partly related to the encouragement given by the priests. The pasawinq in both communities stressed the importance of the support they receive from the priests and the parish council of pasawinq. The dominance of one principle over the other in the four villages coincides with the kind of pastoral policy that is followed by the churches. All these indicators point to a strong power position priests have as regards local leaders and communities.

Priests have several advantages in this respect compared to their evangelical counterparts. They monopolize the preparation and administration of sacraments and the central meanings of the sacraments constitute an important power resource. Next, compared to Pentecostal ministers in particular priests have much more pronounced authority as regards legitimate discourse, such as Bible interpretations. In addition, the Catholic church provides a considerable number of social projects while this capacity - and willingness - on the part of most evangelical churches is very limited. Finally, the Nazarene's church has a rather democratic organization, limiting the power of ministers: they are elected by the local church every two years.

Nevertheless, the power of Catholic pastoral agents and ministers has its limits. First, although the Q'eqchi'es identify with their church, this identification is subordinated to their primary identification as a member of the household and local community. As a result, each minister and Catholic pastoral agent has to gain the confidence of the community before being able to work with its members. This confidence cannot be taken for granted and is not unconditional. Secondly, there is considerable diversity and tension among these specialists which seriously hampers any effort to work out a common pastoral policy towards the Q'eqchi'es. This is certainly true of the Catholic church with its diverse clergy, bishoprics and diverging pastoral policies. The increasing fragmentation of evangelical churches points in the same direction.

Thirdly, either because of their limited numbers or out of conviction Catholic pastoral agents and ministers work through structures of lay leaders which constitute the backbone of their church. The catechists are very sincere in transmitting to their communities what these pastoral agents tell them; especially in Salesian-run parishes these agents actually control the catechists to a large extent. Nevertheless, the fact that even in these parishes the catechists continue to practice customary rituals indicates that they are not mere executors of what they have been told by the clergy.

A similar pattern applies to evangelical church leaders: the importance of Bible-oriented religion is an indicator of their influence, but at the private level many evangelicals demonstrate an important degree of continuity with customary religion. We have come across several quotations from evangelicals who suggest that the power of their leaders is limited and that it is the Q'eqchi'es themselves who decide mainly about what they believe and what they do. In their meetings it does not matter very much whether a minister is present or not. They emphasize individual religious responsibility. Evangelical leaders were certainly unable to convince my respondents of the discursive differences between their churches and the Catholic one. The power of local evangelical leaders and ministers should not be exaggerated.

Referring to the power of the catechists several considerations should be taken into account. The authority they derive from their contacts with priests and religious women is an important resource vis-à-vis other community members. In addition, their "office" has a permanent character, their role in the community has a strong discursive element (Bible explanation, sacrament preparation), and they have access to the Bible and other external meanings. Catechists benefit from intensive religious training and from skills acquired for example in literacy groups. Next, the importance of the Bible-oriented principle is not only indicative of the power of Catholic pastoral agents, but also of the catechists. They play a prominent role in the Catholic part of the public level in Chaabilchoch and Rubelpec. In the latter community being a Catholic is even associated with being a "collaborator" with the catechists. Nevertheless, the fact that they themselves apply a creolizing religious strategy shows that they are more likely to be regarded as part of the community than as externally supported religious leaders dominating the community.

In most communities customary leaders do not have access to external power resources like those of the catechists and local evangelical leaders. Only in parishes where a policy of liberating pastoral work is followed are they authorized to play an important role by the clergy. Elsewhere they rely solely on the authority of age and the willingness of the community to value customary religion. Moreover, the "office" of chinames and membership in cofradías and hermandades is temporary, their influence is mainly practical and they need the confirmation of their "office" by the community. The power of the pasawinq has a stronger basis because their "office" is permanent, their role is discursive (praying and leading customary rituals) and they have the power to expel someone from the community. They did so in Xalihá recently. Those pasawinq who also work as ilonel may have specially important power resources to draw on. They offer a crucial service (cure for illness), have special knowledge about how everything and every "person" should be treated and this knowledge is rather secret. In addition, they are feared because they are suspected of having tuul qualities enabling them to inflict harm.

In any case, the roles customary leaders play in their communities vary and the importance of the customary principle itself is the best indicator of their influence in local communities which means that their influence is particularly strong in Xalihá and Samox. In Chaabilchoch and Rubelpec they play hardly any role at the public level, but they are often called in to lead customary practices at the household level.

In short, the power of religious specialists vis-à-vis the "ordinary" Q'eqchi'es varies from one category of specialists to another; the influence of priests and catechists in particular is considerable. However, the relationship between specialists and "ordinary" Q'eqchi'es is not characterized by one of the parties unconditionally accepting and doing what the other party says. It is a matter of - often implicit - negotiation. Even the effects of conversion to an evangelical church should not be exaggerated. Such conversion has limited discursive consequences and the way converts deal with an evangelical church is not very different from the way they used to deal with the Catholic church. In general, religious specialists are unable to significantly affect the fundamental strategy of the Q'eqchi'es for dealing with their religion, i.e. the selective articulation of pre-modern and modern aspects adopted from indigenous and external sources which they adapt to their symbolic needs in an originally modern framework.

This analysis points first of all to the fact that the concepts of pre-modern, originally modern and contemporary modern can be applied both to the religion of churches and local leaders and to the religion of the "ordinary" Q'eqchi'es. Secondly, there is no reason to assume that the Q'eqchi'es are heading for clear-cut religious modernization. As long as they are able to continue their strategy of selective articulation of pre-modern and modern aspects, there is no reason to suppose that the Q'eqchi'es are unavoidably heading for an ever more modern religion.

Over the last few decades Bible-oriented religion has certainly been reinforced among the Q'eqchi'es because of increasing interventions both by the Catholic and evangelical churches, but it is not farfetched to suppose that this increase has not led to any great decline in customary religion. In Xalihá and Samox there are no indications of the latter; in Samox there has even been a revival of customary religion. In Rubelpec and Chaabilchoch the community mayejak and much of the communitarian character of the patron saint's feast have been lost, but the villagers have retained an important degree of continuity in customary practices and meanings. The differences between Samox and Xaliha on the one hand and Rubelpec and Chaabilchoch on the other are indicative of the fact that churches do play a role in the religious affairs of these communities, but their influence is not strong enough to significantly alter the relative autonomy of the local communities which enables them to continue their religious creolization.

An important effect of the power of these churches is the declining public role of women. In the Salesian-run parishes in particular the catechists tend to dominate not only religious life but all community affairs. The fact that the vast majority of them are men who have a negative attitude towards the "general assembly" has brought about a reduction in the public role of women. Customary leaders are always couples and both the man and the woman decide on their tasks; although the "general assembly" was and still is made up mainly of adult men, I have seen women participating on this level in various communities.

The religious women have been unable to neutralize this effect by organizing women's groups or female catechists. These groups are not expected to play a leading role in the community and even in those cases where there are female catechists they are supposed to work only with women's groups and not to play a leading or discursive role in the celebration of the Word. Women's groups focus on practical skills and on religious instruction which emphasizes existing gender patterns.

6

The Economic Field:
Intervening Agencies and Local Leaders

In the following chapters the focal point will shift from the world of gods and spirits to the material existence of the Q'eqchi'es, or more precisely, to the ways in which they try to reproduce and improve their material conditions. Both focal points do not exclude each other. In the previous chapters we came across several examples of religious representations and practices that are interrelated with economic matters. One of the objectives of this analysis of Q'eqchi' economy is to detect its interrelations with Q'eqchi' religion; however in order to do so, economy and religion must first be distinguished. The analysis of Q'eqchi' economy will start in this chapter with an outline of the main actors and agencies that intervene in the life-world of the Q'eqchi'es and influence their economic strategies. Next, local Q'eqchi' leaders who play a prominent role in the economy of the communities will be presented.

Intervening actors and agencies

The external character - external to the social and geographical units with which the Q'eqchi'es primarily identify - is very pronounced in the case of actors and agencies that intervene in the economy of the Q'eqchi'es. These actors and agencies consist almost exclusively of Kastii who have a difficult task trying to convince the Q'eqchi'es of their good intentions. The Q'eqchi'es have interests that clash with those of several of them such as the landlords.

Landlords

The landlords who own large estates in the Q'eqchi' region show a wide variety of origins and nationalities.[1] There are descendants of Germans, army officers and other whites, Spaniards and North Americans who mostly live in the capital or abroad. There are no Q'eqchi'es among them.

These landlords control approximately one third of the arable land in the region. Their estates can be classified into *haciendas* or cattle ranches, and *fincas* which grow cash crops. Such a finca or hacienda covers at least a few *caballerías*[2]. The main coffee and cardamom growing fincas are to be found in the highlands of the Q'eqchi' heartland, but in the last decades relatively little capital has been invested in them. Just before the war the fincas in Verapaz boasted the highest levels of investment and productivity but by the end of the 1980s, they had dropped to the lowest in the country.[3] Even the railroads and steamships connecting the highlands with the Caribbean seaports have fallen into disrepair. The exceptions are the modern rice growing farms in the lowlands of the Polochic river valley. Cattle raising haciendas are mainly to be found in Izabal, El Petén and the Franja, but in most of these areas cattle raising turned out to be unprofitable and several landlords are selling out.

The cattle raising farms are very labour extensive so few Q'eqchi'es live or work on them. In contrast, the growing of coffee and cardamom does require much labour. The economic strategy of the finca owners is based on the brutal exploitation of the labour force which is organized along semi-feudal lines. The labour force on these fincas falls into two categories: the permanent workers (*mozos colonos*), and temporary labourers (*jornaleros*).

Almost all the mozos are Q'eqchi'es who have no access to land of their own. They live on the finca and work in the coffee or cardamom production a large part of the year. To compensate they are allowed to use a plot of land of a few *manzanas*[4] to grow their basic food crops. These plots are usually the less fertile ones high up the mountain slopes. In addition, they receive a wage of between three and seven quetzales[5] a day except during the coffee harvest period. Some fincas pay just one or two quetzales while the official minimum wage is 11.25 quetzales. The landlords want to exercise strict control of every aspect of the social life of the mozos. Trade unions are strictly forbidden.

This large scale cash crop production has very severe consequences for the Q'eqchi'es. First, the occupation of a large proportion of the best arable land is one of the principal reasons for the serious land shortage in the region. In addition, much of the land controlled by fincas is not used productively. For example the finca of Sasis has a territory of 245 caballerías (11,049.5 hectares). Only nine of these caballerías are used to grow coffee while the 500 families of mozos have some 15 caballerías at their disposal to grow their food crops. As a result, 221 caballerías (9,967.1 hectares) lay fallow. Part of this fallow land is not suited for agriculture, but there is still an enormous potential of fertile land which is held back from the Q'eqchi'es in an area (Carchá) where land scarcity is most severe. In the settlement areas, the land owners leave a large part of their land unused and deny Q'eqchi'es access to it.

Secondly, the pressure on land and the expansion of large landed estates result in countless land conflicts between landlords and Q'eqchi'es, which continue to the present day. Just to give one example, the community of Venecia had been cultivating a piece of land on the finca Panacté, municipality of Panzós, for more than a decade with the consent of the finca owner. Then, the finca was taken over by a new owner; at the same time rumours about the construction of a new bridge and road which would make the finca more accessible, incited the new owner to throw the community off his land. When they refused to leave he sent a band of gunmen to kill four community members on February 6, 1991. The community does not exist any more. Land conflicts are the principal reason for human rights violations in the region.

The export of coffee, cardamom and meat has a positive effect on the country's balance of payments but the Q'eqchi'es see very little of this money. Government investment in the region is very limited and in spite of legal obligations landowners' willingness to invest in such things as health care or education facilities is negligible. For instance, in their efforts to organize primary schools several priests told me they have come up against serious opposition from finca owners even when these schools are externally financed.

The Q'eqchi'es react to this intervention by landlords in various ways. Many communities involved in land conflicts resort to the department of legal assistance of the bishopric of Verapaz but there are also many who, after a while, see no alternative but to leave and look for land elsewhere. Mozos colonos sometimes leave the finca to look for a piece of land in the settlement areas. In recent years many of them have been pushed by the landlords because they want to stem population increase on their fincas and several of them are transforming their fincas into haciendas with much less labour demand. Especially younger Q'eqchi'es leave the fincas, but some mozos colonos do not dare take the risk of leaving. Several of them told me: 'Although we are in a bad situation, we prefer to go on like this'.

The general reaction of those who live outside a finca is to refuse to work for a landlord. They profoundly dislike fincas and landlords. In Xalihá, Samox and Chaabilchoch very few villagers who go to work on a finca once in a while. In Rubelpec where wage labour is by far the most important source of income, only five villagers work on nearby fincas. The villagers even prefer to go to distant places such as the Franja and El Petén to work for other Q'eqchi'es than to work on nearby fincas which pay higher wages during the coffee harvest period. As a result of the Q'eqchi'es' refusal to work as jornalero, the finca administrators have to bring in thousands of families from other parts of the country, mainly from Baja Verapaz and El Quiché, during the coffee harvest. Like the mozos in this period they are paid by the piece, which makes it possible for a family to earn up to fifteen quetzales a day.

Merchants

With respect to trade and commerce in the region, a distinction has to be made between cash crop trade on the one hand, and retail trade in consumer goods on the other hand.[6] The latter is open to Q'eqchi'es and members of other indigenous groups while the former is monopolized by Kastii merchants.

The power of the Kastii merchants who buy cash crops such as coffee, cardamom and rice from Q'eqchi' villagers is considerable. They are able to take advantage of the poor infrastructure and the lack of a properly functioning market system. Most communities are not connected to any road at all and except for the three central towns of Cobán, Carchá and Chamelco there is no functioning local market where the Q'eqchi'es can sell their crops. The types of trucks able to negotiate the existing roads are expensive. Only some of the Kastii in the towns have access to enough capital or credit to buy one and to work as a merchant with a truck, a so-called *camionero*. In the Cobán and Lancetillo areas merchants even use small aircraft to transport cardamom. The Q'eqchi'es have no alternative but to take their crops to the nearest road and wait for such a camionero to pass by, often having to stay there for hours. Consequently, they are very dependent on camioneros.

Moreover, there are clear indications of price agreements and fixing among the camioneros. Such an indication is presented by what happened to the cardamom dryer in Samox. The villagers managed to get a loan of 15,000 quetzales from the state bank, *Banco Nacional de Desarrollo Agrícola*, to build a cardamom dryer hoping to get better prices for their product in a processed form. When they first offered their processed cardamom for sale, no merchant was willing to pay a higher price than for the non-processed cardamom. At present, the dryer is not used any more and the villagers remain with a debt of thousands of quetzales. In addition, many Q'eqchi'es complained that they had recently been cheated by camioneros. The fact that they hardly speak Spanish seriously undermines their negotiating ability.

The fact that these market conditions and the power of the camioneros seriously restrict the opportunities of the Q'eqchi'es to integrate into the market economy, is underlined by the examples of El Petén and Rubelpec. In El Petén the low prices which the Q'eqchi'es receive for their products because of these constraints seriously discourage them to sell their products at all.[7] In contrast, the villagers of Rubelpec have direct access to the market in Carchá which significantly improves their eagerness to develop many market-oriented activities.

When capital and access to markets are available, the Q'eqchi'es are able to make important improvements. Stimulated by the programme of multiplicadores de pastoral social of the bishopric of Verapaz, the villagers of four communities in the Franja Transversal del Norte decided to buy a truck financed by a loan mediated by the bishopric in 1992. This truck has allowed them to take their rice to Zacapa in the eastern part of the country and sell it to the most important rice trader in Guatemala. In this way, the villagers leave out the intermediary merchants and sell their rice at a price of 55 quetzales a quintal. Middlemen offered them 25 quetzales in their own villages. Nevertheless, the general lack of access to capital, poor infrastructure and the absence of a proper market system exclude the Q'eqchi'es from cash crop trade. The resulting dependence on Kastii camioneros seriously affects their profits derived from cash crops production.

INTA

Besides private actors there are several state agencies which intervene in the economy of the Q'eqchi'es. The *Instituto Nacional de Transformación Agraria* (INTA) is the agency in charge of the legalization of land rights in the settlement areas.[8] It is supposed to give out titles to land officially known as *baldío*: a piece of land that can be used for agricultural purposes but which has no private owner and consequently belongs to the state. In addition, INTA has given out *fincas nacionales* to co-operatives. These fincas were confiscated from their German owners during the Second World War and have not been returned to them. Moreover, INTA gives out small plots of land, *lotes*, to households to build their houses. Finally, INTA has two training centres to instruct community leaders, but in 1992 only one of them was operating.

In principle, INTA has two kinds of land titles on offer: the first is called *parcelamiento* and the other, *patrimonio agrario colectivo*. Referring to the latter others names are used as well. In the case of a parcelamiento, INTA gives out fixed plots of land to which no one yet has access. These titles are strictly individual, i.e. only an individual household may receive such a title. At first the household obtains a provisional title upon paying the first ten per cent of the price of the land; the balance has to be paid in yearly instalments over the next ten or twenty year, without interest. In the end INTA is supposed to grant the permanent title. An owner is allowed to sell this permanent title, but those who do this are not allowed to buy any more land from the state.

The patrimonio agrario colectivo title has a mixed communitarian and household character. The Local Development Committee of each community is the one which deals with INTA in order to become entitled to the total amount of land on behalf of the community and allocates specific plots of land to each household. Both the committee and the households receive the titles and these indicate which part of the land belongs to whom. If the household wants to sell its plot, the committee has to approve of the new owner.

These kinds of titles are especially suited to communities that already have access to the land in question and want to legalize this access. First, there is the question of the legal status of the land: whether it has an owner or is a baldío. In the latter case the land has to be surveyed; its quality, characteristics and price, as well as the households who are to benefit from it, have to be established. For all these services the community has to call in and pay an INTA engineer several times. Next, the community pays ten per cent of the price and receives provisional titles. Eventually, after ten or twenty years, when the villagers have paid the full price without interest, INTA should concede the permanent titles.

Especially the patrimonio agrario colectivo scheme sounds reasonable. It responds to the mixed communitarian and household control preferred by the Q'eqchi'es themselves when administrating their own lands (see next chapter). In practice, however, both schemes are very problematic. The parcelamiento scheme has been applied on a small scale in various parts of the Q'eqchi' region, such as in the Polochic valley, along the main road in the Río Dulce area, in Raxruhá and in Fray Bartolomé de Las Casas. Among the beneficiaries there are many Kastii and the plots of land vary from a few manzanas tot one caballería.

These beneficiaries have to face serious difficulties. The parcelamiento projects started several decades ago - as early as 1962 in Raxruhá and Fray Bartolomé de Las Casas - but even according to the INTA spokesmen the concession of land titles is very deficient. Only a small minority have permanent titles and in the Raxruhá and Fray Bartolomé projects, the majority do not even have provisional titles yet. In trying to explain these facts, these spokesmen point to the low earnings which the parcelarios receive for their products, the high prices they have to pay for land and the impossibility of paying off their debts with, among others, the state bank BANDESA. Many of the parcelarios have to sell their land or simply leave after a few years. In the Raxruhá and Fray Bartolomé areas, these problems are aggravated by exhaustion of the land after a few years of cultivation. Even when the parcelarios are successful, each household has insufficient land to give each son enough land to start his own household.

The patrimonio agrario colectivo scheme is not very successful either. The chaotic state of the land registration systems make it very difficult to find out whether a piece of land actually is a baldío, but this fact cannot hide INTA's inefficiency and inertia. In the case of Xalihá, the villagers started to apply for the legalization of their land in 1977. INTA sent officials to survey the land in 1985 for the first time and repeated this procedure twice, the villagers having to pay each time. In 1992 INTA offered only the lotes, but it refused to indicate the total amount of land that had been surveyed and what its price would be. In spite of many visits to the central INTA office in the capital by delegations of the villagers, they still remain without even provisional titles. In the case of Chaabilchoch the procedure has been dragging on in a similar way: the villagers remain even without provisional titles, although they have been paying fifty quetzales per household every year since 1984.

The unlawful - if not corrupt - character of INTA practices is suggested by the Samox case as well. A few years ago an INTA engineer surveyed the land of a neighbouring village. He took away a large part of the land of two Samox villagers who have land titles granted by INTA villagers, and gave it to this neighbouring community. The Samox villagers assume that their neighbours have bribed the engineer. Corruption is also suggested by the fact that communities in the San Luís Petén and Poptún areas have to pay five per cent interest and other costs, such as value-added tax, in the course of the ten or twenty years during which they are paying off the price of their land.

Even payment of the total price is no guarantee of receiving titles. In 1991, 4,000 households in the department of El Petén had paid the final instalment but the president simply refused to sign their titles. In the other settlement areas in Izabal, the Polochic valley and the Franja Transversal del Norte, optimistic estimations by INTA officials hold that half of the communities have provisional land titles while only a small minority have permanent titles. Priests and even mayors in several of these areas are much more pessimistic in this respect. Moreover, even the possession of a permanent land title does not guarantee stable access to land, as several communities in Alta Verapaz experienced. Their permanent titles did not prevent them from being confronted with a landlord presenting a title to the same land granted by the same INTA officials. The landlord has ordered the police several times to destroy the villages and capture their leaders, which is what they have done.

In short, instead of assisting the Q'eqchi'es in securing their land rights, INTA seriously adds to the confusion and insecurity concerning access to land. This situation not only seriously affects their willingness to invest in production, it is a major source of human rights violations as well.

DIGESA and DIGESEPE

The *Dirección General de Servicios Agrícolas* (DIGESA) and its sister organization the *Dirección General de Servicios Pecuarios* (DIGESEPE) are two sub-divisions of the ministry of agriculture aiming at providing technical assistance to small and medium size farmers. DIGESA focuses on agrarian production while DIGESEPE concentrates on livestock raising. DIGESA started to work in the Q'eqchi' region in the early 1970s but for several years, its activities were interrupted by the violence. It returned in 1985 and since then, its officials have been working throughout the region. DIGESEPE has a similar network of offices and employees, albeit on a much smaller scale.[9]

DIGESA extension workers instruct farmers on agricultural techniques such as the use of hybrid seeds, chemical fertilizers and pesticides. They teach them how to improve their food crops and how to diversify their cash crops production of coffee, cardamom, fruits, pepper and tomatoes. Vegetables production is also promoted. The extension workers train the farmers on how to maintain the quality of the soil and the wells on their land. In some communities the extension worker manages a small-scale irrigation project. In order to transmit this knowledge to the farmers, each extension worker works with four or five communities which he visits once a week. He organizes a garden in each community to demonstrate the usefulness of his technology.

Next to the DIGESA officials themselves who work in the local communities, DIGESA runs the programme of *representantes agrícolas* together with DIGESEPE. These representantes are selected by the extension workers from community members. They receive training in the areas already mentioned which the extension workers are promoting as well as on the themes favoured by DIGESEPE employees. The representante is supposed to work in his own community and in one or two neighbouring ones to which he is expected to pass on the knowledge he received from the extension workers. He is supposed to spend half his time on these tasks and receives a wage.

The real impact of DIGESA activities is very limited. DIGESA employees work directly in some 85 communities.[10] They are supposed to work two or three years in each community before moving on to another one. However, the extension workers stressed that it takes this time just to gain some acceptance by a community. A spokesman of the central DIGESA office estimated the total number of communities involved since the 1970s at about 25 per cent higher than the number of communities with which DIGESA officials are currently working. If we add the communities that are only contacted through a representante agrícola to these 107 communities, the total number amounts to 250. Even if these were all Q'eqchi' communities, this would mean that only 15.49 per cent of the Q'eqchi' communities has been reached by DIGESA. In practice, this percentage is even lower because DIGESA officials prefer to work with parcelarios among whom non-Q'eqchi'es prevail.

Moreover, the extension workers admitted that they only work with a minority of farmers within this small minority of communities. Moreover, they complained about the fact that when they stop visiting the community, its members stop practising what they are being taught. This is what happened to the oranges project in Xalihá. The extension worker urged the villagers to dedicate a manzana to plant orange trees and he organized a youth club to look after the trees and oranges. After some months, the DIGESA promoters stopped coming so the youth club disintegrated and no one looks after the orange trees any more. Most of the extension workers told me that it is very difficult to convince the communities to apply the advice they offer.

DIGESA officials attribute the low impact of their work mainly to lack of funds, which makes sense. The low prices which the Q'eqchi'es receive for new products whenever they diversify their cash crop production is another problem. Nevertheless, not only external factors are to blame. DIGESA officials conceive of their work as simply transmitting their knowledge to the communities and show very little interest in the economic strategies, indigenous knowledge and technology of the Q'eqchi'es, let alone in the meanings which the Q'eqchi'es attach to this knowledge and technology. They talk about these techniques in a bantering tone.[11] They make no effort to look for external technology that would complement existing Q'eqchi' technology and strategies. DIGESA officials do not recognize their own shortcomings in this respect. Instead, they blame Q'eqchi' culture for the poor result of their work. DIGESA officials point to the 'idiosyncrasy' of the Q'eqchi'es, their lack of education, 'the way they are', the fact that almost all of them speak only Q'eqchi' and their fearful nature in order to explain their reluctance to 'understand' and accept the instructions offered by DIGESA.

This disparaging way of talking about the Q'eqchi'es not only explains a large part of the failure of DIGESA programmes, it also shows that differences between Kastii and Q'eqchi'es are easily interpreted by the former in racist terms. It also reminds us of the difference between official objectives - to do their work properly - and actual goals - cultivating good relations with superiors to get a transfer to an office with a higher status - common to Kastii staffed agencies as outlined in Chapter Two.

DIGESEPE works along the same lines as DIGESA. It runs several schemes of livestock promotion, such as the selling of chickens and cocks at a reduced price. DIGESEPE's main work is focused on preventing and curing animal diseases. In Raxruhá, DIGESEPE has a special station financed by funds from France and Canada and recently a project was started with the assistance of *Veterinarios sin Fronteras* and a fund of 100,000 US dollars donated by the European Union. It resulted in the training of 52 *promotores pecuarios* whose task is to help the community to raise animals, to provide veterinary medicine and to vaccinate animals.[12] In other areas the representantes are taught the same things.

Other official development agencies

Other state agencies working with Q'eqchi' villages include ICTA, BANDESA, INDECA, DIGEBOS, ANACAFé, Moscamed, *Caminos Rurales* and UNEPAR.[13] The *Instituto de Ciencia y Tecnología Agrícolas* (ICTA) is doing research on crop cultivation and livestock raising to determine which ones are most suited for the existing natural conditions. ICTA mainly provides DIGESA and DIGESEPE with applied technology to be passed on to the local communities. The Banco Nacional de Desarrollo Agrícola (BANDESA) is supposed to provide short term loans to peasants and farmers, but in practice its effectiveness is very limited because it only grants loans to those who have land titles. The *Instituto Nacional de Comercialización Agrícola* (INDECA) is supposed to provide the peasants and farmers with facilities to store their products, but its installations hardly function at all.

DIGEBOS organizes groups in local communities, such as Chaabilchoch and Rubelpec, to plant trees. ANACAFé promotes coffee production and Moscamed is responsible for controlling the *mosca mediterranea* and other insects that damage cash crops and livestock. In Chaabilchoch, two villagers receive a wage for working for Moscamed. Caminos Rurales builds and maintains roads making use of the labour force of local communities. Not far from Chaabilchoch, it is building a road and pays the villagers a wage of 307 quetzales for a month's work. Despite such efforts, roads in the region are few in number and bad in quality. The limited number of communities that have a drinking water system suggests that the impact of UNEPAR, which is responsible for organizing such systems, should not be exaggerated. Recently, Chaabilchoch joined neighbouring villages to build a drinking water system, but UNEPAR sold them a worn-out pump that has never functioned.

The army

The most powerful state agency in the area is of course the army, whose operations have serious economic consequences. In Chapter Two we showed that at the beginning of the 1980s in the conflict-ridden areas, the army disrupted the regional economy and destroyed the economic life of some 100 villages. After that the army concentrated on the reconstruction of these villages within the framework of the "development poles" programme. In the reconstructed villages and in the town of Chisec the army, supported by other state agencies, managed to provide corrugated iron sheets, electricity and drinking water. The army gave "food for work" to those who were forced to reconstruct the villages and the town as part of a reducciones-like scheme (AVANCSO 1992: 177). Apart from these efforts, no special attention has been paid to the area as far as development is concerned.

Para-statal agencies and NGOs

Next to state agencies there are several para-statal organizations and NGOs which intervene in the economy of the Q'eqchi'es. However, compared to other regions in Guatemala the presence of NGOs in the Q'eqchi' region is very limited. Several employees of NGOs with offices in the capital attributed their absence from the Q'eqchi' region to the distance from the capital, the poor infrastructure and the fact that only very few Q'eqchi'es speak Spanish.

The *Federación de Cooperativas de las Verapaces* (FEDECOVERA) and the *Instituto Nacional de Cooperativas* (INACOP) are the two main agencies working with co-operatives in the region. After 1968 the fincas nacionales, i.e. the dispossessed fincas that had not been returned to their German owners after the war, were transformed into co-operatives of the former mozos colonos. FEDECOVERA was founded as a formally independent federation of 24 such co-operatives in the central highlands with a membership of more than 5,500. These are production co-operatives which means that the land is collectively owned and cultivated by their members. Funded by USAID, FEDECOVERA provides technical assistance for agricultural production, has facilities to process and store their products, assists in management and administrative tasks and grants credits to the co-operatives.[14] The para-statal organization INACOP provides similar services to the same as well as to other co-operatives.[15] It mainly grants assistance to agricultural production co-operatives, but also to consumer and credit co-operatives.

Any assessment of the impact of FEDECOVERA and INACOP must unavoidably be influenced by the fact that most co-operatives are in a deplorable state. In any case, neither agency has been able to prevent these co-operatives from ending up this way. Those pertaining to FEDECOVERA present a particularly lamentable picture. Almost all of them have enormous debts, are internally divided and unable to make a profit.

Several explanations of these problems have been put forward. On the one hand, from the start these co-operatives were objects of political strife between political parties, INTA and other government agencies about who was to exercise control over them and, more specifically, who should be appointed as administrator. At the times of massive violence, the army has assumed control of the co-operatives. Motives other than the interests of the co-operatives have ruled their management resulting in lack of efficiency and corruption. On the other hand, the Q'eqchi'es in these co-operatives do not feel very responsible for their operation. We must remember that these co-operatives were formed, not as an initiative of those who became their members, but as a result of government policy. Moreover, the purely collective control over and cultivation of land does not respond to the mixed communitarian and individual forms of land control and labour which the Q'eqchi'es generally prefer (see next chapter).

Two other agencies providing technical instruction are the *Instituto Técnico de Capacitación y Productividad* (INTECAP) and *Vitamina "A"*. INTECAP[16] has been working in the Q'eqchi' region since 1972, but the results of its work are unsatisfying because the participants have to be able to read and write and examinations are in Spanish, all of which preclude a large majority of Q'eqchi'es from taking part in its courses. Vitamina "A" is a USAID financed NGO. It promotes the cultivation of vegetables and instructs women on how to prepare them. Its employees distribute vitamin pills and deworming liquids in 22 villages in the Carchá and Chamelco areas. According to its co-ordinator, ten per cent of the villagers follow the advice of the project employees while the project is still going on. What will happen when the project comes to an end as planned after three years is hard to say.

Their recent establishment makes it difficult to assess the effects of two other agencies as well. *Proyecto Quetzal* and *Defensores de la Naturaleza* focus on economic and ecological matters. These matters are very much interrelated. Because of land scarcity and the very unequal land distribution, ever more marginal lands are cleared for agricultural use. Deforestation increasingly threatens ecological conditions. Apart from DIGEBOS, these two agencies try to preserve the remaining forests on the mountain ranges on both sides of the Polochic valley.

Churches

As mentioned in Chapter Three, churches feel they have a role to play not only in Q'eqchi' religion but in their economy as well. Evangelical churches encourage the Q'eqchi'es to optimize their economic performance. The Mennonite church has small-scale agricultural training and drinking water projects in the Carchá and Fray Bartolomé areas. The Nazarene church runs charity projects to help widows and orphans as well as drinking water projects. However, the evangelical projects are limited in number and scope.

The Salesians have many small-scale economic activities such as making loans to local communities and buying chemical fertilizers at reduced prices. They organize meetings of the villagers to allow employees of state agencies to promote their technology. Moreover the boys who are trained in four Salesian boarding schools to work as teachers in the 500 Salesian-run primary schools[17] are expected to instruct the villagers in their communities on external agricultural technology. The Salesians promote an instrumentalist view of production factors such as land and labour and believe in progress through the adoption of modern technology. Indigenous knowledge is looked down upon.

The Department of Social Pastoral Work of the bishopric of Verapaz as well as several diocesan institutions in El Petén and several parishes promote a variety of economic projects that meet the criteria of liberating pastoral work. According to these criteria the whole community must be involved. The project should help the community solve its own problems, to avoid creating a dependent attitude vis-à-vis external agencies, and to increase its technical and management capacities. External techniques and knowledge are supposed to complement and not replace indigenous knowledge and technology.

In keeping with these criteria, the Department of Social Pastoral Work in Cobán works with communities of displaced people who came down from the mountains after hiding from the army. It has secured or purchased land for these people, delivered materials to build houses and community halls, developed productive projects, and it has provided technical assistance. In addition, the Department is involved in the Yalpemex settlement project involving several hundred refugees who returned from Honduras in 1991.

Apart from these integrated projects focusing on those who have returned after hiding inside or outside of the country, the Department has several projects in other communities which have been affected by violence. These communities suffer not only from the physical impact of destruction but from its social effects as well. A considerable number of communities remain divided between those who returned after having spent several years in the mountains, and those who remained behind and had to stay in army camps for several months. In these communities the Department has developed several projects that are meant to encourage the various factions in these communities to overcome their mutual distrust by working together in practical ways. Only in the parish of San Martín (Cobán) has the Department developed these kinds of projects in 32 communities.

In 1988 the Department created an office to provide legal assistance to the countless communities involved in land conflicts. Communities can rely on the office for legal support to claim their rights in accordance with Guatemalan law. This service has created high expectations among the Q'eqchi' communities and every day there are representatives of local communities visiting the office. The office regularly sends its employees to the INTA headquarters in the capital to investigate land issues and to accelerate and monitor bureaucratic procedures. The office's possibilities are limited, though, because of legal restrictions imposed by Guatemalan law. In the end a successful outcome depends on government institutions such as INTA and its funds for granting loans to buy land are limited. These limitations have created some disappointments on the part of some communities. The Vicariate of El Petén has its own lawyer who visits the parishes every two months.

Another initiative of the Department is the creation of a network of multiplicadores de pastoral social which link local communities to the Department. The multiplicadores are trained by the Department in approximately three courses of several days every year. These courses have three standard elements. First, the official ecclesiastical sources that deal with social problems are presented, such as the official social doctrine of the church and the letter of the Guatemalan bishops' conference called *El Clamor por la Tierra* of 1988. Here the bishops severely condemn the appalling inequality of land distribution in Guatemala as well as the exploitation which goes on in the estates of the landlords. They call for a drastic land reform.[18] A second element of the courses refers to the rights of the Q'eqchi'es as Guatemalan citizens in accordance with Guatemalan law and the Universal Declaration of Human Rights. The fact that most of the Q'eqchi'es are not familiar with these rights still encourages the state and landowners to abuse them. As a third element, the multiplicadores are taught practical technologies such as how to make natural fertilizers or how to avoid doing harm to ecological conditions.

The multiplicadores project started in 1990. Two years later it had established a network of representatives of more than one hundred local communities. The multiplicadores found the courses to be very positive; in some cases they were even able to stimulate their communities to take practical action. Nevertheless, the project has its limits. The parishes run by the Salesians do not participate. Problems have also arisen with authorities in several areas because the villagers are becoming aware of their rights. The Catholic church is the only institution that can create the space for the development of such a network of representatives of local communities to deal with delicate subjects such as human rights and social injustice, but its margins for doing so remain limited.

An additional social task in which the diocese of Verapaz is engaged is the running of a boarding school called *Centro de Formación II* in San Juan Chamelco. In a 150 days period, about 120 boys receive training in technical skills such as carpentry, bricklaying and shoemaking. After passing the final examinations, they are offered a loan to enable them to start a workshop in their community of origin. This centre is financed by foreign aid, owned by the Ministry of Urban and Rural Development and managed by the church. It shows that, where possible and desirable, the bishopric is willing to engage in joint efforts with the state.

Local economic leaders

The economic actors and agencies already discussed not only intervene in the local communities directly, their influence is also mediated by local leaders. These leaders play a prominent role in the economic life of the community and deal with the intervening actors and agencies. They can be subdivided into committees and individual leaders. The most important committee is the Local Development Committee, or Improvement Committee.

Local Development Committee

The *Comité de Desarrollo Local* (Local Development Committee) is a result of the policy of president Vinicio Cerezo who, in 1987 and 1988, tried to set up a nation-wide network of development committees at the national, regional, departmental, district council and local community levels. It was meant to become the local executive agency for development policies formulated within this network (Inforpress Centroamericana 1988: 113).

In practice, in many communities its predecessor, *the Comité Pro Mejoramiento* (Improvement Committee), was simply renamed the Local Development Committee, and the existing practice of one committee looking after the common economic interests of the community went on under another banner. The local communities have been able to turn this government initiative to their own advantage, which has certainly been enhanced by the fact that the network of development committees at the levels indicated above has died a silent death. There are simply no policies coming out of this network to be transmitted to the communities.

The committee usually consists of a president, a vice-president and three or four other members who are elected by the local community. They have to ensure that at least some members of the committee are able to read and write and speak Spanish in order to deal with intervening agencies. In Chaabilchoch, Samox and Rubelpec the members of the committee stay on as long as they want to, but in Xalihá the community elects its members every few years.

The committee is in charge of important matters that concern the community. First, in communities formed in the last few decades that have organized their land within a patrimonio agrario colectivo scheme, such as Chaabilchoch, Samox and Xalihá, the committee represents the community in its dealings with INTA. It meets INTA officials, holds the land titles and has to approve land sales within the community. Secondly, in these communities the committee assigns the various plots of land to individual households. It usually does so during the formative years of the community and afterwards, it sees to it that conflicts are settled and that newcomers are discouraged to establish themselves. The committee can be very harsh in this respect. In Samox it gave the one evangelical household only half the land to which it is officially entitled. A man from another household had to accept a loan from a co-operative in La Tinta to cover the expenses of treating his wife's illness. He did not repay in time and the co-operative wanted to take away two of his manzanas. The committee refused to accept this, paid his debt and took all his land. In Xalihá the committee gave only 18 *cuerdas*[19] to a villager who recently returned after living in Belize for twenty years whereas the average household in Xalihá has access to about 300 cuerdas.

A third task of the committee in these communities is to organize collective work on community land. Chaabilchoch has no community land which is dedicated to agricultural purposes, but the committee in Xalihá has reserved between five and ten manzanas for cultivation by the community in addition to the plots that have been assigned to the households. Samox has 0.87 manzana of such community land. Cash crop production on these community lands has allowed the villagers of both communities to buy a considerable part of the materials to build an attractive church. However in recent years, the committees in both communities have been unable to mobilize the villagers to do this community work because their two presidents are highly conflictive persons. In Xalihá the villagers chose someone to become president because he was one of the few villagers who spoke Spanish, but neighbours do not help him to plant his maize or to build his house. Besides, there are rumours about the supposed disappearance of 4,000 quetzales of community funds. In Samox the president simply refuses to step down from his post.

In the Q'eqchi' heartland communities that have a long history, and in the communities within the parcelamiento projects with individualized land rights, the tasks of the committee concerning land issues are much more limited. However, the committee may have other tasks as well which include mobilizing the men of the community to clean and maintain the trails and the community buildings and to supervise other committees that are dedicated to special tasks. There are drinking water committees in all the villages I visited though only Samox and Rubelpec have a functioning drinking water system. In Chaabilchoch there is a road construction committee which recruits the men of the village to work in the nearby Caminos Rurales project. Rubelpec has committees for the co-operative, the bakery, the DIGEBOS project, electricity and the construction of a community hall.

The co-operative in Rubelpec started eleven years ago as an initiative of the villagers themselves and since then it has proved to be sustainable and profitable. It is a consumer co-operative which means that it buys groceries in the nearby towns and sells them to the villagers. It also has a grounding mill to make maize flour. It employs two men on a permanent basis and they have a strong influence on what goes on in the co-operative. The committee that manages the co-operative in Rubelpec is elected every two years by the members of the co-operative. There are some 60 members who have to pay 50 quetzales to become a member. At the end of the year, INACOP officials come to do the bookkeeping, profits or losses are shared by the members. In recent years it has had to face competition from private grocery shops.

The co-operative shows that the villagers are willing to make the best out of market integration. This conclusion holds true for both men and women. Several years ago the women in Rubelpec started their own bakery in the co-operative building and some of them received training by INTECAP employees on how to make bread. However at the moment, the bakery is no longer very successful. The people in the community do not like the taste of its bread, there is some discord among the women who run the bakery and several leading men, including those who run the co-operative, oppose the work of these women. This public role of women meets with resistance.

Recently, DIGEBOS organized a committee in Rubelpec to take charge of a reforestation project. There is a group of fifteen villagers who meet every week with a DIGEBOS official. They run a small nursery garden to grow pine and eucalyptus trees and the villagers are supposed to plant the larger trees on their land and take care of them. Members of the DIGEBOS committee claim that some 5,000 trees have already been planted.

Individual leaders

In addition to the various committees there are several individual leaders who influence the economic practices and representations of the Q'eqchi'es and who are related to intervening agencies. The most important of these are the representante agrícola, the veterinarian promoter, representatives of NGOs such as Vitamina "A" and the multiplicador de pastoral social.

In the communities that I studied in detail, only Rubelpec has a representante agrícola. He works for both DIGESA and DIGESEPE in this village as well as three nearby communities and receives a wage of 300 quetzales a month. As part of his DIGESA work, he encourages the villagers to cultivate vegetables, to plant their maize and beans in furrows and increase the number of plants per square metre, to build pigs sties and chickens coops and to use chemical fertilizers. Two households offered him a few cuerdas to lay out a demonstration garden. His DIGESEPE work focuses on the vaccination of animals, to cure animal diseases and he promotes two projects focusing on raising chickens and cows. The representante agrícola is also the co-ordinator of the Vitamina "A" project. He co-ordinates a group of eleven voluntary workers who work in as many sectors of the community. They encourage the households in their sector to build latrines, take hygienic measures, grow vegetables and take vitamin pills and deworming liquids. They hold meetings with these households every two weeks.

In Chaabilchoch there are three veterinarian promoters who encourage livestock raising. They have been trained by Veterinarios sin Fronteras and DIGESEPE in Raxruhá and French co-ordinators of the programme have visited the community several times in recent years. Like the representante agrícola in Rubelpec, these promoters vaccinate and cure sick animals.

7

The Economic Field:
Practices and Strategies of the Q'eqchi'es

Whatever the influence of intervening actors and agencies or local leaders, in the end the Q'eqchi'es have to rely on themselves for economic survival. This chapter focuses on their ways to secure such economic survival. It starts with discussing the common denominators of economic practices in order to provide the groundwork for delineating the general lines of their economic strategies. In addition, the ways in which these strategies are related to their religion will be outlined. The economic practices which will be presented include: organization of access to land, labour, subsistence production and market-integration, external inputs, consumption and savings, and economic stratification among Q'eqchi' households.

Organization of access to land

The general pattern of access to land includes three elements. First of all, there is the community land administered by the local development committee. Until recently the committee in Xalihá and Samox organized the joint tilling of this land. In Chaabilchoch and Rubelpec no community land is tilled, but there is land which has been used for building churches, a community hall or a co-operative or that serves as a football pitch. Secondly, there are common waste lands. These lands belong to the community, but are not used for cultivation or building. They are the least fertile, most difficult to work on because of the rocky soil or steep slopes. Nevertheless, these lands do play an important role in the local economy. They are used to collect firewood, wax and copal pom. The villagers graze their cows, bulls and horses on these lands and they are an important source of building materials. Sometimes the villagers use them for hunting wild animals, and wells are sunk on them.

Thirdly, there are plots of land that are used by individual households. These lands include plots on which houses have been built, those that are used for agricultural purposes or that are lying fallow at present. Most of the household lands are used for agricultural purposes in a shifting pattern of cultivation. This pattern is rather complicated. It includes plots of land on which cash crops such as coffee and cardamom have been cultivated for several years because these crops have a cycle of between three and seven years. Next, there are parcels on which crops with a much shorter cycle, such as maize, which has one or two harvests each year, are cultivated. In addition, some plots are left fallow in order to recover their fertility after being tilled for one or more years. The pattern of land rotation responds to both the need to cultivate a variety of crops and the requirements of fertility recovery.

Levels of market-integration, population pressure and scarcity of land determine how intensively or extensively this pattern is followed. In Xalihá the rotation scheme is very extensive. On average each piece of land is left fallow for three or four years. The villagers do not apply this rotation pattern to a fixed and circumscribed total amount of land and the household lands are not staked out clearly. Due to the relatively low levels of population pressure and market-integration this extensive scheme is common in most of the settlement areas of El Petén and Izabal. In these areas it is not uncommon to find households with access to up to one caballería, but because of poor infrastructure and adverse market conditions they till a small proportion of it.

In Rubelpec, on the other hand, fallow land is scarce and the rotation scheme is applied in a framework of a near permanent cultivation. Here every villager knows exactly which plots of land he or she has access to and this access is regulated in individual land titles. Intensive forms of land rotation are common in villages close to the central towns of Cobán, Carchá and Chamelco. These areas are marked by high population pressure, severe scarcity of land and relatively easy access to markets. Market access may encourage villagers to dedicate part of their lands to cash crop production.

In terms of scarcity of land and intensity of the rotation pattern Chaabilchoch and Samox occupy an intermediate position between Xaliha and Rubelpec. Table 7.1 shows the differences in the average household lands in four villages. It also expresses the different intensities of application of the land rotation pattern in these communities in terms of the percentage of the household land that was actually tilled by themselves or by others and the percentage of the household land left fallow in 1992. These differences in scarcity of land and intensity of the land rotation pattern coincide with differences in population pressure and access to markets.

Table 7.1: average land use patterns at household level in four villages (in manzanas and percentages)

Average land use per household	Xaliha	Chaabilchoch	Samox	Rubelpec
Tilled	3.78	6.62	4.34	0.97
	(20.58 %)	(41.40 %)	(58.02 %)	(50.26 %)
Leased out	0	0.46	0.07	0.35
		(2.88 %)	(0.94 %)	(18.13 %)
Left fallow	14.59	8.91	3.07	0.61
	(79.42 %)	(55.72 %)	(41.04 %)	(31.61 %)
Total average land per household	18.37	15.99	7.48	1.93
	(100 %)	(100 %)	(100 %)	(100 %)

Calculations based on relevant data provided by 40, 39, 39 and 64 respondents in the villages of Xaliha, Chaabilchoch, Samox and Rubelpec respectively.

Differences in access to land are noticeable not only between the various communities, within these communities there are considerable differences as well. In Xaliha these differences are not due to any real scarcity of land, although limits on the available land are becoming discernible. In the other three villages all the arable land has been allocated to the households - except for the land that is directly administered by the committee - and the differences between these households are considerable. In each of these communities there are households with no land at all whereas in Chaabilchoch, Samox and

Rubelpec the largest land-holding households have 31.25, 20 and 15.63 manzanas respectively. In Rubelpec in particular this maximum is remarkable given the fact that the average size of household plots is only 1.93 manzanas. Rubelpec also has 19 households who have no land at all.

Of course, the quantity of land of each community or household is important, but equally important is its quality or fertility. In Xalihá fertility varies considerably between the lower and higher parts of the village. Rice grows very well in the former and very poorly in the latter. The opposite is true of maize, but the average maize production per manzana (19.49 quintales) is well above the standard measure used by the Department of Social Pastoral Work in Cobán for fertile lands (12 quintales per manzana). In Chaabilchoch the land is very suited to maize production, but this is not the case in Samox and Rubelpec. However, cardamom and coffee grow quite well in Samox.

The household can compensate for its limited access to fertile land by using external inputs to improve the productivity of its land. It may also resort to renting or buying land from others within the community or elsewhere. The villagers of Xalihá do not need to own or rent land elsewhere or to rent land in the village. They do not lease out land either. In Chaabilchoch the households with few or no lands rent land from other households and ten villagers rent land in a nearby community, but the land scarcity is not severe enough to prevent some 20 outsiders coming to the village to rent one manzana each. In both Samox and Rubelpec the majority of households rent land (26 and 68 respectively) and no land is leased out to outsiders. Almost all the villagers of Samox rent or own plots of land in the lower part of the Polochic valley. In Rubelpec most villagers rent in the community, but some rent or have bought land in the Polochic valley and the Franja Transversal del Norte. The land which is rented or bought is mainly used to grow maize. Those with no land or a relatively small plot rent land in order to secure their maize production.

Renting land takes place on three different terms. In the first case land is not considered to be a commodity and no reward at all is given to the owner. In the second case it is considered to be a commodity: the renting of land is exchanged for something else. In Samox two respondents give part of their cardamom production or lease out a piece of their land on which cardamom can be produced in exchange for renting land in the valley which they use to produce maize. A common way to compensate the renting of land is to clear another piece of land for the owner. In the third case land is not only commoditized but also valued in monetary terms. The one who rents pays money.

Concerning rental deals Samox and Rubelpec constitute the extremes with Chaabilchoch in between. In Samox rental deals are predominantly monetary while in Rubelpec only a small proportion are. In Rubelpec most rental deals are commoditized though a significant proportion are concluded in terms of personal favours between members of the same kinship line. Even in Samox personal relations continue to play an important role: the villagers can only rent land in the valley if they have a good personal relation with the person they rent from. Moreover, in every village it is the responsibility of the community to provide each household with access to at least a small piece of land to grow their maize on, whether as property or rented from others. As a result, every household has some access to land, either inside or outside their community, owned or rented. In short, rental agreements are not standardized. The Q'eqchi'es deal with rented land in mixture of personalized, commoditized and monetarized terms.

In most of the Q'eqchi' villages the land is controlled in a mixed communitarian and individual household way. The pieces of community land and the common waste land are administered by the committee. Individual households have free access to the common waste land in addition to the specific plots of land which have been allocated to them. In Xalihá, Chaabilchoch and Samox the committee interferes in household plots in cases where the household wants to sell land or is not able to fulfil its obligations. In these communities the committee is quite influential. The committee in Rubelpec, however, has very little to do with land issues. It does not interfere in land conflicts and has no influence on land transactions. As a result it has not been able to keep several Kastii from buying quite large plots of land in Rubelpec which they use in a very extensive way. The high level of individualization of land control in Rubelpec has thus aggravated the land shortage the Q'eqchi' villagers have to face. One of them expressed regret for this individualization in these words: 'We all have our lands, but perhaps this is a sin because all of us will die equal'.

Labour

As with land use and land control there is a balance between individual households and the community as regards labour. Each individual household performs certain tasks but others are carried out jointly. In terms of jointly performed activities a distinction can be made between labour that is done by the whole community on the one hand and labour done by groups of ten to twenty villagers on the other. In the former case the whole adult population is recruited to carry out tasks that are the responsibility of the community. In the latter case a group of villagers joins the man or woman of the household to do work for the benefit of that household. The next day or occasion the same group joins the man or woman of another household. In short, three forms of labour can be distinguished: individual, group-wise and communitarian.

Division of labour within the household

Among the various villages there is quite some variation regarding the division of labour between men and women within the households. Nevertheless, all of them share common features. Women look after the children, keep the house clean, wash the clothes, prepare the food, make kitchen utensils, fetch water and firewood, and take care of the birds (chickens, ducks, turkeys) and the smaller food crops (beans, chillies). Women also take a hand in clearing the land and harvesting maize - widows may perform these tasks - but they are never allowed to plant maize.

All these activities are performed by individual women. In general women are supposed to focus on activities within the household, but they are also involved in activities that entail market-integration to a greater or lesser extent. In Xalihá men take the quantities of chillies and birds that are not consumed within the household to the market in San Agustín Chahal; but in Chaabilchoch and Samox quite a few women sell these products at the nearest market and buy grocery products there. The involvement of women in market-oriented activities is relatively high in Rubelpec. They buy firewood from traders, for example, because the common waste land does not provide them with sufficient firewood. The chickens raising project supported by DIGE-SEPE aimed at selling these birds in nearby San Pedro Carchá is a women's activity. The same holds true for the production of fine huipiles and they sell their products in the same nearby town. The women of several households go to this town to select cardamom for wage labour. They are also quite heavily involved in clearing land and harvesting maize because many men are away for a large part of the year working as travelling merchants or wage labourers.

In short, the involvement of women in market-oriented activities is most pronounced in Rubelpec and least developed in Xalihá, with Samox and Chaabilchoch in between. Almost all these activities are performed on an individual basis. Women work in a communitarian way when, for example, food has to be prepared for a community feast. The same activity is done group-wise by women when men perform a particular task as a group as well.

Men are mainly responsible for tilling the land, grow the main food (maize) and cash crops (cardamom and coffee), take care of the larger animals (pigs, cattle, horses), sell cash crops and animals, work for wages and carry out most of the commercial activities. They also build the houses, make the furniture and take care of most of the contacts with the outside world. In doing so the men practise a variety of labour forms. We have already come across the communitarian labour in which until recently the adult male population of Samox and Xalihá was engaged tilling community land. The local development committee and other committees also recruit men for other purposes such as building churches or village halls, and the so-called *faenas*. Once every few weeks the paths, the football pitch, the school and other community buildings have to be cleaned and maintained. Other male tasks that will be discussed in the pages that follow include clearing land, planting and harvesting maize, cultivating cash crops and building houses.

Clearing the land

Land clearance is a heavy task. After selecting the piece of land to be cultivated, the Q'eqchi'es cut down the trees and bushes with their machetes and axes. After that they spread out the material cut down and let it dry. They take away useful materials, make fire breaks and burn the rest. They do this at the beginning of the main maize cycle in March or April. If there are to be two maize crops the land to be used in the second cycle is cleared at the same time. Table 7.2 below outlines the various labour forms that are practised during land clearance and the percentages of households engaged in each of these forms in four villages. This table shows that there is considerable diversity in the forms of labour which the various respondents within the same village practise in clearing their lands. Some work in a group while others prefer to clear individually or with the help of some day-labourers whom they pay.

Moreover, there is considerable difference between the various communities in this respect. In Xaliha group-wise labour is relatively strong while in Rubelpec there is significant use of wage labour. Chaabilchoch and Samox occupy an intermediate position between these two villages. Such diversity of labour forms used in land clearance is common to most Q'eqchi' communities. However, the issue has not been settled finally. In Samox there is discussion among the villagers about whether clearance work should be done individually or group-wise. Rented land is always cleared individually.

Planting and harvesting maize

By contrast, Table 7.2 also shows that maize planting is almost always done group-wise. This is common to almost all the Q'eqchi' villages. Only villagers who are in conflict with the rest of the community, such as the president of the committee in Xalihá and his father, have to plant individually. Even maize planting on rented lands is done group-wise in Samox and Rubelpec, but not in Chaabilchoch.

Table 7.2: labour forms practised in clearing land, planting maize and harvesting maize in four villages in percentages of respondents

Activity	Labour form	Xalihá	Chaabilchoch	Samox	Rubelpec
Clearance	Group-wise	55.00	30.77	5.40	5.88
	Individual	42.50	48.72	86.49	64.71
	Individual and hired wage labourers	2.50	20.51	8.11	29.41
Planting maize	Group-wise	95.00	94.88	94.88	95.59
	Individual	5.00	5.12	2.56	-
	Individual and hired wage labourers	-	-	2.56	4.41
Harvesting maize	Group-wise	92.31	43.24	5.72	14.92
	Individual	7.69	29.73	80.00	52.24
	Individual and hired wage labourers	-	27.03	14.28	32.84

The same table shows that there is a diversity of labour forms used in harvesting maize similar to that which was observed in land clearance, albeit with more emphasis on group-wise labour and on hiring wage labourers. This diversity is apparent both in the pattern for households and as regards differences between the villages. However, the issue of labour forms to be applied in the case of harvesting maize has not been decided definitely yet. In Chaabilchoch ten of the sixteen respondents who told me they harvest group-wise said they do so only when they have a big harvest. On rented land they harvest individually. In Samox the villagers used to harvest group-wise, but because of disagreement among them they started to harvest individually. In Rubelpec relatively more villagers harvest group-wise than in Samox, but those who harvest individually are more convinced that this is what they ought to do. Consequently, as in the case of land clearance Xalihá and Rubelpec constitute the opposite extremes with Chaabilchoch and Samox in between.

The cultivation of cash crops

When coffee is produced only as a food crop, the woman of the household takes care of it. Where coffee is produced as a cash crop the man does the job individually and, when needed, he hires wage labourers. The same pattern, i.e. individual labour and when needed hiring mozos, is used in the cultivation of all cash crops including cardamom. The only exception is rice. The villagers of Xalihá began cultivating this crop a few years ago and at present production has reached 769.84 quintales. In Xalihá rice is mainly a cash crop: an estimated 72.90 per cent of the harvest is sold. However, all those who produce rice in considerable quantities (more than three quintales a year) plant and harvest it group-wise. DIGESA officials confirmed that in the Río Dulce area rice cultivation is also done in a group-wise manner. In Xalihá the use of group-wise labour to plant rice is related to the fact that rice and maize are planted at the same time, so the inclusion of rice with maize planting makes sense for practical reasons.

The amount of wage labour involved in cash-crop production varies considerably from village to village. In Xalihá no wage labourers at all are hired. By contrast, in Samox 45.24 per cent of the households hire wage labourers for their coffee and cardamom harvest and pay 8159.50 quetzales as wages. Ten villagers work as wage labourers for other villagers. In Chaabilchoch 43.59 per cent of the households employ wage labourers in their cardamom harvest and pay 16,165 quetzales in wages. Ten villagers work for other villagers and some fifty Q'eqchi'es from other areas also come in to work in Chaabilchoch. In general households with a relatively high yearly income in both villages hire these labourers while those with relatively low incomes perform wage labour. A few years ago many more labourers were hired in both villages. In Rubelpec hardly any wage labourers are employed in cash crop production because there is not much production of this kind. However, quite a number of villagers employ wage labourers in clearing land, harvesting maize and building houses.

The hiring of wage labourers suggests a high level of commoditization of labour in cash crop production; however, personal relations continue to play a role in wage labour. For example, in Samox there is a considerable difference between the average wages that the villagers pay to fellow villagers - Q. 7.87 a day - and those they pay to Q'eqchi'es from elsewhere - Q. 4.79 a day.

House building

House building is another heavy job that has to be done once in a while; the frequency of which depends on the kind of building materials they use. The labour forms they practise are as diverse as in the case of land clearance and harvesting maize. Some work group-wise, others work alone while still others hire wage labourers. Moreover, there is also considerable diversity between the villages. In Xalihá almost everyone performs this task group-wise while in Rubelpec and Samox a large majority either work individually or hire wage labourers (85.29 and 85.00 per cent of the households in Rubelpec and Samox respectively). Chaabilchoch occupies an intermediate position.

Subsistence production

The Q'eqchi'es' economic practices have two basic aims. On the one hand there are the activities of the household or community that focus on the cultivation of crops, the raising of animals and the fabrication of articles that are consumed by the household or community itself. These activities enter into the category of subsistence production. On the other hand the household or community engages in activities intended to earn money or exchange goods with others. These activities include the cultivation of cash crops, the sale of animals, trade activities and commercial artisan production.

Almost all the households engage in the same repertoire of subsistence production. Even many urban households hold on to this standard repertoire using their gardens or a piece of land on the outskirts of the town. They produce maize, black beans, chillies, coffee, cocoa, fruits such as bananas and *yuca* and vegetables such as *huisquil*. They always have birds such as turkeys, ducks and chickens and sometimes one or more pigs; sooner or later they all find their way into the mouths of household members. Most of the cooking utensils and furniture are made within the household.

Maize is by far the most important subsistence crop. It is used to prepare the main ingredients of the diet, such as tortillas, tamales and atol. Moreover, it is used as fodder for birds and pigs, and part of the maize production is reserved as seed for the next planting. However, not all the maize that the household consumes is produced by the household without external inputs and not all the maize that the household produces is actually consumed by that household. Maize is also bought and sold which means that maize production and consumption do not stay exclusively within the limits of the subsistence sphere. Nevertheless, most of its production and consumption maintains a predominantly subsistence character. The average production, sale and purchase of maize per household as well as the average maize consumption per capita in four villages are listed in Table 7.3. Maize consumption refers to the maize that is used for human consumption, fodder and seed.

Table 7.3: average production, sale and purchase of maize per household and average maize consumption per capita in four Q'eqchi' villages (in quintales)

Maize	Xalihá	Rubelpec	Chaabilchoch	Samox
Production per household	52.51	27.68	28.01	14.60
Sale per household	6.85	3.81	2.42	-
Purchases per household	0.17	6.97	3.91	13.87
Consumption per capita	8.17	5.13	4.62	4.39

Source: these data were collected in interviews with 40, 39, 39, and 57 households in Xalihá, Chaabilchoch, Samox and Rubelpec respectively.

Of course, the production of maize per household depends on the quantity and quality of the household's land and on the climatic conditions. In the higher parts of the Q'eqchi' heartland, including Rubelpec, the climate permits only one harvest of maize each year while the lower areas, including Xalihá and Chaabilchoch, allow the Q'eqchi'es to have two crops of maize. These two crops a year on a relatively large expanse of fertile land allow the villagers of Xalihá to have a relatively high maize production per household. They are able to sell part of their maize and dedicate a considerable part of their maize to feeding a few hundred pigs, most of which are sold. This fodder partly explains the relatively high level of maize consumption per capita. In the other three villages the number of pigs per household is much more limited.

Another part of the explanation is that the villagers do not like to sell maize. According to the elderly villagers they should not sell maize 'because it will cry if we do so'. In addition, bad market conditions do not encourage them to optimize the selling of maize. The possibility that the Xalihá villagers could produce more maize than they actually do cannot be ruled out.

The other three villages have more or less the same maize consumption per capita, but to do so they have to resort to buying maize. The villagers of Rubelpec and Chaabilchoch both sell and buy maize; this is due to the fact that some are able to sell while others have to buy and to the lack of storage facilities. After the harvest they have to sell part of their maize because they cannot keep large quantities of it until the next harvest. Consequently, some months before this next harvest they have to buy at a much higher price. Chaabilchoch, Samox and Rubelpec are all net maize "importers".

In order to maintain this level of human maize consumption the villagers of these three communities have to resort to buying land elsewhere or to renting land on which maize can be cultivated. The villagers of Samox are able to produce around half the maize they need for consumption only in this way because the land in their own village is not suited to maize cultivation. In Rubelpec even access to rented land or land owned elsewhere is not sufficient to cover their maize consumption needs. On their limited amount of land just one harvest is possible. They compensate for this limited access to land by using considerable quantities of chemical inputs.

In short, the Q'eqchi'es try to produce themselves a considerable proportion of the maize quantities they consume, even if this entails renting or buying land elsewhere or resorting to large quantities of external inputs. They are willing to use money they have earned from market-oriented activities to achieve this objective. Several respondents who were not able to produce enough maize and had to buy the majority of the maize they needed told me they felt very sad about that.

Market-oriented production and activities

Subsistence activities take place within the household and the community; market-oriented practices relate the household and local community to outsiders. In Xalihá the circulation of goods within the community remains very limited. By contrast, in Samox, Chaabilchoch and Rubelpec some maize is sold among the villagers, there are some who sell grocery articles and medicines to fellow villagers, there are some who work as carpenters selling furniture within the village and there are others who complement their income by working for other villagers. In other words, in these three villages economic relations between the households have become commercialized to some extent. Nevertheless, even there market-oriented activities are mainly directed towards actors outside the community. The limited exchange of commodities between households points to a low level of division of labour among them.

The most obvious form of market-oriented production consists of selling the surplus of food crops and animals that are raised primarily for consumption. This holds true for the surplus of maize, pigs, chickens, turkeys, beans, chillies, cocoa, fruit and other subsistence products. The flexible use of these products - if they cannot be sold at a good price they can always be consumed - is one of their attractive aspects. The same holds true for rice production. It is used mainly as a cash crop, but can also be consumed. Nevertheless, other market-oriented activities do not show any continuity with subsistence production, such as the production of cardamom.

In order to assess the market-oriented performance two standards will be used: "gross product" and "net income". The former refers to the products and services the households have sold minus the costs of production, expressed in quetzales. For example, from the amount of money the households earned by selling cardamom the costs they incurred by hiring wage labourers in the cardamom harvest, transport costs and the costs of chemical inputs have been subtracted in order to reach the gross product of cardamom. Payments to INTA have also been included in the total gross product calculations.

The net income subtracts from the gross product the investments that would have to be made to be able to achieve the same production in the following year or years. For example, the amount of money made by selling a cow has been included in the gross product, but in order to reach the net income of cow raising the price of a calf has been subtracted. I do not know whether all those who sold a cow actually bought such a calf, but to get a good indicator of economic performance I assume they did. Moreover, in the net income the money spent on buying maize has been subtracted from the gross product because that allows me to relate net income to its consequences for subsistence production; this gives a more adequate indicator of economic performance. Take for example two households which are able to earn the same amount of money by way of market-oriented activities. One is able to do so together with producing sufficient maize for its own consumption while the other has to buy a lot of maize to reach the same maize consumption level. The performance of the former household must be evaluated in more positive terms than the latter. These differences become visible in my net income calculations. The average gross product and net income per household, in total and per main product or activity, in four villages are listed in Table 7.4.

Table 7.4: gross product and net income per household and per main activity or product in four villages (in quetzales and percentages)

Village	Item	Gross product	Per cent	Net income	Per cent
Xalihá	Total	1571.21	100	1451.21	100
	Pigs	453.24	28.85	453.24	31.23
	Rice	451.87	28.76	451.87	31.14
	Chillies	214.52	13.65	214.52	14.78
	Maize	184.14	11.72	180.88	12.46
Chaabil- choch	Total	3361.00	100	2941.40	100
	Cardamom	2185.99	65.04	2185.99	74.32
	Cattle	402.67	11.98	181.85	6.18
	Wage labour	342.23	10.18	342.23	11.63
Samox	Total	3473.31	100	2774.88	100
	Cardamom	2547.67	73.35	2547.67	91.81
	Coffee	515.57	14.84	515.57	18.58
Rubelpec	Total	2100.37	100	1684.20	100
	Wage labour	1048.36	49.91	1048.36	62.25
	Trade	401.83	19.13	401.83	23.86
	Huipiles	252.89	12.04	252.89	15.02

Source: based on interviews with 40, 39, 39 and 51 households in Xalihá, Chaabilchoch, Samox and Rubelpec respectively.

Raising pigs and cultivating rice are the two main income generating activities in Xalihá. As in most remote areas the popularity of raising pigs is related to the fact that pigs can walk all the way to the nearest road where the Q'eqchi'es wait for a camionero to pass. Cash crops present more transportation problems. Rice has the advantage that it allows the swampy lands of the village to be used for agricultural purposes. The fact that it has been taken up as a crop only in recent years means that the gross product and net income levels of the villagers used to be considerably lower. The fact that the villagers abhor wage labour is expressed in its low contribution to both gross product (1.98 per cent) and net income (2.14 per cent).

Chaabilchoch is performing much better in market-oriented activities; both its average gross product and net income per household are more than twice as high as in Xalihá. In Chaabilchoch by far the most important income earner is cardamom. When the villagers sell the estimated 1740 quintales they produce, the amount of money they receive is even much higher than the figures of this table. Transportation costs, the wages they pay to mozos and other costs have been subtracted from this amount to reach these figures. A few years ago both the gross product and net income from cardamom were much higher, but prices have dropped in recent years and due to the drought last year the volume of production has diminished considerably. The drought affected each household's cardamom production differently, depending on the kind of land and the point in the cardamom cycle where the drought struck. There are considerable differences in cardamom production between the households.

Cardamom production requires wage labour. Most of the demand for wage labour is met by Q'eqchi'es who come in from the central highlands to work for the Chaabilchoch villagers. Wage labour is also an important source of income for the relatively poor villagers of Chaabilchoch. However, more than eighty per cent of total earnings from wage labour comes from working for state agencies such as Caminos Rurales and Moscamed. The road construction project close to the town of Chajmaïc produces most of this income, which suggests that when this project ends the amount of money earned in this way may decrease again. In any case, the willingness to perform wage labour is much greater in Chaabilchoch than in Xalihá.

The relatively high level of cash crop production allows the villagers to develop a number of other activities. For example, there are three villagers who transport persons and cardamom from the village to the town of Chajmaïc using boats with outboard motors. However, after reviewing calculations with them we discovered that the profit they make is very limited. The fact that they enjoy navigating with their boats is more important to them than the money they make. Two villagers had to sell their boats because they were not profitable. A similar picture emerges regarding commercial activities. Several villagers trade in grocery articles, but many villagers have failed to make this trade profitable. The decreasing net income from cardamom has caused the local demand for consumer goods to shrink.

As a consequence of cultivating cardamom the villagers of Chaabilchoch have to buy maize and rent land on which to cultivate maize. These costs make up a considerable part of the difference between gross product and net income. The same difference is even more pronounced in Samox; there the villagers have to spend even more money on buying maize and renting land on which to cultivate maize. The gross product per household in Samox is higher while the net income per household is lower than in Chaabilchoch. Nevertheless, in both villages cardamom production is by far the most important income raiser; in Samox this is mainly complemented by coffee cultivation.

Lower prices for cardamom and coffee have affected these income figures in Samox in the same way as in Chaabilchoch and due to a cardamom and coffee disease the production in volume has decreased significantly in recent years. I estimate the average gross product and net income from cardamom per household a few years ago as 4762.31 quetzales at current prices, i.e. 86.93 per cent higher than in 1991-1992. Of course, these figures become lower if we take into account that greater cardamom production would entail higher costs such as wage labour, but in any case gross product and net income have decreased significantly in the last few years. As in Chaabilchoch this decrease differs from household to household and has involved a reduction in commercial activities such as selling grocery products.

The gross product and net income from wage labour are much more limited in Samox than in Chaabilchoch, but this difference is mainly due to the fact that the villagers in Samox perform very little wage labour for state agencies. Actually, the income the Samox villagers earn by doing wage labour for other villagers is higher than in Chaabilchoch. In Chaabilchoch most of the demand for wage labour is filled by wage labourers from outside the village, while in Samox most of this demand is satisfied by Samox villagers.

In contrast to the other three communities the villagers of Rubelpec do not earn most of their money by selling cash crops, but from wage labour and commercial activities. This difference is due to two principal factors. First, the villagers do not have access to sufficient land to cultivate both cash crops and their main food crops and they clearly give priority to producing maize for their own consumption. This means that there are few pieces of land left for cash crop production. Secondly, the villagers have access to a functioning market in the nearby town of San Pedro Carchá which encourages them to develop other commercial activities.

Wage labour is the most important income earner. An estimated 77 households have one or more members who engage in wage labour at some time every year; only eight of them find work within the village. Most of the income earned from doing wage labour is actually earned in the town of San Pedro Carchá (55.81 per cent) by working for the municipality and other state agencies, selecting cardamom (exclusively women's work) and by working as truck drivers. An additional 14.22 per cent of wages come from working in the cardamom harvests in places like Chaabilchoch in the north. Only 9.85 per cent is earned on nearby fincas: the villagers do not like to work on fincas.

The second way the villagers can earn income is by setting up a small shop in the village or, much more importantly, leaving the village to work as travelling merchants in the Polochic or Franja Transversal del Norte areas. Some have even set up shops in Raxruhá or Chahal. They trade in grocery items, clothes, shoes, kitchen utensils, machetes and similar products and buy these articles in Carchá or Cobán. 42 Households have one or more members who work in this way.

Another important means of making money is exclusively women's work: they weave huipiles of white fibre, add embroidery to the blouses and sell them in the market in Carchá. The knowledge needed to do this has been transmitted from mother to daughter and there is no interference by any external agency in this textile production. Textile production is very limited among the Q'eqchi'es, unlike other ethnic groups in Guatemala, but Rubelpec is the exception where it adds significantly to gross product and net income.

The data regarding these four villages confirm more general economic patterns in the region. In the central highlands the villages try to maintain their subsistence agriculture by using external inputs such as chemical fertilizers or renting land in other areas. They complement this subsistence agriculture with several market-oriented activities and products such as wage labour in the Franja Transversal del Norte and nearby towns and work as travelling merchants. In addition, they produce limited quantities of coffee and beans to be sold on the market. On the other hand, in the settlement areas in the lowlands fertile land is not the scarcest element, but opportunities for becoming involved in profitable market-oriented production or activities are very rare. In these areas the households produce sufficient maize and other food crops for their own consumption without external inputs. However, market-oriented activities are limited to selling any surplus of maize and beans, and the production of rice, cows and pigs. In the intermediate areas, called *tierra templada*, the households are able to maintain their subsistence economy and complement this production by cultivating cash crops (cardamom and coffee) and by raising some cattle. They make use of wage labourers coming from the central highlands. Their crucial problem is stable access to their lands.

External inputs

To some extent the Q'eqchi'es make use of external inputs in their production. The willingness to accept such inputs is directly related to how the villagers perceive Kastii who offer them the inputs. It was already pointed out that when the Q'eqchi'es are confronted with any Kastii they first need to develop relations of trust with this person. Provided such relations can be established they are willing to see whether his or her proposal or technology may be useful. The decisive moment comes after the Kastii stops coming: will they continue to apply his or her advises or stop doing so?

There is considerable variation in the meanings the Q'eqchi'es attribute to the Kastii. In Xalihá most of my respondents (28) expressed fear towards all Kastii in rather strong words such as: 'The Kastii only want to command us and do not respect us'. Only nine respondents said that they did not fear the Kastii. In Samox the numbers of respondents who expressed fear and those who did not fear the Kastii are equal (16), but state employees and merchants do frighten almost all of them. In Chaabilchoch a majority of respondents (25) rejected the idea of fearing the Kastii; only 13 told me they feared them. In Rubelpec 17 respondents admitted that they feared the Kastii while a majority of 51 respondents denied feeling any fear in this respect. Most of the latter (34) told me that they need not fear them any more. In short, there is a scale from relatively high to little fear from Xalihá to Samox to Chaabilchoch and Rubelpec.

This scale coincides with the level of acceptance of external inputs. In Xalihá the villagers buy only calves and machetes from outsiders and in the previous chapter the failure of the DIGESA project was discussed. They hardly use chemical fertilizers; the only input they accept is the vaccination of their animals by a DIGESEPE employee. In Samox the villagers accept the same limited number of inputs as in Xalihá. The only production input the Samox villagers obtain in significant quantities from Kastii is *gramoxone*, a chemical product for disinfecting the land. In contrast to the Q'eqchi'es of Xalihá the villagers of Samox use an average 0.94 litres of this input per household on which they spend an average 32.12 quetzales per household.

The villagers of Samox had various negative experiences with external agencies. UNICEF officials broke their promise to deliver tubes for building a drinking water system. However, the clearest example of the villagers' distrust towards such agencies is provided by the cardamom and coffee disease, which appeared for the first time in 1985. According to the villagers the appearance was related to two facts: it started after Moscamed dropped boxes with large insects from an aeroplane and after ANACAFé came to teach them how to improve coffee production. In the eyes of the villagers the appearance of these agencies has something to do with the start of the disease. The villagers do not resort to government agencies to find a remedy either. DIGESA employees once told them which pesticides to use, but these pesticides turned out to be very expensive and they could not stand the smell. The villagers considered government agencies to be part of the problem, not part of the solution.

The fact that the same agency - Moscamed - the one the villagers of Samox hold partly responsible for the disease in their crops, is able to recruit several villagers in Chaabilchoch to work for it and to convince the villagers of that community to accept its services indicates the difference in acceptance of projects and external inputs between Samox and Chaabilchoch. The Caminos Rurales project in Chaabilchoch has already been mentioned. The three veterinarian promoters trained by DIGESEPE and Veterinarios sin Fronteras are quite popular in the village and there is a DIGEBOS group. Moreover, the villagers buy calves from a nearby Kastii hacienda administrator and use a considerable quantity of gramoxone (1.43 litres per household) on which they spend 42.69 quetzales per household.

Even more external inputs are accepted in Rubelpec. The villagers use an average 0.34 litres of gramoxone per household and spend an average 117 quetzales per household on chemical fertilizers: 2.25 quintales per household. In addition, there is considerable intervention by government agencies and NGOs in Rubelpec. There is a DIGEBOS group; INTECAP has trained the women who run the bakery and INACOP does the bookkeeping for the cooperative. There is a group of five women who have made a contract with DIGESEPE: they buy a little chicken at a price of 2.75 quetzales, sell the adult bird for 25 quetzales and buy special fodder from DIGESEPE. The same agency encourages a group of eight men to raise cows. They have received a loan of 24,000 quetzales for a period of 18 months at 30 per cent a year interest. They buy calves at a price of 450 quetzales, rent a meadow for 2,200 quetzales a year and sell an adult cow after 18 months for 1,500 quetzales. Four years ago they started this project and they now have twenty cows.

DIGESA began to work in Rubelpec in 1987 with a group of 50 men and a women's group of 30 members. According to the representante agrícola these efforts met with much distrust initially. He managed to overcome this distrust, but after a few years the DIGESA officials stopped coming and the groups disintegrated. The promotion of vegetables production was also supported by another agency called *Desarrollo de la Comunidad*. In 1991 Vitamina "A" took over the vegetable promotion and according to the project co-ordinator between 40 and 60 households participate and have a vegetable garden.

In brief, three projects have focused on vegetables promotion and one of them is still active in the village. Indeed, vegetable cultivation has developed to a considerable extent. Of my respondents 45 per cent told me they cultivate at least some relatively new vegetables for their own consumption. Of course, it is hard to say whether they do so as a result of these projects, but the percentage is high compared to other communities where hardly any of these vegetables are cultivated. However, the decisive moment comes when the

Vitamina "A" officials stop coming to the village. Will the villagers go on cultivating vegetables? The fact that the DIGESA project ended when DIGESA employees stopped coming does not give much hope in this respect. The sustainability of vegetable production still has to prove itself.

The relatively open attitude of the villagers of Rubelpec towards external inputs and project proposals is not only related to their relatively low distrust towards Kastii; their proximity to the markets in the central towns enables them to evade the frustrating impact of merchants in other parts of the region. They are in a position to integrate into the market on better terms. However, even the villagers of Rubelpec reject specific inputs such as hybrid seeds and pesticides as well as the repeated proposals by DIGESA that they change their maize planting practices in order to improve the production per square metre.

Consumption and savings

Calves are among the inputs the Q'eqchi'es purchase outside their community. The raising of cows and bulls contributes 165.00 and 166.00 quetzales to the gross product per household in Xalihá and Rubelpec, but after subtracting the prices of calves a much more limited contribution to net income remains (51.25 and 66.00 quetzales). The fact that there is hardly any price difference between calves and adult animals in Samox means that the villagers hardly raise any cows or bulls. In Chaabilchoch cattle raising is more profitable due to the fact that the villagers maintain good contacts with the manager of a nearby hacienda who pays them a favourable price for their animals.

However, cows and bulls are not only raised for making money in the short run, they are also used as a means of investing savings. Cows and bulls present no storage problem; they can be fed using plants from the waste lands; and when the household needs cash they can be sold. Several households who sold an animal did so because someone was ill: they needed to buy medicines.

Table 7.5: gross product per capita in four villages (in quetzales and US dollars)

Gross product per capita	Xalihá	Rubelpec	Chaabilchoch	Samox
Quetzales	280.13	349.23	526.42	535.41
US dollars	56	69	105	107

Figures in US dollars are calculated using an exchange rate of five quetzales to one dollar.

The average household is not able to save much. The amounts of money per capita the Q'eqchi'es in these four communities are able to make are very limited, as Table 7.5 shows. A comparison with the national gross domestic product per capita, which was 904 US dollar in 1991 (Inter-American Development Bank 1993: 109), shows that despite their differences the villagers in these communities are very poor, even by Guatemalan standards. Of course, the picture becomes less black if we take into account the fact that these figures do not include subsistence production within these communities. On the other hand, the net income per capita in these communities - which is a better indicator of the amount of money they are able to spend - is even lower than the gross product per capita: 51, 56, 92, and 85 US dollar in Xalihá, Rubelpec, Chaabilchoch and Samox respectively.

This picture of severe poverty is confirmed by the available statistics for the *región norte*, which includes the population of the departments of Baja and

Alta Verapaz. In this region 76 per cent of the population live in extreme poverty and another 14 per cent live in poverty (Instituto Nacional de Estadística 1988). The first category refers to those who do not have sufficient income to buy basic food nor have access to a minimal level of goods and services. The latter category is able to buy food, but not the minimal level of goods and services. Again, this income refers to income in money; it does not take into account the fact that many Q'eqchi'es are able to produce their basic food themselves. Nevertheless, actual poverty remains very severe.

Economic stratification

The Q'eqchi'es are not only very poor, there are considerable differences between the villages and between the various households within each village. The distinction between subsistence production and market-oriented production will be used as a starting point for measuring the degree of economic stratification within the communities.

Concerning subsistence production it is impossible to take into consideration all the food crops and other items that are produced and consumed within the household, but I do have the details for maize production and consumption. From the point of view of economic stratification maize consumption is more important than maize production because what matters is what the households can actually do with the results of their activities. Of course, maize consumption is not just an indicator of subsistence production because part of the maize some households consume is bought and the maize some households consume has been produced using inputs they have bought. Nevertheless, most of the maize that is consumed is produced by the households and together with net income differences maize consumption differences give a quite accurate picture of economic differences between the various households.

As was discussed above, maize consumption refers to the maize the households dedicate to human consumption, to feeding their animals and that they reserve as seed. The standard I use is the one provided by the agricultural extension workers in the Department of Social Pastoral Work of the bishopric of Verapaz. According to this standard one person consumes one *libra* (453 grams) of maize each day; a pig needs 2.5 libras of maize as fodder while chickens, turkeys and ducks eat two-thirds of a libra. Large animals such as horses and cows are not given any maize as fodder. The standard is relatively high for pigs and birds; in practice they need less fodder because they walk around and look for complementary food in the surroundings of the house. The quantity of maize the Q'eqchi'es need to reserve as seed depends on the amount of land they use for maize cultivation.

Next to the limited quantities of maize needed to reserve as seed, human consumption is the first priority and what is left over is used as fodder. Taking these considerations into account five categories of maize consumption can be defined. Into the first category (category I) come those households which do not have enough maize even for human consumption. A second category (category II) consists of those households who have just enough maize for human consumption. A third category (category III) is made up of those who have more than enough to feed themselves but not enough to feed their animals. Into a fourth category (category IV) come households that have enough maize to feed themselves and their animals. The last category (category V) consists of those who have more than enough to feed both themselves and their animals. The numbers and percentages of households that enter into each category in four villages are listed in Table 7.6.

Table 7.6: spread of maize consumption per household in four communities (in number of respondents and percentages per category)

Categories maize consumption	Xalihá	Chaabil-choch	Samox	Rubelpec
I	-	3 (9.37 %)	8 (22.86 %)	4 (7.55 %)
II	10 (38.46 %)	12 (37.50 %)	9 (25.71 %)	9 (16.98 %)
III	4 (15.38 %)	8 (25.00 %)	2 (5.72 %)	6 (11.32 %)
IV	11 (42.31 %)	5 (15.63 %)	9 (25.71 %)	4 (7.55 %)
V	1 (3.85 %)	4 (12.50 %)	7 (20.00 %)	30 (56.60 %)
Total respondents	26 (100 %)	32 (100 %)	35 (100 %)	53 (100 %)

The data of this table point to the conclusion that stratification in terms of maize consumption goes from low to high from Xalihá to Chaabilchoch and to Samox. In Rubelpec stratification has also reached a high level, but these data may give a distorted impression because the villagers of Rubelpec have relatively few pigs and birds to feed. Thus, when a household has more than enough for human consumption it enters into category four or five much more easily than in the other villages. Nevertheless, the fact that 92.45 per cent of the respondents in Rubelpec have sufficient maize to feed themselves while they buy relatively little maize (see Table 7.3) shows that in spite of the fact that they have very little arable land at their disposal (1.55 manzana per household each year) they give importance to producing a large part of their maize themselves. On the other hand, the fact that 46.16 per cent of the households in Xalihá are able to feed themselves and their animals given the high numbers of their birds and pigs without buying much maize underlines their remarkable maize production.

After dealing with the need to provide enough maize for consumption the other necessity has to be addressed: earning enough money to cover other needs. The most suitable criterion to apply in this respect is net income. The differences in average net income per household between the various communities were outlined above in Table 7.4. In Table 7.7 below the spread of net income of the households within these four communities is listed. It shows first that there are considerable differences in terms of net income stratification between the various villages. This level of stratification varies from low to high from Xalihá to Rubelpec to Chaabilchoch and Samox. Secondly, it makes clear that there are very substantial net income differences between the various households within each community. In Samox there is a household with a negative net income of -762.23 quetzales while the "richest" household has a net income of 12951.60 quetzales; even in Xalihá the "poorest" household has a net income of only 240 quetzales while the "richest" has a net income of 3692.50 quetzales.

140 'We are Children of the Mountain'

However, part of these differences in Xalihá, Chaabilchoch and Samox are due to incidental factors. In Xalihá rice production contributes considerably to the net income (31.14 per cent) but not for all households. Some started to cultivate rice when I held my interviews so their rice production has not been included in my calculations and they ended up in the lower net income categories. Probably after a few years, when they will all have started to produce rice, net income differences in Xalihá will have reduced significantly.

Table 7.7: spread of net income of households in four communities (in number of households per category)

Net income categories in quetzales	Xalihá	Rubelpec	Chaabilchoch	Samox
XII. 6750 or more			2	2
XI. 6000 - 6750			2	2
X. 5250 - 6000			4	3
IX. 4500 - 5250		5		3
VIII. 3750 - 4500		1	3	1
VII. 3000 - 3750	3	4	3	3
VI. 2250 - 3000	6	7	2	6
V. 1500 - 2250	7	6	9	4
IV. 750 - 1500	10	8	7	4
III. 0 - 750	13	14	6	6
II. -750 - 0		4		4
I. -750 or lower		1		1
Total respondents	39	50	38	39

Incidental factors also play a role in net income differences in Chaabilchoch and Samox where the drought and the cardamom and coffee disease have affected the various households in differential ways. Without these incidental effects net income differentiation would have been much more limited.

Q'eqchi' economic strategies and religion

> 'We have to give thanks for our harvest, burn candles and copal pom and eat together, and not just cut down trees, take the crops from the land and earn money.'

This quote from a Samox villager points to the fact that Q'eqchi' economy is not just about an instrumentalist use of production factors in order to optimize profits. Some economic practices make sense from an instrumentalist point of view, others do not. Economic practices are subject to meaning-making, which opens up the possibility for religion to influence them. This section has two objectives. First, it will outline the Q'eqchi'es' economic strategies based on the preceding discussion of their economic practices. Secondly, it will discuss the ways these strategies are interrelated with their religion. I shall focus on "interrelations" between economy and religion emphasizing mutual reinforcements rather than unilateral influences from one vis-à-vis the other.

Subsistence and market-integration

From my analysis of subsistence production and market-oriented activities two central conclusions come to the fore. First, agriculture remains the basic economic activity and the Q'eqchi'es are willing to engage in non-agricultural activities provided they are able to reproduce at least a minimal agricultural basis. Secondly, the Q'eqchi'es want to become involved in market-oriented activities, to produce cash crops or to raise animals for the sake of selling them provided they are able to secure their subsistence production. Almost all of them produce a large part of the food crops and animals that they consume, even when it requires them to rent land or to buy inputs to increase the productivity of the land. In the latter case the market is instrumentalized in order to be able to reproduce their subsistence agriculture.

The desire to balance first agricultural and non-agricultural activities and secondly subsistence and market-oriented production and activities is a central aspect of Q'eqchi' economic strategies. It makes sense for two profane reasons. On the one hand, the Q'eqchi'es have to engage in market-oriented or non-agricultural activities because they cannot produce themselves all the things they need. They have to earn money to buy these things. Moreover, they want to become involved in such activities to improve their material situation. On the other hand, these activities can become very risky because they involve becoming dependent on Kastii which in the experience of the Q'eqchi'es is very problematic. Consequently, Q'eqchi'es wish not to become too dependent on market-oriented or non-agricultural activities and to retain the basic aspects of their subsistence agriculture.

Nevertheless, this profane logic is complemented by clear religious reasoning. The Q'eqchi'es themselves clearly differentiate between production for their own consumption and practices which focus on making money. In Chapter Four it was pointed out that this distinction has a religious background: customary religion is intimately linked to subsistence agriculture. Just to summarise the argument, customary religion specifies a social and geographical unit in which there are direct relations between the Tzuultaq'a and the local community, i.e. not mediated by the market. The Tzuultaq'a provides food and other items that the Q'eqchi'es consume, and "alien" objects and animals are not accepted by the Tzuultaq'a as sacrifices. Only activities within the subsistence sphere such as cultivating maize and house-building provide occasions for performing customary or substitution rituals. The land the villagers of Samox rent in the Polochic valley and on which they cultivate maize is included in the area that is marked by the four local mountains which the pasawinq visit when performing their mayejak. By way of emphasizing the thirteen central Tzuultaq'as in their mayejak the villagers of Rubelpec are able to relate this ritual to the land which they rent for subsistence purposes in distant parts of the Q'eqchi' region.

In this way customary religion provides a strong symbolic or meaningful support for the priority given to the reproduction of subsistence agriculture before entering into market-oriented or non-agricultural activities. Customary religion is closely related to the Q'eqchi'es' desire to optimize maize production for their own consumption. This basic aspect of their economic strategies holds both for communities in which customary religion is dominant and for villages in which it has been adapted to Bible-oriented religion.

Moreover, customary religion also stresses the difference between themselves - those who are related to the Tzuultaq'a - and the Kastii - outsiders on whom they become dependent when involving themselves in market-oriented activities. Thus customary religion relates to the Q'eqchi'es' cautious attitude to market-integration. For example, in the explanations the villagers of Samox give for the cardamom and coffee disease distrust of Kastii is linked with customary interpretations. They relate the appearance of the disease to intervention by Moscamed and ANACAFé in their village and to the villagers' neglect of their ritual obligations towards the Tzuultaq'a.

By contrast, Bible-oriented religion plays an important role in reducing this distrust towards Kastii and as such encourages the Q'eqchi'es to become involved in commercial relations with them. Moreover, in Chapter Four the positive attitude of Bible-oriented religion to economic improvement was discussed with reference to the motivations of Q'eqchi'es to become catechists or to convert to an evangelical church. Bible-oriented religion advocates the avoidance of "vices" that might impair their economic performance and impels them to work hard. Bible-oriented religion has no direct relationship with market-oriented economic activities such as customary religion has with subsistence economy, but Bible-oriented religion encourages the Q'eqchi'es to optimize their market-oriented activities.

Selectively adopting external inputs

Another basic characteristic of the Q'eqchi'es' economic strategies is their selectiveness in adopting external inputs and accepting projects offered to them by outsiders. In the previous section it was shown that hybrid maize seeds and new methods of planting maize are rejected by everyone in the four communities. On the other hand, the curative services offered by the representante agrícola or veterinarian promoters in co-ordination with DIGESEPE are accepted by almost all the villagers. The acceptance of gramoxone, chemical fertilizers and vegetables cultivation techniques is variable.

One of the considerations the various Q'eqchi'es have is that the adoption of external inputs and projects should not make them too dependent on Kastii. As a result, the Q'eqchi'es reject hybrid seeds and most of them do not use chemical fertilizers. They have their own varieties of maize seeds, each adapted to specific soil conditions and altitude. One of the disadvantages of hybrid maize seeds as compared to their own varieties is that the Q'eqchi'es cannot use part of the crop as seed for the new maize cycle. They would have to buy hybrid seed at every new cycle, which would make them very dependent on Kastii who sell these seeds. Kastii also virtually monopolize the sale of chemical fertilizers and together with the fact that these products are expensive this monopoly makes the Q'eqchi'es think twice before adopting them. In three of the four communities the villagers decided not to use them while the village in which chemical fertilizers are used has better access to the market; this enables them to avoid monopolies.

Another important factor in this respect is the question of who takes the initiative. The fruitful co-operation between the co-operative and bakery in Rubelpec and INACOP and INTECAP respectively is clearly related to the fact that it was the villagers themselves who took the initiative to start these projects and only afterwards sought assistance. The Q'eqchi'es' willingness to engage in projects or to accept external inputs in the end depends greatly on whether these projects or inputs serve to meet one or more of the basic elements of their economic strategies. The vaccination programme for animals has surely had the opportunity to prove its usefulness. Gramoxone turned out to benefit agricultural production at relatively low costs. However, profitability is just one element that the Q'eqchi'es take into consideration. The fact that the villagers of Rubelpec overcame their reservations and use chemical fertilizers is not only related to their access to nearby markets, but can also be explained by the fact that these fertilizers enable them to meet their basic objective of themselves producing a considerable part of the maize they consume. In Rubelpec this objective can only be met by using chemical fertilizers.

All these profane considerations make sense to the Q'eqchi'es in deciding to accept or reject external inputs, but their religion is also involved in these matters. First, customary and Bible-oriented religion influence the ways the Q'eqchi'es perceive Kastii and thus their willingness to accept external inputs they can only acquire from Kastii. There is not only a coincidence between the level of trust of Kastii on the one hand and the level of acceptance of external inputs and of willingness to engage in projects offered by them on the other. Both levels go from low to high from Xalihá to Samox to Chaabilchoch to Rubelpec. In the first two villages the customary principle dominates while in the latter two the Bible-oriented principle is dominant.

Secondly, the Q'eqchi'es are not willing to accept external technology or inputs that contradict the religious meanings they attribute to important elements of their economic strategies. For instance, the fact that the Q'eqchi'es do not adopt hybrid seeds is not due only to reluctance to become very dependent on Kastii. In the eyes of the Q'eqchi'es life is provided to them by the Tzuultaq'a and God through the maize that grows on the former's skin. It is imbued with a spirit which has to be reactivated in the planting rituals. The adoption of hybrid seeds would seriously disrupt this logic.

To give another example: several extension workers were surprised that the Q'eqchi'es are unwilling to give up their group-wise method of planting. The men who plant the maize stand in a row and then move forward making holes with a stick and planting the seeds. The distance between two holes is thus determined by the distance between the men. In order to increase the number of plants per square metre DIGESA employees tell the Q'eqchi'es to give up this group-wise planting method, insensitive to the fact that this way of planting is essential to the Q'eqchi'es' collective presentation of themselves to the Tzuultaq'a and God.

Dealing with labour

The meaning attributed to maize planting is just one of many examples of customary religion influencing labour forms. In the previous section a distinction was made between individual, group-wise and communitarian forms of labour. Individual labour refers to tasks that each household performs individually and from which only that household benefits. In cases where the labour of which the individual household disposes is insufficient to fulfil such tasks, wage labourers are hired. Hired labour is treated as a commodity: as something that is exchanged for something else (money, land, other labour) between households. It is a production factor instrumental in achieving maximum production or profit for the individual households. Communitarian labour is done jointly by the whole male or female population of the community and the community as such benefits from it. In this case someone performs labour as a service to the community without any exchange relations involved. As a result, this labour cannot be conceptualized as a commodity.

Group-wise labour is a special case. It refers to tasks from which the individual household benefits but which are done by the women or men of several other households and not just those who belong to the same kinship line. For example, from maize planting only one specific household benefits, but other men join the man of this household to plant his maize. This group-wise labour is not dealt with as a commodity. Clearly, group-wise labour embodies an element of reciprocity. In maize planting, one neighbour helps the other plant his maize and the next day the other reciprocates. However, the logic for performing group-wise labour does not stem from this reciprocity, but is provided by customary religion. Customary religion holds that the fulfilment of specific tasks that belong to the household depends on a contract with the Tzuultaq'a and God who require the villagers to present themselves as a community rather than as individual households.

Customary religion portrays this contract in a practical and reciprocal way; thus communitarian and group-wise labour can be seen as a "commodity" in terms of an exchange with the Tzuultaq'a and God but not in terms of an exchange between human beings. In the case of maize planting group-wise labour becomes one of the obligations the Q'eqchi'es have to meet in order to receive a good harvest from the Tzuultaq'a and God. Group-wise labour is exchanged for a good harvest. In short, the "commoditization" of labour within the relation between the Q'eqchi'es and the Tzuultaq'a entails the non-commoditized character of labour within the relations between the Q'eqchi'es. Customary religion makes this paradox possible and even necessary.

On the whole, where customary religion is relevant - mainly in subsistence activities - the Tzuultaq'a wants to be addressed in a communitarian or group-wise way which means that communitarian or group-wise labour is practised, labour is not commoditized and the community mediates between the households and the Tzuultaq'a and God. The personalized view of maize and houses in customary religion excludes an instrumental way of dealing with them. By contrast, in those cases in which customary religion has no relevance - mainly in market-oriented activities - individual labour is practised, extra labour is hired in and an instrumentalist or commoditized logic holds sway. All this may seem rather abstract, but it will be made explicit in the pages that follow as regards the various tasks that are performed in an individual, group-wise and communitarian way.

The Q'eqchi'es practise communitarian forms of labour in cases such as keeping paths and community buildings clean, constructing such buildings and tilling community lands. It is obvious that these community tasks should be performed in a communitarian way which entails non-commoditized labour. By contrast, the cultivation of cash crops by individual households prompts the Q'eqchi'es to work individually and to pay for extra labour. The commoditization of labour in this framework coincides with the fact that the cultivation of cash crops is not complemented by customary rituals.

The absence of these rituals has to do with the fact that the main cash crops, i.e. cardamom and coffee, have a cycle that covers several years; there is no fixed time when they have to be planted and there is an extended period of several months during which the coffee and cardamom can be harvested. In brief, there are no specific times of year which may serve as apparent occasions on which to perform rituals. However, the absence of customary rituals from cash crop production is most of all related to the fact that the Q'eqchi'es consider these crops to have an "alien" origin and destiny which escapes the logic of concluding a contract with the Tzuultaq'a. Of course, in their mayejak rituals the villagers of Samox ask the Tzuultaq'a for a good harvest of coffee and cardamom and they conceive of these crops' diseases as a lesson from the Tzuultaq'a, but even they do not perform rituals at specific moments related to these crops and they do not consider coffee and cardamom to have a spirit. The idea of life as granted by the Tzuultaq'a to the villagers does not apply in the case of cash crops so there is no need to present themselves in a communitarian or group-wise way to the Tzuultaq'a. Consequently, individualization and commoditization of labour can take place.

By contrast, maize planting is done group-wise by almost everyone and labour is not treated as a commodity. There are no practical reasons for doing so because there is no equipment involved: doing the job group-wise does not result in any time or energy saving compared to each man planting his maize individually on his "own" plot. The respondents consider planting maize to be a cheerful activity. They enjoy doing it as a group in a relaxed atmosphere. They told me this cheerful atmosphere is necessary for the maize to grow well. There is continuity between the vigil the night before the planting and the group-wise work on the land. Both elements serve the need to reinforce and reactivate the life of the seed and to present themselves as a group representing the community to the Tzuultaq'a and God. To the Q'eqchi'es religious and economic aspects of maize planting are inseparable.

Practical reasons for working group-wise do make sense in the case of building a house, which can be done more effectively in a group than individually. However, for the same reasons as those mentioned regarding maize planting, group-wise labour does not make sense from the practical point of view in the case of land clearance and maize harvesting. These three activities - land clearance, maize harvesting and house building - occupy an intermediate position between the extremes of cash crop cultivation and maize planting. These activities clearly belong predominantly to the subsistence sphere and to the tasks of individual households. Land is cleared mainly for maize cultivating. For cardamom and coffee production a piece of land has to be cleared only once every five to seven years. Many of the building materials are fetched from the waste lands. Both maize and the house are imbued with a spirit emanating from the Tzuultaq'a. Consequently, one would expect to find group-wise labour, dealt with in a non-commoditized way and the performance of customary or substitution rituals.

However, the picture is mixed as regards these three activities: some work group-wise while others work individually and - if necessary - hire labour. There are two explanations for the fact that they do not all work group-wise and treat labour in a non-commoditized way. First, customary religion may be relevant to these activities but its importance is not as compelling as in the case of planting maize. Obviously, the need to fulfil one's obligations to the Tzuultaq'a while harvesting maize is less pressing than when maize is being planted when the Tzuultaq'a still has to be convinced of the Q'eqchi'es' dedication to fulfil their part of the contract. In addition, there is no need to jointly reactivate the spirit of maize during its harvest and b'antioxink rituals are much less flowery than the planting rituals. In Chaabilchoch twenty per cent of respondents even do not perform any b'antioxink rituals at all. The situation regarding land clearance is similar to maize harvesting: the need to carry out one's obligations to the Tzuultaq'a is not as pressing as in the case of planting maize.

Secondly, in the case of land clearance the fact that not everyone works group-wise can also be explained by the fact that communitarian mayejak rituals or individual mayejak rituals or substitution rituals have already taken place immediately before this work. Several respondents told me that because of these preliminary rituals they feel that they have already paid attention to the Tzuultaq'a before the land clearance. A similar argument may be valid in the case of harvesting maize and house building: several Q'eqchi'es consider the performance of the relevant rituals to be enough. There is no need to confirm this ritual attention again through group-wise labour.

In any case, the fact that several respondents told me that they were not sure which labour form to use for these three activities confirms the conclusion that they are caught in a dilemma between the fact that customary logic is not as pressing for these activities and the fact that this logic is still relevant. This dilemma has encouraged some respondents to let an instrumental and commoditized treatment of labour take over.

Customary religion is also related to the division of labour within the household. It confirms the existing division of labour between men and women. For example, only men are allowed to plant maize (see Chapter Four). However, Bible-oriented religion plays a similar role in affirming this division of labour by way of its moral requirements. This affirmation is the only example of Bible-oriented religion exercising any direct influence on labour issues. The general pattern of religion influencing labour issues is of customary religion demanding a non-commoditized and group-wise or communitarian form of labour because of its relevance to subsistence activities. In the absence of this relevance an instrumental or commoditized logic shapes labour.

Dealing with land

Land control patterns show a similar mixture of individual and collective forms. Individual households and the community share control over the land. Some communities emphasize community control; others communities stress household control.

In line with customary logic one would expect community control to be founded in customary religion, but at present the relation between customary religion and communitarian land control is not as obvious as in the case of customary religion and communitarian or group-wise labour. The tilling of community lands and the cleaning of trails and squares, for example, are not accompanied by customary rituals. In the past this relation was much more obvious. The so-called *yuwa' ch'och* or "chief of the land" used to supervise all land issues and was one of the leading pasawinq. In recent decades the Local Development Committee has taken over his land control tasks.

Nevertheless, customary religion continues to underscore communitarian aspects of land control. At present the mayejak rituals in particular continue to express the idea that land is a community matter. The Tzuultaq'a wants to be addressed by the community as a whole at a mayejak in order to ensure good harvests on all the lands the community has access to. The communitarian way of presenting themselves to the Tzuultaq'a coincides with the obligation of the community to provide each member with at least a small piece of land to cultivate maize. In short, customary religion provides a meaningful support for communitarian land control and for treating land in a personalized way on those occasions when customary religion is relevant. On other occasions, when customary religion has no relevance, the Q'eqchi'es treat land in an instrumental way and as a commodity. For example, they are willing to pay money to INTA for access to their lands and would clearly buy more land if they had the money to do so.

Economic individualization and stratification

The rewards of economic activity go primarily to individual households. In this sense the economic strategies of the Q'eqchi'es give particular emphasis to the interests of individual households. As a result, economic stratification reaches quite a high level in the communities, but in some more than in others.

There are several factors that influence this level of economic stratification. First, there is access to sufficient fertile land to cultivate maize and cash crops. The relatively easy access to land with a high maize fertility explains the relatively low level of stratification in terms of maize consumption in Xalihá where almost everyone is able to produce a considerable amount of maize. Access to sufficient fertile land to cultivate maize does present a problem to several households in Samox and Rubelpec who enter into the lowest categories of maize consumption. In Rubelpec those with little access to fertile land for cultivating maize not only see their level of maize consumption affected, but also their net income because they have to buy considerable quantities of maize and fertilizers.

Moreover, differential access to land with high cardamom fertility is an important factor in Chaabilchoch and Samox influencing net income differentiation. In Chaabilchoch those with land with low maize fertility have the possibility of renting land elsewhere, and the villagers of Samox who have good relations with Q'eqchi'es in the valley can do the same. In the case of land with low cardamom fertility the same escape valve is no option because cardamom has a cycle of about six years and land is rented on a yearly basis.

The access to fertile land is determined by several issues such as the scarcity of land, the moment of settlement in the community, the splitting up of land afterwards between sons and membership of the Local Development Committee. In Xalihá these last issues are not very important because of the relatively low level of land scarcity and the fact that lands have not been allocated in a definite way to each household. In Rubelpec access to land is very differential, but it is not related to the moment of settlement or membership of the Local Development Committee because the latter has no influence on land issues and the households belong to kinship lines that have probably been there for ages already. In Samox and Chaabilchoch there is no fertile land available any more. In these communities those who came in at the moment the community was founded and those who maintained a position within the Local Development Committee have the best lands.

Another factor that particularly influences net income is the willingness, need or ability to go into market-oriented activities. On the one hand, bad market conditions and the fact that they do not like doing wage labour is clearly one of the factors that explains the relatively low level of stratification in terms of net income in Xalihá. On the other hand, the much higher level of net income differentiation in Rubelpec is related to the relative eagerness - and the need to do so - of the villagers to go into retail trade and perform wage labour. Differences in the number of household members who are able to do so have a considerable effect on the net income differences per household.

However, the effects of economic stratification are alleviated by mutual assistance between households. I have no details on the quantities of products, services and money involved in mutual aid, but I have the impression that considerable exchanges take place in this respect. Probably the most important of these exchanges occur between households within the same kinship line. Both elements - the one encouraging further economic stratification and individualization and the other alleviating its effects, encouraging redistribution of resources and stressing communal responsibility - form part of the economic strategies of the Q'eqchi'es.

Religion plays a role in both elements. Bible-oriented religion encourages the Q'eqchi'es to optimize their economic performance. Consequently, where some villagers are more open to Bible-oriented religion than others, this religion may contribute to increasing economic stratification. In fact, there is a close relationship between economic performance and the role Bible-oriented religion plays in the lives of individual Q'eqchi'es. In Chaabilchoch and Rubelpec the leading catechists such as ministros and instructors have above average net incomes. In Rubelpec the six respondents with the highest net incomes (categories VIII and IX of Table 7.7) are all either leading catechists or leading members of evangelical churches.

Moreover, among those with the lowest net incomes in Rubelpec there are several who have a serious drinking problem. Drinking may not affect agricultural production very much, but in activities that require discipline such as wage labour it may have a much more negative effect. The woman of the man in one of these households told me: 'Guillermo used to pray a lot before he went to buy and sell merchandise and his profits were high. But now he does not earn much money any more. He drinks a lot, goes to another woman and does not pay attention to God any more'. The intimate relationship between God, moral behaviour and economic success is apparent in her words.

A similar positive relationship between the importance of Bible-oriented religion and economic performance is strongly suggested by the fact that in Chaabilchoch the evangelicals in general do very well in terms of net income. Their average net income (3914.83 quetzales) is more than one thousand quetzales higher than the average for all the households. Of the eight highest net income earning households five belong to an evangelical church. They do well in spite of the fact the evangelicals have hardly any access to the Local Development Committee.

This relation between Bible-oriented religion and doing well in market-oriented activities may involve two causalities. On the one hand, Bible-oriented religion may encourage individual Q'eqchi'es to do their utmost to earn money. On the other, those who perform well in market-oriented activities may be attracted to a form of religion that legitimates these activities. Of course, these causalities are not mutually exclusive.

Simultaneously, both customary and Bible-oriented religion may counteract the effects of economic stratification. Both encourage the Q'eqchi'es to help their fellow villagers who are suffering from a bad harvest or illness. Bible-oriented religion is related to, for example, the Catholic women's groups who visit households with some kind of problem. Evangelicals consider such visits and mutual assistance to be one of their central practices. Customary religion limits the effects of economic stratification by encouraging the community to see to it that every member has access to land.

8

Q'eqchi' Economy and Modernization

The objective of this concluding chapter on Q'eqchi' economy is to relate the analysis of the previous two chapters to the concepts and questions discussed in Chapter One. I will first try to classify the basic characteristics of Q'eqchi' economic strategies into pre-modern, originally modern and contemporary modern terms. The room for manoeuvre the Q'eqchi'es have to carry through these strategies is limited by intervening actors and agencies and material factors. These limitations, the kind of influence these actors and agencies exert on the Q'eqchi'es and their power to do so will be discussed next on the basis of the material presented in Chapter Six.

Q'eqchi' economic meanings and practices in a modernizing framework?

Regarding all the aspects of the economic strategies of the Q'eqchi'es outlined above I hold that they articulate pre-modern and modern elements in a creolizing way. They fundamentally want to reproduce pre-modern elements of their economy, and provided this condition is fulfilled they engage in all kinds of modern economic activities. However, these activities must not be allowed to disrupt fundamental elements of their pre-modern economy and related religious meanings.

There are multiple examples in which this fundamental principle is expressed. First, the Q'eqchi'es engage in (modern) market-oriented agricultural and non-agricultural activities provided that they are able to reproduce their (pre-modern) subsistence agriculture. The Q'eqchi'es have various reasons to do so, such as the need for drawing on a variety of activities and avoiding risks to secure a sustainable and viable livelihood. We have seen in the previous chapter that Q'eqchi' religion plays an important role in this respect too. Q'eqchi' households are quite flexible about combining various elements, but they always look for such a combination of pre-modern subsistence agriculture and modern market-oriented activities.

Secondly, the Q'eqchi'es selectively adopt and adapt external and scientifically developed (modern) technology and other modern elements introduced by way of projects on certain conditions. This adoption must not make them too dependent on Kastii, which confirms the (pre-modern) fact that trust in persons instead of in expertise systems plays a crucial role in technology transfer. In addition, modern inputs must support basic elements of their economic strategies if the Q'eqchi'es are to be convinced of the need to adopt them. It is not just the profitability of the inputs that plays a role here; modern elements such as chemical fertilizers are used by the villagers of Rubelpec, for example, to achieve their objective of themselves producing as much as possible of the maize they consume, i.e. to reproduce their (pre-modern) subsistence agriculture. Moreover, if modern inputs are to be accepted they must not contradict essential (pre-modern) customary religious meanings which the Q'eqchi'es attribute to basic elements of their strategies.

Thirdly, the Q'eqchi'es combine both (pre-modern) communitarian and group-wise labour with (modern) individual labour. They deal with labour both as a non-commodity (pre-modern) and in an instrumentalist and commoditized (modern) way. Just as the relevance of customary or Bible-oriented religion depends on the occasion, the various labour forms and treatments of labour are also occasion-specific. The relevance of customary religion largely determines which form or way of dealing with labour is practised.

Fourthly, the various forms of land control and the way the Q'eqchi'es deal with land show the same mix of pre-modern and modern elements. The various communities I studied show a balance of communitarian (pre-modern) and individual household (modern) control of land. As in the case of labour their treatment of land in a personalized and non-commoditized (pre-modern) or instrumental and commoditized (modern) way depends on the occasion.

Finally, the various communities exhibit various levels of economic stratification, but all are seeking to strike a balance between economic performance on the part of the individual households (modern) and the communitarian (pre-modern) responsibility they feel for those who are suffering the effects of illness or a bad harvest. This sense of responsibility alleviates the effects of economic stratification.

In short, the Q'eqchi'es are not just on the pre-modern side; they usually talk about economic matters in secular and profane ways and sometimes are eager to improve their economic situation. The introduction of cardamom production is one of several examples in this respect. Before the 1970s no Q'eqchi' had ever produced cardamom. When some large landowners started to produce this product in the 1970s and when prices were high, the first Q'eqchi'es followed suit. Since then cardamom production has become one of their most important sources of income. However, the Q'eqchi'es are not completely on the modern side. Their priority is to secure the reproduction of fundamental aspects of their existing and pre-modern economic practices and meanings before entering into modern experiments.

The characteristics that have so far been classified as modern fit both the categories of originally and contemporary modern as discussed in Chapter One. However, in line with Giddens it makes sense to characterize the articulation or creolization of pre-modern and modern elements as typical of an originally modern condition. This characterization is supported by the fact that religion and economy are interrelated among the Q'eqchi'es in a combination of pre-modern and modern ways. On the one hand, the direct ways in which customary religion is related to almost all the pre-modern aspects of the five features discussed should be qualified as pre-modern. It is intimately linked to subsistence agriculture, to communitarian, group-wise and non-commoditized labour, to a non-commoditized conception and communitarian control of land, to redistributive practices within the community; and it underscores the Q'eqchi'es' selectiveness in adopting external inputs. Customary religion and economy are inextricably intertwined when the former is relevant. On these occasions representations of nature (the land) and social relations (the community cultivating the land) have a religious character.

On the other hand, Bible-oriented religion is not related to Q'eqchi' economy in a direct way. This relation is mediated by the religiously based moral impetus to work hard and put one's life in order, and by encouragement to overcome distrust of Kastii. Bible-oriented religion allows for a profane interpretation of land and other production factors and a commoditized and instrumentalist logic holds sway.

In the light of this mixture of pre-modern and modern ways of interrelating religion and economy, does it still make sense to interpret Q'eqchi' religion and economy in terms of separate fields, which is a feature of an originally modern condition? I think it does. To begin with, in the case of Q'eqchi' economy and religion there is a separation between religious and economic institutions and leaders, despite the fact that many religious specialists claim that they have a responsibility in economic matters as well. Moreover, these specialists and institutions propagate an understanding of religious and economic matters mainly in their own terms. Perhaps the main exceptions are the Pentecostal churches which portray social reality as the arena for the struggle between God and Satan, both with their adherents. One might expect that the separation between economic and religious practices and meanings within the framework of a society differentiated into fields would be mainly expressed in the discourses of the specialists. Among the "ordinary" Q'eqchi'es one might expect that this separation would not have the same clear-cut traits.

The distinction between religion and economy among the Q'eqchi'es is confirmed by the fact that the emphases on pre-modern or modern aspects in religious and economic matters do not simply coincide in the four villages. Of course, the dominance of customary religion is associated with low levels of trust in Kastii and low levels of acceptance of external inputs while Bible-oriented religion is related to relatively high levels of both trust in Kastii and acceptance of external inputs. Moreover, in the community in which the villagers most clearly emphasize pre-modern economic elements in relation to modern elements - Xalihá - the customary principle predominates while the community with the highest level of acceptance of modern economic elements - Rubelpec - the Bible-oriented principle is dominant. However, the villagers of Samox and Chaabilchoch exhibit similar levels of pre-modern and modern elements in their economic strategies but in the former village the customary principle dominates, while in the latter the Bible-oriented principle is dominant. Chaabilchoch is even stronger on pre-modern elements such as non-commoditized and group-wise labour and the levels of economic stratification are lower than in Samox.

There is a relative autonomy of religion and economy vis-à-vis each other. On the one hand, the emphasis on pre-modern or modern elements in religion not only depends on a similar emphasis in economy; it is also influenced by the kind of pastoral policy implemented by religious specialists and their power resources. On the other hand, the emphasis on pre-modern or modern elements in economy is not only related to a corresponding accent in religion; it depends also on factors such as varying opportunities to become involved in profitable market-oriented activities, differential necessity to become involved in non-agricultural activities because of land shortage and the variable power of intervening agencies and actors promoting modern elements.

In short, the Q'eqchi'es' economic strategies articulating pre-modern and modern elements are located in an originally modern context of an economic field which has limited but real autonomy vis-à-vis the religious field.

The influence of intervening actors and agencies and local leaders

This economic field includes not only the Q'eqchi'es themselves, but also intervening actors and agencies which limit the Q'eqchi'es' room for manoeuvre to pursue their strategies. Moreover, there are also local Q'eqchi' leaders who have an impact on the economic strategies of the "ordinary" Q'eqchi'es. In the following pages the influence of these intervening agencies and actors and local leaders will be classified in terms of modernization and their power to exercise this influence will be discussed.

Negative and destructive

A first category of intervening actors and agencies consists of those whose influence is predominantly negative and destructive. This category includes the army, the merchants, the landlords and INTA. The army is without doubt the most powerful intervening agency. It can and often is willing to use military force; it is well-organized and it controls the civil administration. Its influence is purely negative: it has destroyed some hundred communities, it forces men to waste their time on military service and is one of the causes of the lack of civil security.

At first glance one would say that the influence of the merchants and landlords is modern. Without the presence of merchants the Q'eqchi'es would be unable to sell their cash crops and animals. The wide variety of nationalities of the landlords and the fact that their products are exported to various parts of the world point to a modern globalizing economy. A closer look, however, reveals a different picture. The merchants seriously limit the Q'eqchi'es' profits from market-oriented production. They take advantage of the absence of a modern and properly working market system. As a result, the Q'eqchi'es' are discouraged from engaging in market-oriented production and other modern activities and from adopting modern inputs in their production provided by these merchants.

Unlike the German finca owners at the beginning of this century most of the present landlords maintain a very low level of investment in their estates. Several landlords I spoke to gave me the impression that their principal interest is not to maximise profits, but to have a source of security and status in Guatemalan society. This pre-modern characteristic of a society marked by stratified differentiation (see Chapter One on Luhmann) is confirmed by the kind of labour relations on the fincas. To be sure, in the course of the present century the abolition of the habilitación system and the vagrancy laws which legitimized forced labour, points to a more capitalist character of labour relations. Nevertheless, labour relations on the fincas retain strong semi-feudal characteristics. These include the plots of land given in usufruct to the mozos colonos which enable the finqueros to pay very low wages, the child labour of jornaleros during coffee harvest periods and the landlords' desire to control every aspect of "their" mozos colonos lives, to limit their access to education and health care and keep out trade unions. Because of these features it is very difficult to speak of a Junker-model of transition towards capitalism.

Moreover, the fincas and haciendas constitute one of the main causes of the shortage of land in the region, which seriously limits the lands the Q'eqchi'es can dedicate to cash-crop production. This holds particularly true for villages in the Q'eqchi' heartland. The same destructive effects result from the land conflicts many landlords force upon the Q'eqchi' villages and the Human Rights violations these conflicts entail.

The power resources landlords and merchants dispose of are considerable. They include access to capital and modern technology, contacts at the national and international level, status and, if necessary, army backup. The merchants make use of the absence of a properly functioning market system. In brief, landlords and merchants seriously hamper the Q'eqchi'es' abilities to successfully pursue their economic strategies, especially their opportunities for becoming involved in modern and profitable economic activities.

INTA exercises a similar influence. It is supposed to promote modern ownership relations, although the patrimonio agrario colectivo scheme involves a balanced land control by the community (pre-modern) and households (modern). However, its land title programmes have had very little success and INTA has contributed to a state of insecurity concerning access to land with the resulting Human Rights violations. INTA discourages Q'eqchi' local communities to invest in modern market-oriented production because of their insecure access to land. Almost all the Q'eqchi' communities in the settlement areas - about half of the total Q'eqchi' communities - have to deal with INTA concerning a crucial economic asset: their land.

Limited modern influence

There are other intervening agencies that have some modernizing impact on the Q'eqchi' communities. These agencies include DIGESA, DIGESEPE, ICTA, INDECA, BANDESA, ANACAFé, Caminos Rurales, Moscamed, UNEPAR, INTECAP, DIGEBOS, INACOP and FEDECOVERA. They provide the villagers with scientifically developed technology, encourage the use of external inputs such as pesticides and chemical fertilizers, encourage the Q'eqchi'es to maximise market-oriented production and individual labour forms, offer them opportunities for wage labour and other non-agricultural activities, promote an instrumentalist approach to land and labour and assist in management and administrative tasks. All these elements can be categorized as modern. Next, there are agencies such as Vitamina "A" and Defensores de la Naturaleza which promote both pre-modern (vegetable and maize production for their own consumption) and modern (cash crops) elements. These agencies show at least some sensitivity towards Q'eqchi' culture and economic strategies.

These development agencies have few power resources to draw on. If necessary, the local communities can do without their services. Moreover, the Q'eqchi'es do not take the trustworthiness of their staff members and the usefulness of their expertise for granted. Of all the agencies DIGESA is the one which disposes of by far the most extensive network of offices and employees. However even DIGESA officials, as we have seen, have access to only a small number of Q'eqchi' households. The cases of DIGESA and the FEDECOVERA co-operatives make clear that the intervention by these agencies rarely takes into account essential aspects of the existing economic strategies, culture and indigenous knowledge of the Q'eqchi'es. They just try to deskill and reskill the Q'eqchi'es and make no effort to link their inputs to the existing economic strategies of the Q'eqchi'es themselves, which seriously reduces the impact of their work.

In short, the modern impact of these agencies differs from one community to another, but on the whole the Q'eqchi' communities maintain a considerable autonomy towards these agencies and remain very selective in adopting modern inputs and technology offered by them.

Churches

A clear modern influence is exercised by the Catholic pastoral agents who practise the concept of sacramentalist pastoral work. This is shown by their instrumental conception of nature and social relations, their social projects emphasizing market integration and the adoption of external inputs, their promotion of scientifically developed technology and disqualification of indigenous knowledge. They express a strong belief in progress and encourage individual believers to improve their economic performance. The latter holds true for most of the evangelical churches as well.

An important part of the work of those who practice liberating pastoral work is to counteract the negative impact of other actors and agencies. The Department of Social Pastoral Work in Cobán works with those, such as the internal refugees, who suffer from army violence. The legal assistance granted by this Department and by the Vicariate of El Petén concentrates on the victims of land conflicts caused by landlord interventions and INTA inertia or complicity. The instruction to the multiplicadores de pastoral social on human rights is a reaction to the state of lawlessness created by the Guatemalan state.

However, liberating pastoral work does not just react to the damaging effects of others. It tries to exercise an influence in which pre-modern and modern elements are combined. Pre-modern elements in the concept of liberating pastoral work include its anti-capitalist position and its distrust of market integration but these elements are not emphasized any more. Pastoral agents who apply this concept advocate community control of land and communitarian labour forms. They try to optimize the use of the communities' existing resources rather than advocating the adoption of external inputs.

They offer modern inputs and scientifically developed technology only when these elements complement or support the Q'eqchi'es' existing strategies. The modern elements these pastoral agents promote are the rule of law as expressed in the legal assistance to Q'eqchi' communities, the condemnation of human rights violations, instructing local communities on how to claim their rights, and calling for reforms that would enable the farmers and peasants to modernize economically (land reform).

In their efforts to influence the economy of the Q'eqchi'es the various churches in the region have important advantages. They can build on the relations of confidence they have established in religious matters, and on their network of catechists and other local leaders. Even more important, churches provide religious legitimation for the economic practices they promote. However, relations of confidence between church leaders and local communities are not unconditional. Nor does having influence on the religion of the Q'eqchi'es automatically lead to influencing their economic strategies.

Local economic leaders

Local leaders such as the representante agrícola are "brokers": both in terms of the framework of relations between the local community and intervening actors and agencies and in terms of articulating pre-modern and modern elements. On the one hand they represent intervening agencies and are responsible for transmitting to the local communities the modern inputs these agencies promote. On the other hand, in their own household economy they practise the same basic strategy of articulating pre-modern and modern elements with slightly more emphasis on the latter. For example, the Local Development Committee was brought into being as a modern initiative by the state to augment its influence in the communities. However, the same committee promotes such pre-modern elements of Q'eqchi' economic strategies as community control of the land and joint cultivation of community land.

The importance of these communitarian activities, the number of other committees to be supervised and the question of whether the committee has a role to play in land title issues are clear indicators of the power of this committee. In Samox, Chaabilchoch and Xalihá it does play such a role in land title issues, but in communities in a parcelamiento project or in the Q'eqchi' heartland - like Rubelpec - the committee's role in land issues is limited.

Membership of the committee can be a source of power in the community. In Chaabilchoch several respondents told me that the committee members picked out the largest and best plots of land for themselves when allocating plots of land to individual households. Moreover, in three of the four local communities the average net income of committee members is considerably higher than the average net income of all community members: see Table 8.1.

Table 8.1: average net income of committee members and community members in four villages in quetzales

Villages	Average net income committee members	Average net income community members
Xalihá	1396.88	1451.21
Rubelpec	2700.01	1684.20
Samox	4039.44	2774.88
Chaabilchoch	4103.85	2941.40

These figures would seem to indicate that in Samox, Chaabilchoch and Rubelpec committee members derive economic advantage from their membership, but it may also be the case that those who do well in economic terms are chosen as committee members. These figures may also point to the fact that the community members who first settled in the community managed to get access to the best lands and formed the committee simultaneously. This could be the case in Chaabilchoch and Samox, but not in Rubelpec because this community has a long history. I suggest that in communities in which the committee members can stay on as long as they like there is a relationship between economic performance and committee membership (Samox, Chaabilchoch and Rubelpec), while in the one community in which the members of the committee are elected every few years there is no such relation (Xalihá).

Strategies and power

The overall balance of the influence of intervening agencies and actors tips towards the negative side. In implementing their economic strategies the large majority of Q'eqchi'es are seriously hindered by most of them. In addition, material conditions such as erosion and the decreasing fertility of the land have caused them serious problems. These problems are intimately related to land shortage which has forced the Q'eqchi'es to work their land over intensively, to start cultivating marginal lands and to cut down trees.

A good example of land shortage creating ecological problems can be found in the Polochic valley. The river has always flooded the lower parts of the valley during the rainy season, but the flooding problems have increased greatly in the last two decades. The Q'eqchi' communities which first settled in the valley were later expelled to make way for haciendas. The Q'eqchi'es thus had to look for lands on higher slopes of the Sierra de las Minas. They cut down the vegetation which caused the rain to bring down increasing quantities of soil. As a result, the quality of the land on the slopes is degrading and increasing quantities of mud are washed into the river. This mud created sediment in the lower parts of the valley and made it increasingly difficult for the river water to find its way to lake Izabal. The flooding problem has become increasingly acute and prevents fertile lands from being cultivated.

Another material problem that threatens to hamper the Q'eqchi'es' basic economic strategies is the fact that the limits of the agrarian frontier have become visible. Until recently the aim of many Q'eqchi'es to reproduce themselves as farmers could be met by migrating to the Petén and Izabal. Consequently, the agrarian frontier was pushed in a northern and eastern direction, but the end of this escape valve is near. What will happen when there is no more land available and what the consequences will be for the economic strategies of those who are left with insufficient land is difficult to say.

Nevertheless, up till now, despite the material conditions and negative influence of intervening actors and agencies, most of the Q'eqchi'es have had limited but real room for manoeuvre to practise their basic economic strategies. It has been possible to classify the basic aspects of Q'eqchi' economic strategies as well as the influences exercised by intervening actors and agencies in pre-modern, originally and contemporary modern terms. However, after classifying both these strategies and influences in these terms and evaluating the power of these intervening actors and agencies and the Q'eqchi'es' room for manoeuvre to pursue their strategies, we are left with no reason to suppose that the Q'eqchi'es are heading unavoidably towards modernity.

First, the intervening actors and agencies are not pushing them inevitably in a modern direction: their modernizing influence is rather limited and the impact of most of them is on the whole rather destructive especially on the modern aspects of Q'eqchi' economy. In addition, there are few grounds for expecting any process towards a Junker-style road to capitalism on the basis of the existing landed estates. Secondly, the Q'eqchi'es own economic strategies do not focus on full-blown modernity either. They continue articulating modern and pre-modern aspects as part of a creolizing and flexible strategy. There is no reason to expect a peasant road to capitalism either as long as they are able to continue their drive to reproduce their subsistence agriculture, to maintain some level of community control over land and labour forms, to go on being selective in adopting external inputs and to limit the effects of economic stratification.

The combined effects of the influence of material conditions and of intervening actors and agencies and the economic strategies of the Q'eqchi'es themselves point to a very specific economic configuration which combines particular pre-modern and modern elements.

9

Conclusions, Considerations and Reflections

The final chapter of this book is dedicated to answering the central research questions using my analysis in Chapter Five and Chapter Eight. Based on the conclusions the central concept of creolization, both as an act of meaning-making and as a social process, will be discussed in the following sections. This concept will first be related to the ways in which the Q'eqchi'es process information and structure their discourse. Secondly, the social conditions of creolization among the Q'eqchi'es will be discussed. Thirdly, the growing importance and risks related to creolization in the contemporary globalizing context will be dealt with.

The Q'eqchi'es and modernization

The *Leitmotiv* of this book has been an attempt to relate the traits of the Q'eqchi'es' social reality to the meanings that are attributed to the concept of modernization in the literature. Having made explicit the meanings of the terms pre-modern, originally modern and contemporary modern and having discussed Q'eqchi' religion and economy, some conclusions can be drawn.

To begin with, the Q'eqchi'es' practices and meanings in the religious and economic fields as well as the influences of intervening actors and agencies in these fields can be classified as pre-modern, originally modern and contemporary modern. There is a basic concordance between the meanings attributed to the three terms and elements of the Q'eqchi'es' religion and economy. My data and information on the Q'eqchi'es can be translated into the academic language of modernization.

Moreover, I hold that the meanings that these three terms point to touch the heart of the problems, dilemmas and issues the Q'eqchi'es have to deal with regarding their religion and economy. These meanings relate to a personalized view of nature and a commoditized treatment of land and labour. They point to communitarian rituals vis-à-vis the Tzuultaq'a and to individual moral responsibility towards God. They deal with the need to "solve" in a symbolic way the Q'eqchi'es' dependence on nature and the reinforcement of Bible-oriented *Selbstzwang*. They relate to personal trust as a key issue of social communication and the need to settle land rights. They deal with the combination of subsistence and market-oriented production. They are about both indigenous and scientifically developed knowledge. They deal with both the spirit of maize and the price of cardamom, etc. All these crucial elements of the religion and economy of the Q'eqchi'es refer to the central meanings of the terms pre-modern, originally modern and contemporary modern. The relevance of the meanings attached to them in the case of the Q'eqchi'es shows that these terms can be meaningful outside of the Western world. The issues and problems implied in these three terms are not just Western phenomena, they point to crucial processes of life on the peripheries as well.

But in the light of the relevance of these three terms in the case of Q'eqchi' reality how are we to conceptualize modernization and to understand its role within this reality? In this respect I propose to use the concepts of "structure" and "agency" as metaphors, as two different but complementary perspectives from which to look at social reality. "Structure" points to the social relations and discourses that influence, or "structure", the practices and meanings of specific social actors. The "agency" point of view highlights the ability of the social actors themselves to partially supersede, either intentionally or non-intentionally, these structuring influences by way of meaning-making and modifying their practices.

In an analogous argument I would say that the themes and dilemmas raised by modernization "structure" the religious and economic problems and issues which the Q'eqchi'es face in their daily lives. The Q'eqchi'es are influenced by intervening actors and agencies; they draw on their own traditions and are conditioned by their natural context as they face problems and dilemmas of modernization that set the agenda of their religion and economy. In Chapter Five and Chapter Eight it has been shown that the problems, dilemmas and paradoxes regarding the relations between pre-modern, originally modern and contemporary modern traits are central to the Q'eqchi' religion and economy.

However, setting the agenda is not the same as determining what the Q'eqchi'es do and think. There are three main reasons which suggest that the Q'eqchi'es are not simply being forced into a unidirectional process from a pre-modern to an originally or contemporary modern condition. First, in Chapter One it was stressed that modernity and modernization are phenomena that are themselves about dilemmas, paradoxes and contradictions rather than linear developments and unequivocal forces and factors. There are no development laws that force social actors to trade in pre-modern elements for originally and contemporary modern aspects.

Secondly, intervening actors and agencies are not just forcing the Q'eqchi'es into a clear-cut modern direction. In Chapter Five and Chapter Eight it was made clear that these actors and agencies do not only exercise a modern influence; some of them partially obstruct any scenario heading for more modern characteristics (landlords, merchants, INTA). Others are very inefficient in promoting modern elements (DIGESA, DIGESEPE) and yet others also promote pre-modern elements (clergy applying the concept of liberating pastoral work). Modern globalizing influences hardly reach the Q'eqchi'es directly. They take on localized forms and reach the Q'eqchi'es through intermediary actors and agencies that intervene in their life-world and thus become embedded in local interfaces with their specific interests, power relations and forms of communication. The outcome of this "filtering" by intermediaries is surely not an unequivocal reinforcement of modern features.

Thirdly, even if the influence of these intermediaries were unambiguously modern, the analysis of Q'eqchi' religion and economy has shown that they are not able to determine the Q'eqchi'es' practices and meanings. The Q'eqchi'es have a limited but real capacity to decide themselves on what to do and think. The agenda set by modernization is complemented by the creolizing "agency" of the Q'eqchi'es themselves. Their creolizing way of dealing with modernization, articulating modern and pre-modern elements, means that if it is up to them they are not heading in an unequivocally modern direction.

In using the concept of creolization to characterize the Q'eqchi'es' ability to respond to modernizing problems and issues, I have extended the original meaning which Hannerz attributes to this concept. He writes about creolization in the sense of the articulation or mixing of aspects stemming from the endogenous cultures of social actors on the one hand and elements coming to them from global flows of meanings on the other.[1] I would say that creolization is not only about the articulation of endogenous and exogenous, internal and external elements, but also of pre-modern, originally modern and contemporary modern aspects. Thus I use the term in a wider sense than the merely cultural one and I locate it in the framework of an analysis of power relations.

Other concepts that are available to express this articulating way to deal with such problems include "syncretization", "synthetization", Latour's "hybridization" and Lévi-Strauss' "bricolage" (see Chapter One). The term "syncretization" has the disadvantage that it expresses both social science's and theological aspects and can hardly be rescued from any discussion about whether this religious mixing is good or bad. The term "synthetization" supposes that the articulated elements used to stand in opposition to each other as thesis and anti-thesis, which I do not want to suggest concerning pre-modern and modern elements. Latour's (Latour 1993) term refers mainly to a supposedly modern condition whereas I want to call attention to the articulation of pre-modern and modern elements. Lévi-Strauss' (Lévi-Strauss 1962) "bricolage" is too general because it points to the articulation of all kinds of meanings whereas I explicitly want to focus on pre-modern and modern, on indigenous and external elements. In the light of the disadvantages of these alternative terms I prefer to use the concept of creolization.

The capacity of the Q'eqchi'es to articulate their selective (re)invention (see Hobsbawm, Ranger 1983; Roosens 1989) of tradition with selectively adopted and adapted external elements from intervening agencies, to combine the selective continuation of pre-modern elements with selectively adopted and adapted modern aspects, means that they do not just stick to a defensive orthodoxy. On the contrary, they are quite aggressive where learning Spanish for example is concerned. They clearly want to learn this second language and are not worried about a possible "loss of identity" connected to this learning. They opt for bilingualism without depreciating their own *na'leb'*, or culture.

In short, the concepts of modernization and creolization are very useful for understanding Q'eqchi' religion and economy, but only after the concept of modernization has been modified. Despite the importance of Bible-oriented religion and cardamom sales over the last few decades, for example, there is no reason to assume that some unequivocal process of modernization in the sense of the trading in of pre-modern elements for originally or contemporary modern aspects is taking place among the Q'eqchi'es. Consequently, I would dispose modernization of any evolutionist perspective and characterize it as a set of problems, dilemmas and paradoxes that deal with the relations between pre-modern, originally modern and contemporary modern elements and which set the agenda of processes of social change. The literature on pre-modernity and modernity, in which I have incorporated the issues raised by globalization and post-modernist authors, does circumscribe and underline basic problems and dilemmas of actors such as the Q'eqchi'es. Their world is not characterized by free-floating and contingent processes which can go in any direction. Modernization sets the agenda of these processes and the Q'eqchi'es adopt a creolizing method of dealing with this agenda.

Creolization and discourse

Creolization is intimately related to the character of the discourses of the Q'eqchi'es and to the ways in which their minds process impulses that reach them from the surrounding world. In order to understand this relationship, a short side-step into cognitive anthropology may prove to be fruitful. The current theory of cognition called "connectionism" holds that the human mind basically works along various networks of association.[2] Every impulse, such as an observation or a thought, simultaneously activates various meanings and emotions which in turn activate other emotions and meanings thereby following extensive networks of association. Our mind principally works through the parallel processing of information activating multiple networks of association of meanings and emotions rather than obeying fixed propositions, explicit rules or sentences. These connections between meanings and emotions are inculcated or learned by way of experiences and explicit learning. The more these connections are confirmed, the stronger the associations become and the more directive these associations are for processing future information or impulses.[3] Needless to say the various emotions and ideas that are activated in a parallel way may lead to contradictory feelings, ideas and actions.

The results of association may be expressed in discourse and some actors may be interested in structuring this discourse in a rational way. Rationalization in this respect means making the discourse as coherent and consistent as possible, freeing it from emotional appeals and decontextualizing its meanings. Some may claim absolute or decontextualized validity of this discourse and thus try to force others to process relevant data in a similar serial rather than parallel way. Thus associations become singular and proceed in a unilinear manner evading possible contradictions. Whatever the context, an impulse that is considered to be relevant activates a rational sequence of meanings, of prescribed thinking, which cuts off other kinds of associations.

In bringing this short outline of connectionism to bear on the Q'eqchi'es, several relevant issues come to the fore. To begin with, the ways in which the Q'eqchi'es deal with their religion and economy express a strongly associative character and very little rationality. To be sure, almost all my respondents were able to indicate specific meanings when I asked them about particular practices. Q'eqchi' religion and economic strategies have an explicit dimension next to an implicit one. In addition, there is some level of rationalization involved in the fact that the villagers tried to adapt the meanings of the dominated religious principle to the dominant one. However, they always talked about meanings in a contextualized way, associated meanings and emotions to specific occasions, showing emotional aspects, without wanting to relate all these meanings in consistent or rational narratives.

The associative character of the Q'eqchi'es' discourse is expressed, for example, at a "general assembly" meeting in a village. Everyone raises his or her ideas and feelings, only to some extent interrelated in sequences, but not in a clearly rational manner. They bring up relevant ideas and emotions in a rather loose way: i.e. in very short sentences and even loose words and names without indicating in what way any expression was related to the previous one. Finally, someone stands up to propose a decision without bringing together all the opinions in such a way that the proposal would be a rational conclusion. A proposal becomes a decision the moment someone is able to sense the direction of consensus. If this intuition is wrong the meeting just goes on.

Another good example of the associative nature of the Q'eqchi'es' discourses is presented by their explanations of ecological degradation. Depending on the context they attributed the decreasing fertility of their lands to Kastii interventions, to their failure to pay attention to the Tzuultaq'a, to population pressure and to the unequal land distribution. Drawing their attention to the fact that they were now giving a different explanation to the one they mentioned before, they always replied with the well-known *'Chi junil'*, 'It is all the same'. In their eyes one explanation does not rule out another and they show little interest in contradictions between these explanations.

The fact that emotions and meanings are often mixed in their discourse is clearly expressed in the way they talk about the rituals they perform towards the Tzuultaq'a. I could not escape the impression that the awe-struck expression in their eyes and voices on these occasions was intimately related to the fact that these rituals serve their objective of "resolving" their feelings of anxiety and uncertainty in an unpredictable natural setting.

On the other hand, rationalized discourses reach the Q'eqchi'es through flows of meaning stemming from the global context.[4] There is the example of the rationalized work of theologians, confirmed by and radiated from religious institutions in Rome, Geneva or the United States and claiming religious authority vis-à-vis the Q'eqchi'es. Scientists who develop technology are usually very pleased when their technology is applied in far-away corners of the world such as the Q'eqchi' region. However, global flows of meaning do not reach the Q'eqchi'es directly, such flows are transmitted to them by intermediaries. The latter - priests, religious orders, bishoprics, parishes, ministers, Kastii staffed development agencies - not only "filter" these meanings through their own cultural frameworks and policies, they also adapt these meanings to local circumstances. For example, ICTA provides DIGESA with applied technology, the clergy practising liberating pastoral work "inculturate" the Gospel into local cultures accepting some level of synthesis, and even the Salesians and ministers have to preach in the local language.

Moreover, these intermediaries have to work through structures of local leaders such as catechists and representantes agrícolas. Their success in working with these local leaders depends on whether meanings can be contextualized and related to specific occasions such as the next preparation of young couples for married life, or taking care of coffee plants. Either these intermediaries have little success in this respect - the example of hybrid seeds - or the contextualization of meanings in the training of local leaders requires that the meanings are "lifted out" of the rationality of the official discourses. The transfer of meanings from intervening agencies to the Q'eqchi'es has a fragmented character: isolated practices and meanings are transferred to the Q'eqchi'es in isolated training sessions without their interconnecting rationality becoming obvious to the Q'eqchi'es.[5]

The loss of a considerable part of the rationalizing character of official discourses is matched by the selective ways in which the Q'eqchi'es adopt and adapt elements from these official discourses. This loss of interconnecting rationality means that the elements they adopt are liable to become reworked and adapted to local needs by the Q'eqchi'es. An example of this reworking and selection is presented by the conversion of Q'eqchi'es to an evangelical church. They feel attracted to specific meanings, such as the emphasis on moral behaviour which supports and legitimates their decision to reorganize their lives. They respond to these elements without embracing the whole official discourse with all its rational consequences for each and every association in their life. Another example constitutes the fact that Q'eqchi'es only adopt chemical fertilizers when they need to do so to maintain their subsistence production whereas the state's main objective in promoting fertilizers is to increase cash-crop production. In short, global flows of meanings may have an asymmetrical character and the discourses "flowing" in this way may have rational features, but their multi-staged character involving various interfaces at various levels means that before these discourses reach the Q'eqchi'es they have lost a considerable part of their rationalizing and compelling or forceful character.

The associative rather than rational character of the ways in which the Q'eqchi'es deal with their religion and economy should not be confused with any notion of irrational thinking or not making sense. For example, based on the assumption - which as such cannot be controlled - that the landscape has a personal nature, customary religion makes perfect sense in trying to "resolve" the Q'eqchi'es' relations of dependency with their natural environment.

This making sense on the part of the Q'eqchi'es is very much encouraged by the fact that each community faces a minimum level of religious and economic pluralism. Even in Samox and Xalihá, where there are hardly any evangelicals and where the priests promote the integration of customary leaders and catechists, the villagers are confronted with evangelical churches in nearby communities to which they feel the need to respond. As a result, both Bible-oriented and customary practices and existing economic practices are not just non-expansive, self-regulating rituals and practices linked to a rather implicit "common sense" which tends to reinforce long-term stability (Hannerz 1992: 127-133, 137). Pluralism rather prompts the Q'eqchi'es to reflect both upon elements offered to them by intervening agencies, and upon their endogenous practices and meanings. They take practices and meanings out of the realm of the taken-for-granted and are encouraged to deal with religion and economy in their lives in a rather explicit way.[6] Pluralism stimulates a rather expansive kind of religion and economy among the Q'eqchi'es. This expansiveness may not be rational, but it is clearly reflexive. It impels them to be active meaning-making actors in a globalizing world.

This reflexivity needs some qualifications. Next to the general reflexivity of all human action, Giddens writes about two specific forms of reflexivity: a traditional and a modern one. In traditional reflexivity actions are mainly examined in the light of tradition, while in modern reflexivity these actions are reflected upon in the light of incoming knowledge, linked to the trust in professional expertise (Giddens 1990: 36ff). From the perspective of his definitions reflexivity among the Q'eqchi'es has both pre-modern and modern dimensions because they reflect on their practices in the light of both their customary meanings and incoming knowledge.

Association and creolization

The associative ways of reflexivity of the Q'eqchi'es have important consequences for their creolizing efforts. The act of creolization involves the articulation of the endogenous and the exogenous, the pre-modern and the modern, and thus the articulation of continuity and change.

To begin with, in line with Strauss' and Quinn's discussion of connectionism (Strauss, Quinn 1994: 289-292) one would expect that their ways of reflexivity working through multiple associative networks enable the Q'eqchi'es to guarantee an important degree of continuity. These associative networks, adapted to specific occasions and circumstances, tend to be self-reinforcing. The more impulses there are that lead to the activation of these networks with more or less satisfying results the stronger the connections of these network become. For example, when the performance of rituals at the time of maize planting is followed by an abundant harvest the Q'eqchi'es will be inclined to believe more strongly in the logic of customary religion. This reinforcement is especially strong when not only meanings are activated, but also emotions are aroused such as the feeling of relief for a good harvest.

In addition, the processing of impulses through existing networks may easily keep disconfirming evidence from arising. For example, if the maize fails to grow well despite having performed their rituals the Q'eqchi'es may feel that they have not performed these rituals with enough dedication or in a sincere enough way rather than considering customary rituals to be superfluous. Pasawinq are particularly ready to bring up this argument. Moreover, associative networks come about not only in practical experience, but also through deliberate teaching in combination with incentives and disincentives. The effects of formal education among the Q'eqchi'es are limited, but processes of education also take place between parents and children and in some places between pasawinq and other community members.

Finally, networks of association are not created in social isolation and the experience of sharing part of the activated meanings and emotions with others further confirms these networks. Especially pre-modern or customary meanings have strong communitarian features among the Q'eqchi'es and require a high degree of sharing. The moment this shared character cannot be guaranteed, customary practices such as the mayejak and the patron saint's feast become problematic (see Rubelpec and Chaabilchoch). By contrast, when these rituals are performed in a communitarian and satisfactory way their shared character reinforces the Q'eqchi'es' positive attitude towards them.

Of course, the durability of existing networks of association is stronger among elderly people than among younger ones. The latter have a more open attitude towards the new, the exogenous and the modern in general, whereas the former are more cautious and suspicious. A similar differentiation can be made between "ordinary" community members and brokers and between villages further away from or closer to urban centres. Although I have not focused much on these differences, I have the impression that women are more cautious in this respect than men. Nevertheless, associative networks guarantee some level of continuity in the case of all the Q'eqchi'es. Strauss and Quinn stress that networks of association can be overlain with other and stronger patterns of connections, but they do not completely disappear.

This associative way of reflexivity not only guarantees a basic level of continuity, it also embodies an important degree of flexibility. Strauss and Quinn emphasize the loose character of these networks which enables the actors to react in a flexible way to the particulars of any given event. The influence of different meanings and emotions activated by the particular features of any given situation can lead to different outcomes from one situation to the next (Strauss, Quinn 1994: 285, 287).

My appearance as a researcher (exogenous, unknown, moderately modern) presents a good example of multiple perspectives from which to approach something or someone new. Existing networks of association and interpretation were clearly inadequate to provide the Q'eqchi'es with a satisfying answer as to what to think of me. I was foreign to them, so belonged to those outside of the units they identify with, but was I to be treated as a Kastii? I talked to them about projects and development, but did not belong to those rare species of development workers. I was sent by the bishop to do my job in their village, as my letter with a nice stamp suggested, but then again, I was not a priest, so what was I? I was doing research that might benefit the policies of the Department of Social Pastoral Work and improve its services towards local communities, but what was their own community going to gain from my work? I was to write a book about them, but what is the use of books and who might read this book? In all the villages I worked in the Q'eqchi'es had these and similar doubts the first few times I visited them. I do not know what the reasons were that finally convinced almost all of them to co-operate and to place their trust in me, but the introduction by the priest turned out to be crucial and the fact that my work could be seen as proof that the bishop was taking an interest in their way of living and their problems surely helped a lot.

Different outcomes are possible from the point of view of different perspectives to approaching the new and unknown based on various networks of association. Existing associative networks of contextualized meanings and emotions may not be directly relevant to the new and unknown, but their flexible nature and embodiment of multiple perspectives allow the actor some room for manoeuvre in extending these networks, reworking meanings, and reflecting creatively upon what to think, to feel and to do in the face of the new and unknown. Flexible association enables the actor to find a balance between continuity and change. Here we touch on the heart of creolization.

The alternative, rational or serial processing of impulses, leaves the actors much more limited room to respond to the new and unknown in a creolizing way. A rational discourse not only requires the separation of meanings and emotions, its decontextualized nature causes contradictions between individual meanings to become apparent and requires the actor to eliminate these contradictions. It demands unequivocal meanings and unilinear associations resulting in singular perspectives from which to approach the new and unknown. It forces a single logic upon the actor's meaning-making and practices and tends to seriously curb the actor's flexibility and creativity in responding to something new. It tends to force actors to make a choice between the one and the other, between continuity and change, between the pre-modern and the modern. For example, if the Q'eqchi'es were to adopt the discourse of the Salesians in a rational all-encompassing way, which claims that customary rituals are contradictory to the Gospel, a creolizing effort in terms of combining continuity and change would become impossible. It would obstruct any positive evaluation of their own reinvented tradition and any articulation of this tradition with new religious practices and meanings.

In short, two stimulating factors play an important role in enabling the Q'eqchi'es to articulate the endogenous and the exogenous, the pre-modern and the modern. The first factor is the predominantly associative nature of their reflexivity. The second is the selective transmission of meanings from intervening agencies to the Q'eqchi'es, in the process of which these meanings become "lifted out" of the rationality of official discourses. However, these are not the only factors that influence the creolizing capacity of the Q'eqchi'es. This capacity has also to be understood in terms of strategies and social relations.

Creolization and social relations

Looking at creolization from a social perspective the decisive question is whether the actors concerned have the power to go on adopting and adapting elements stemming from both endogenous and external, both pre-modern and modern sources, for their own benefit. It requires some level of autonomy in decision-making. In the case of the Q'eqchi'es this autonomy is especially relevant to the local community and in this respect they have much to fear from the landlords, finca administrators, merchants, army officers and state officials. Since colonial times, the social and cultural survival of the Q'eqchi'es has depended on their determination and capacity to retain the economic, social, political and cultural autonomy of their local communities in the face of incursions on the part of the state and other intervening agencies and actors. The state in particular has repeatedly tried to pull them into an urban and national arena. The colonial reducciones, the INTA policy of concentrating their lotes in village centres and the counter-insurgency efforts of the army in creating model villages, have more in common than state spokesmen would be willing to admit.

Moreover, the army policy of concentrating as many people as possible in ethnically mixed communities aims at the destruction of identification with local or ethnic categories and the creation of some sort of national identity. The same can be said of the army's efforts to exercise ideological influence on the survivors of violence. In addition, the contents of the material used in many official educational programmes betray a similar intention which, in my view, is one of the major reasons for the failure of many of these programmes. These materials reflect government ideas about national identity and hardly coincide with what the Q'eqchi'es want to learn.

There is little doubt that these efforts of the state contradict the cultural identity of the Q'eqchi'es. In the ways they "map" their life-worlds, there is no such thing as a national cultural identity waiting for them to be embraced. To them, national state agencies have to be treated with a great deal of caution because their intentions rarely coincide with specific Q'eqchi' strategies. For example, not only is the state unable to enforce its laws in the Q'eqchi' region, in cases of land conflicts it appears as a major accomplice in illegal violence. Q'eqchi'es do not just reject any urban or national influence, but it seems that at least most of them consider it wise to retain their communal autonomy.

Are we dealing, then, with another version of the "closed corporate community" which Eric Wolf wrote about? He claimed that as a reaction to the expansion of large estates encroaching upon Indian lands and labour from the Seventeenth century onwards, Indian communities in Mesoamerica adopted a closed and corporate character. This defensive character was designed to ensure communal jurisdiction over land, a restricted membership, the maintenance of a religious system and mechanisms for the redistribution or destruction of surplus wealth generated by members of the community; moreover it would uphold barriers against the entry of goods and ideas from outside of the community (Wolf 1957, see also Smith 1990b: 19-20).

I agree with Carol Smith when she confirms the corporate character of local Indian communities. Indians identify primarily with their local community and they basically want to retain the relative autonomy of their community vis-à-vis the state. However, the determination to retain local autonomy is not linked to keeping the community closed, but to the wish to selectively engage in external communications and exchange. Moreover, Wolf's concept tends to reify colonial institutions within the local community without giving due consideration to the transformation of these institutions through history (Smith 1990b: 3, 13, 17-21). In the case of the Q'eqchi'es, there have been important institutional transformations taking place since the Seventeenth century and up to the present day, but their attitude towards external influences has probably always been one of selective openness. Originally, many of the religious practices and meanings that are now classified as costumbres, and many customary institutions, have an external origin. The saints, the patron saint's feast and the chinames and cofradías were selectively adopted and adapted in the past to constitute basic elements of customary religion today. Creolization among the Q'eqchi'es has probably been of all times.

In a later article Wolf made several qualifications to his concept. He emphasized the need to pay attention to internal divisions, that the boundaries between Indians and non-Indians are contested and not static and that many closed corporate communities have disappeared in the Nineteenth century. He wrote that his basic aim was to criticise interpretations which draw a direct line from the pre-Columbian past to the Indian present and to call attention to historical factors influencing Indian communities (Wolf 1986).

Nevertheless, by claiming a basic continuity from the Seventeenth century onwards, Wolf comes close to essentialist interpretations, which tend to pinpoint Indian cultures or identities to one specific period or to reduce them to one specific constitutive quality. I would say that the Q'eqchi'es are not just the autochthonous champions of resistance - as Guzmán Böckler and Herbert claim (Guzmán Böckler, Herbert 1970) - that their culture is not just the internalization of exploitation and oppression - as Cabarrús claims (Cabarrús 1979: 60, 73-76, 109) - and that they are not just threatened by "ladinoization" as many present-day advocates of the Indian cause fear. They are not romantic fighters against modernity nor can they find relief only by wholeheartedly taking over modernity. All these essentialist interpretations conceptualize Indian cultures either as something essentially desirable and authentic or as reflections of backward social structures. In both cases, Q'eqchi' culture appears as an essentially static phenomenon which is either threatened to disappear or needs to be transformed radically. The creolizing capacity of the Q'eqchi'es emphasizes the dynamic character of their culture and identities and thus refutes any such static and essentialist simplification.

Social conditions of creolization

As has been stated above, this creolizing capacity of the Q'eqchi'es depends on the maintenance of the relative autonomy of their local community and of their households. The disappearance of this relative autonomy of decision-making at these two levels would, first of all, disrupt the continuity of most of the existing economic and religious practices since these two units bring together the Q'eqchi'es to perform almost all of these practices. Secondly, any creolizing effort would become impossible because these units constitute the social conditions within which the processes of decision-making about external and modern influences take place. The articulation of both continuity and change depends on the relative autonomy of these two units.

What happens when this basic condition of creolization becomes seriously threatened is demonstrated by those Q'eqchi'es who were the victims of army violence. Most of those who have been lucky enough to survive have either left their community for good - refugees who went to Mexico and those who fled to the outskirts of the town of Cobán - or have returned to their places of origin only to find their former community in a state of disruption, mutual fear and distrust. In both cases Q'eqchi' community life among Q'eqchi'es has generally disappeared. Many of them have even lost their homes and relatives.

This disappearance of community life not only undermines much of their existing identity constructions but also, in particular, the foundation of many pre-modern aspects of their economy and religion. This holds true, for example, for the communitarian aspects of land control, labour and redistribution of resources. Wilson has made clear that among these Q'eqchi'es, customary practices such as the mayejak and customary institutions such as the chinames face many difficulties to survive; even the Tzuultaq'a has lost much of his or her role in their universe (Wilson 1995: 68, 243-247). This not only refers to those who have left their places of origin, but also to those who returned.

In a violence-torn rural context, hardly any new or modern economic activities have taken the place of pre-modern ones, and the picture which emerges is that of rather desperate and individualized Q'eqchi'es trying to survive. On the matter of religion, many Q'eqchi'es have turned to an evangelical church, but it remains to be seen whether modern religious practices and meanings offered by these churches have a lasting impact on their meaning-making in these circumstances. The Catholic church faces serious difficulties when it encourages these violence-torn communities to even perform the celebration of the Word.

In short, the experience of war-torn areas confirms the idea that there is a close relation between the loss of relative autonomy, especially by the local community, and its creolizing capacity. These experiences leave the Q'eqchi'es in a kind of no man's land between a collapsing mixture of pre-modern and modern aspects on the one hand, and the lack of modern alternatives on the other. It remains to be seen whether war-torn communities will be able to restore some level of autonomy and creolizing capacity in the future.

Except for the violence-torn communities, generally speaking the local communities maintain a circumscribed but real room for manoeuvre and local autonomy to continue their creolization. This may be valid at a general level, but it does not rule out the possibility that the influence of specific agencies and actors may have particular consequences. Sacramentalist pastoral work has a negative impact on the continuation of the so-called "general assembly" and emphasizes the power of the catechists. The reinforcement of the role of male catechists limits the public role of women. Landlords seriously curb the relative autonomy of the communities of mozos colonos in every way. The introduction of several churches within a single community makes it much more difficult for this community to speak with one voice.

On the other hand, these encroachments on the relative autonomy and decision-making capacity of the local community may be reflections of an already weakened internal structure and sense of cohesion. How far these encroachments on the internal structures of the communities will go in the future is hard to predict, until now they have not been successful in undermining the decision-making and creolizing capacity of the local communities in which I have worked in a decisive manner.

Of course, exogenous influences do not reach all Q'eqchi'es in a similar way or with the same intensity. Factors that make a difference in this respect include the distance towards the urban centres, the level of trust or distrust towards Kastii and the kind of pastoral policy followed by churches. In particular local leaders who operate as brokers with their many urban contacts are among those who are subject to the greatest exogenous influences. One would expect among them the highest level of adoption of such influences, but it is precisely among urban Q'eqchi' catechists and teachers that one finds the strongest efforts to reinvent tradition, to take their costumbres and history seriously. Among them, the endeavours to produce texts and radio programmes in the Q'eqchi' language, to introduce specific customary practices in standard Catholic rituals and to contact organizations of the indigenous movement in the capital are the strongest.

Apparently the stronger the exogenous influences, the more compelling the desire to reinvent traditions and to promote a Q'eqchi' or even Maya ethnic identity. Among urban brokers in particular, ideas about a multicultural society and a Q'eqchi' "imagined community" criticising the concept of the nation-state are becoming popular. The Q'eqchi'es may hardly exist as an ethnic group but there is no reason to rule out their potential for becoming one.

Creolization and globalization

The relative autonomy and creolizing capacity also has to be understood in the light of the pace and intensity of the influences which external actors and factors exercise on the Q'eqchi'es. This is where globalization comes in. As flows of people, meanings, images, ideas, capital, goods and technology span the globe and reach actors such as the Q'eqchi'es, their creolizing capacity is increasingly required as well as placed under strain. Confronted with these widening flows, such actors increasingly have to face up to the necessity of making sense out of new meanings, ideas, people and goods, to relate this sense to their endogenous meanings and practices, and to decide what should be done with the new and unknown. Implicit or rather non-reflexive ways of dealing with the new and endogenous may become increasingly insufficient as the explicit and reflexive dimensions of creolization are emphasized.

In addition, it does not seem far-fetched to suppose that when the pace and intensity of the new and unknown reaching them as a result of global flows become too high, the social conditions and meaning-making dimension of creolization may reach their limits. The decision-making capability within the local community and household and the capacity of association and articulation may have to "surrender" in the face of an overwhelming "invasion" of the new or the modern. I speculate on purpose here and use some imaginative terms because, to my knowledge, no systematic comparative research has been done to determine where the limits of creolization are to be found and what happens in social, cultural and psychological terms after those boundaries have been crossed.

It has to be stressed that global flows reach the Q'eqchi'es from a polycentric and polyvocal global scene. The religious centres from which they originate can be found in Rome, the headquarters of congregations in various European and North American towns, and various places in the United States from which evangelical churches have radiated all over the continent. Other flows connect the Q'eqchi'es with coffee consumers in Europe and the United States, with Arabs who use cardamom in their cuisine, with European and

North American donor agencies, with research centres all over the world working on technological aspects of agricultural production and with universities in England or the Netherlands who send researchers to the Q'eqchi'es. Those linked to these centres do not speak with one voice. Pentecostal and Catholic missionaries, or various scientists for that matter (see Note on Methodology), are not the only ones who emphasize their differences.

This polycentric and polyvocal character of the global scene does not just pose threats, it also opens up new opportunities. Specific external influences - churches emphasizing the Biblical idea of equality before God and several agencies offering access to education - have significantly improved the self-assuredness of the Q'eqchi'es. Moreover, in the last decade, NGOs made up of Indians who successfully completed higher education have emerged to speak out. Stimulated by such events as the commemoration of the colonization of the continent five centuries ago, the Nobel price awarded to the K'iche' Rigoberta Menchú as well as the United Nations decade of indigenous peoples, many such groups have come to the fore.

They have developed contacts and alliances not only with similar groups in other parts of the continent, but also with NGOs and international and multi-national organizations such as the International Labour Organization. The flows through these contacts, including financial ones, allow these groups to work quite independently from the Guatemalan state, if only the latter would keep its repressive claws from them. These groups have relatively few organizational connections with the Q'eqchi'es, but their existence may open up perspectives in the future for the Q'eqchi'es to increasingly deal directly with more global contacts, bypassing the Guatemalan state. This would take away much of the pressure which the state exercises on Q'eqchi' communities. Globalization is not only about risks but also about new openings and chances.

On the other hand, these global flows are marked by basic asymmetrical features (Hannerz 1992: 219); they have a multi-staged character involving various interfaces before they reach the Q'eqchi'es and reflect asymmetrical power relations. These asymmetrical power relations justify the rescue of the centre-periphery framework of analysis from dependency theory. However, one can only do so after having stressed the very differentiated nature of these relations between actors and agencies at a multiplicity of levels. Therefore I prefer to talk about centres and peripheries in the plural.

Even more, in recognizing asymmetrical power relations, we do not necessarily have to adopt a basically dialectical model of interpretation. Those in power not necessarily harm the interests of those with fewer power resources at their disposal or "destroy" their culture and economy. Neither does such a recognition impel us to conceive of the latter as compliant victims of or resistance fighters against oppression of those in power. We do not need to adopt an oppression/manipulation versus resistance/compliance opposition as we find, for example, in the cultural imperialism thesis. Indeed, the Q'eqchi' region does not remain free from Western consumer practices and the expansion of evangelical churches with their origins in the United States has incited many to talk about cultural imperialism. However, behind the sale of Coca Cola one does not need to see a deliberate intention to destroy Q'eqchi' culture and evangelical churches cannot just be interpreted as a conspiracy.

To be sure, the influence of the Guatemalan army, for example, is clearly antagonistic to the interests the Q'eqchi'es, but the same can hardly be said of other the clergy practising liberating pastoral work. To be sure, Q'eqchi' communities involved in land conflicts do conceive of INTA and the landlords as their adversaries, but we cannot conclude from this that their ways of dealing with intervening actors and agencies in general make sense in terms of compliance or resistance. Their ability to maintain their relative autonomy towards these agencies and their determination to improve their situation vis-à-vis the Kastii by enlarging their access to resources without entering into conflict or competition, do not make sense in these terms. Compliance is not an appropriate term because the maintenance of their relative autonomy is clearly not in line with the objectives of the state, while their intention to enlarge access to resources can hardly be seen as compliance either. In addition, the avoidance of conflict does not stem from any approval of existing social conditions.

On the other hand, the Q'eqchi'es do not simply refrain from open conflict because they are aware that this would just lead to more bloodshed. The awareness that they would taste defeat in open conflict is certainly present among many of the Q'eqchi'es and I argue in Chapter Two that they feel they do not have the resources to defend themselves against the Kastii; however this awareness is not the main reason for abstaining from violent or open opposition. This would imply that if they had sufficient power resources at their disposal, they would enter into such conflict, which is highly speculative.

Such resistance thinking is refuted by the fact that many Q'eqchi'es told me in confidence that they wish to improve their situation but not against or at the cost of the resources held by others. They clearly want their children to live a better life than they do, but they do not conceive of this desire in terms of opposition to the Kastii. They express their distrust towards the Kastii in stronger or weaker terms, but their basic aim is to meet them on equal terms in a climate of harmony. They do not link their own improvement with concessions of power or resources from the Kastii. Even those respondents who were involved in land conflicts expressed themselves in these terms.

In my view, efforts to force these intentions and ideas into categories of either compliance or resistance miss the point. Of course, any exogenous researcher "with his or her heart in the right place" cannot escape feelings of rejection and denunciation about the ways in which many Q'eqchi'es are forced to live, and reasons to denounce cases of social injustice abound. These feelings and reasons do not just stem from the large gap between what the researcher is used to and what he or she is confronted with in the Q'eqchi' region, especially when the researcher has boarded his or her plane in a relatively comfortable place in North America or Western Europe. Many events such as the bloodshed which the army has inflicted on thousands of Q'eqchi'es are wrong by any standard.

Given such facts and feelings, one can understand why researchers adopt a dialectical framework of analysis and interpret the practices and meanings of the Q'eqchi'es in terms of compliance or resistance. However, after taking a closer look, I hold that this is not how the Q'eqchi'es predominantly deal with, for example, their religion and economy. Creolization is clearly related to power relations, and the relative autonomy of the local community and household is an essential condition for creolization of the Q'eqchi'es; however it does not follow from these considerations that their creolization can be understood in terms of compliance or resistance. Is the maintenance of endogenous or pre-modern forms, such as the belief in the Tzuultaq'a or the practice of group-wise labour, an act of resistance against powerful intervening agencies?

Is the selective adoption of technology offered by DIGESA for example an act of compliance? Such interpretations try to impose a rather essentialist interpretation and simply do not make sense.

In short, the centres-peripheries framework does make sense in interpreting processes of globalization and creolization because they highlight the importance of power relations associated with these processes, but this framework should not be confused with a dialectical model or a revival of the cultural imperialism thesis. The often paternalistic attitude of those advocating this thesis is expressed in the fact that they often attribute very little power to the oppressed in non-Western areas. They portray the latter as mere passive victims of cultural duplicity and political manipulation. In addition, they criticise those who buy hamburgers in Guatemala since they should not do so. Social actors in non-Western areas are expected to refrain from adopting the Western meanings and practices the advocates of the thesis criticise.[7]

Moreover, by claiming that the actions and meaning-making of the non-Western actors can only be guided either by resistance or by compliance the advocates of the cultural imperialism thesis imply that the powerful are able to set the agenda of the oppressed to a very large degree. As far as the Q'eqchi'es are concerned, I contend that intervening agencies and actors are able to influence the Q'eqchi'es to an important extent; however the latter retain a circumscribed but nevertheless real room for manoeuvre to construct and implement their own strategies and agendas. As long as they are able to maintain their local relative autonomy the Q'eqchi'es do not care much about asymmetrical power relations as such.

While adopting the centres-peripheries framework I do not argue that the two basic ways of dealing with modernization - creolization and fundamentalism - would coincide with this opposition. Probably, both creolization and fundamentalism can be found at all levels and in all the regions of the world. Advocates and opponents of relativization can be found both at the centres and at the peripheries. The creolizing way accepts the relativization of one's own culture and endogenous forms in order to articulate them with exogenous forms. The act of merging counteracts fragmentation and disintegration, while the products of these mergers themselves constitute something new that cannot be reduced to the original categories. As such, these products contribute to foster further differences.

The fundamentalist way intends to reject relativization and opposes the exogenous and the modern while making an absolute claim about the value of its own culture and endogenous forms. In this manner the fundamentalist way emphasizes the particular and tries to stress the difference with others. However in reality, fundamentalism cannot avoid accepting an important degree of modern and global influences. Robertson argues that fundamentalist leaders tend to capitalize on distinctively modern diagnoses of the discontents produced by modernity. He also holds that their anti-global position is in itself an aspect of the process of globalization which moulds their ideas and features (Robertson 1992: 170). In his analysis of Islamic fundamentalism Gellner emphasizes that it has come up in the context of clear modern phenomena such as urbanization, political centralization, incorporation in a wider market and labour migration. It represents a shift from Folk Islam to High Islam, the latter expressing originally modern features such as the central role of scriptures and doctrine and a puritan attitude (Gellner 1992: 2, 15-22).

In this respect, both fundamentalism and creolization foment both a degree of difference and a degree of sameness, both end up with an articulation of the pre-modern and the modern, the indigenous and the external. The balance between the pre-modern and the modern, between the indigenous and the external, may vary in time and space and the same may be said about the differences between creolizing and fundamentalist ways of dealing with modernization, but these variations cannot be forced into essentialist oppositions between "North" and "South", between "developed" and "underdeveloped".

Note on Methodology

'If you go to the Q'eqchi'es to write a book about them and someone else does the same, you always end up with two different stories.' These are my own words on the very first page of this book; they do not just make up a hypothetical statement, but refer to a matter of fact. In 1987 and 1988, the anthropologist Richard Wilson did his fieldwork in the Q'eqchi' region and since then he has produced a respectable number of books and articles on the Q'eqchi'es (see Bibliography). His work contrasts in quite a number of aspects with my own results and conclusions, so in the light of the discussions on restudies in anthropology and methodological issues I think it is worthwhile to draw some parallels between the methods Wilson applied and the conclusions he reached at, and my own methods of data collection and results.

To begin with, our fieldwork projects have had quite a lot in common. Wilson worked in the Q'eqchi' region about four years before I did my fieldwork, a time difference too short for fundamental changes to have taken place. Next, the time he spent in the region, some sixteen months, does not differ very much from the two years I spent there. In addition, he also did not dedicate all his time to one or two villages but worked in several areas of the region, including the Cobán, San Pedro Carchá and Cahabón areas. Moreover, he did not stay very long in the same community, but visited several communities several times for relatively short periods. As he writes: 'This enhanced my picture of religious and cultural diversity...' (Wilson 1995: 5). My experiences were similar.

There is no doubt that his fieldwork allowed Wilson to bring in a harvest of very rich material on important aspects of the lives and life-worlds of the Q'eqchi'es. In particular his discussion of the consequences of the experiences of massive violence for the religious life and community structures of the Q'eqchi'es (Wilson 1991; Wilson 1995: 206-260) are excellent contributions to the anthropology of violence and of Human Rights violations. Also his detailed approach and presentation of various indigenous ways of conceptualizing and curing illness (Wilson 1995: 115-157) are impressive and, just like mine, his experiences were quite participatory in this respect as he also had to fall ill. These discussions are very complementary to my own work.

Nevertheless, the problems I have with his work relate to two basic issues: representativity of data and style of presentation. The former issue refers to questions such as to what extent is it possible to draw general conclusions about the Q'eqchi'es based on the particular and specific, but always limited and incomplete material one has collected. The latter topic in particular is about subjectivity and politics, about personal ways of expressing oneself and the effects one would like to generate among the readers.

Regarding representativity, Wilson is not very explicit with respect to the relevant methods he used in order to be able to write about the Q'eqchi'es as such except for the fact that he worked in several areas of the region. Questions such as whether his particular fieldwork experiences reflect some level of common ground among the various Q'eqchi'es in various circumstances are left open in his work. Nevertheless, he repeatedly writes about the Q'eqchi' population as a whole.

My own starting point was similar, i.e. to write a well-founded book about the Q'eqchi'es as such. As was mentioned above, the Bishop of the diocese of Verapaz and officials of diocesan institutions invited me to do my research and they were mainly interested in data on the Q'eqchi'es, not just on one or two villages. However, I was aware from the start that significant research on religious representations and practices, for example, ought to focus on local communities. How to relate such a focus with the kind of knowledge my "sponsors" were interested in? I was faced with a macro-micro dilemma.

In order to deal with this problem I divided my fieldwork into two stages. In stage one I mapped the whole Q'eqchi' region in terms of geographic, demographic, economic, social, health care, educational, political and religious characteristics. I subdivided the region into 27 areas in all of which I interviewed spokespersons who had an overview of at least some of these characteristics in their area. These spokespersons included priests, religious women, catechists, evangelical leaders, extension workers, health care workers and teachers. Very little reliable statistical material was available.

From this first stage the variables and selection criteria arose in order to select a number of local communities to study in further detail in the second stage. Because I had a clear overview of the whole Q'eqchi' region and the most important variables in mind, I was able to determine which communities represent the most common variations in the region. On this basis eight local communities were selected and studied, four of which feature prominently in this book. By way of systematically comparing the experiences of the various households within and between these communities, I was able to reach at a certain level of representativity of my data. They allowed me to deduct the main characteristics and variations of the Q'eqchi' religion and economy without pretending to cover all or even most of the details of religious and economic practices and meanings each Q'eqchi' is performing or constructing. For the applied variables and the limitations of this representativity see Chapter Two.

The initial construction of a regional overview greatly helped me to evaluate the representativity of data I collected subsequently in the various communities. There are many indications in Wilson's work which suggest that this is exactly what he was missing. He collected data mainly in the violence-ridden areas and among leaders such as catechists and urban "brokers", but frequently generalizes his findings and writes about the Q'eqchi'es in general. I may refer to my analysis in Chapter Two to claim that the experiences of these particular Q'eqchi'es in these specific areas do not constitute "typical" cases, that is, they do not allow us to say something well-founded about the Q'eqchi'es in general. Of course, experiences of violence are very pertinent and fundamentally shape the lives of those who have become involved in such experiences in many ways. Nevertheless, those involved originate from some one hundred local Q'eqchi' communities whereas the total number of Q'eqchi' communities amounts to 1,600.

There are many instances in his work in which Wilson generalizes about the Q'eqchi'es as a whole based on these very a-typical experiences. For example he asserts that the civil patrols, in which until recently adult men were forced by the army to spend one in every ten days walking around in the community with some rifles, would have taken over local power in a despotic way marginalizing others leaders (Wilson 1995: 239-240, 247). He emphasizes the institutional and ideological influence of the army on the local communities (Wilson 1995: 251-252). He holds that there are only few villages left which collectively celebrate the mayejak (Wilson 1995: 68). He writes that chinames and pasawink have disappeared from community life (Wilson 1995: 247). He states that the majority of Q'eqchi' men are engaged in day wage labour on the fincas (Wilson 1995: 24, 47-48). All these statements contradict my own data regarding areas with less explicit experiences of violence collected through fieldwork in villages and through interviewing spokespeople with a regional overview. The latter respondents confirmed that what these statements refer to only holds true for war-torn communities.

Moreover as I have outlined above, there is no such thing as a clear contradiction between catechists on the one hand and pasawink on the other, the former promoting only an individualistic and market-oriented agriculture, bringing about a radically new world-view and suppressing the customary knowledge system while the latter would only support subsistence production and oppose modernity, as Wilson holds. He does acknowledge the mediating role of the catechists between external, institutionalized power and the community, but he still writes about a rapid switch in religious and moral frameworks, a radically new world view, a sea change in identity, and '... an inner clash, a volcanic conflict of two worlds that both exist within [them - hs]' as a result of the changes they have provoked in the local communities (Wilson 1995: 178-180, 192, 199, 296). Only urban "brokers" may come anywhere close to such a qualification.

To be sure, the original catechists programme in the 1970s and the continuing programme of the Salesians have introduced important changes into local religious life, but because Wilson does not see the continuity of customary practices and meanings, even among Salesian-trained catechists, he overemphasizes discontinuity. His classification of Q'eqchi'es into "traditionalists", promoters of "orthodoxy" and those working in the "indigenist revitalization movement" misses the crucial point that in practice all of them articulate meanings and practices from various sources. My data point to their creolizing capacity selectively combining elements from different sources that only in a decontextualized way (for example to the researcher) seem to contradict each other. Problems in articulating such elements may appear to be acute especially among "brokers", but their experiences cannot be generalized to refer to all Q'eqchi'es. In the case of my respondents it was not the conflictive or the clash which came to the fore.

Because Wilson does not pose problems of continuity and discontinuity in a systematic way and because he maintains an apparent but implicit predisposition for rational reflexivity he misses the point when he opposes a supposedly Western analysis in terms of unequal access to the land and extension of the agro-export economy on the one hand and the view of pasawink on the other hand pointing to the breakdown of relations between the Q'eqchi'es and the conscious environment as explanations for ecological degradation (Wilson 1995: 290-291). As I have shown above, from the point of view of the Q'eqchi'es' associative reflexivity such explanations need not to be exclusive or contradictory.

Of course, the differences between his analysis and mine not only stem from different methodologies, but also partly relate to different subjectivities. One the one hand our own subjectivities enable us to understand human affairs in the first place while at the same time leading to different understandings by different people. Researchers are no exceptions in this respect. Wilson might qualify my analysis of creolization as a rather romantic story - which I vehemently reject of course - while I think that he has a predilection for sweeping statements and eye-catching assertions without always being able to found and demonstrate his claims with sufficient data. Moreover, he repeatedly mixes up various levels of analysis - the Q'eqchi' areas that have suffered from massive violence, the department of Alta Verapaz which includes not only Q'eqchi'es but also other ethnic groups, the Q'eqchi' region which goes beyond the department of Alta Verapaz and the indigenous population of Guatemala as a whole - using material from one level to demonstrate something while suggesting that it also holds true for another.

Just to give an example of unfounded sweeping statements: Wilson claims that during the times of massive violence the Catholic clergy actively endorsed their congregation's decision to support the insurgents (Wilson 1995: 215). His assertion that there would have been congregations that decided to support the guerrilla movement is not only refuted by explicit statements the clergy concerned made to me in confidence, it is also quite irresponsible to write such a thing while some of the priests and religious women concerned still work in the region. His claim that there were Marxist missionaries working with the Q'eqchi'es ten years ago (Wilson 1995: 263-264) shows that he is not very familiar with what religious discourses and pastoral methods of the Catholic church are all about (see Chapter Three).

To give another example: regarding the same period of violence Wilson writes about the rebels operating within an infrastructure of solid support, about the mass incorporation of the Q'eqchi'es into guerrilla ranks, and about widespread insurrection (Wilson 1995: 211, 222, 230, 258) without providing any data regarding the Q'eqchi'es that might support his view. He even points to Mgr. Flores Reyes who said that twenty thousand people went into hiding in the mountains. Wilson presents the bishop's words suggesting that these people incorporated into the guerrilla ranks (Wilson 1995: 222), while the same bishop told me several times that their hiding in the mountains must not be interpreted in this way (see Chapter Two).

One more example which demonstrates that Wilson not always makes the effort to painstakingly and carefully build up his argument refers to a Q'eqchi' movement called *Qawa' quk'a*. The idea of this movement was to encourage local communities to replace products that they used to buy by items they are able to produce themselves using indigenous technology and local materials (see Wilson 1993: 124-125). Wilson sees this initiative as a proof of the Q'eqchi'es retreating into economic conservatism, a revival of traditionalism, a strategy of autarky and a reaction to market-integration (Wilson 1995: 284-293). This movement Qawa' quk'a had a short-lived existence of just a few months in only a few places, which seriously questions Wilson's sweeping statements.

In short, as I wrote above, two social scientists always end up with two different stories after finishing their fieldwork in the same region and focusing on the same people, but that does not take away the fact that based on the rules of the game one story may still be more plausible and credible than the other.

Notes

Chapter one

1. For an advocate of this thesis see Hamelink 1983, for a convincing critique on it see Tomlinson 1991.
2. See Hettne 1990: 234-241. In line with Hettne I do not agree with Frans Schuurman (Knippenberg, Schuurman 1996: 63*ff*) who makes a distinction between development and progress. He attributes normative connotations to the concept of progress and perceives development as any process of social change. I would say that in development studies literature and in the practice of development work the concept of development is almost always used in a normative way. It is rather the social incarnation of the philosophical concept of progress.
3. In modern conditions time is no longer linked to a particular place. It can now be organized in agendas and time-tables that allow a complex society to function (Giddens 1990: 17-19).
4. Social relations are "lifted out" of the local context. Individual actors can now engage in social relations with other actors many miles away (Giddens 1990: 21-22).
5. Robertson 1992: 31, 143. His statement is not very convincing because his own periodization of globalization would easily fit any periodization of modernity (Robertson 1992: 58-60).
6. In this sense Friedman portrays Robertson's approach to globalization in the cultural sense as the identity space of modernity (Friedman 1995: 71).
7. According to Giddens (Giddens 1990: 21) this "lifting out" is especially emphasized in the present context of globalization, but it starts at the very beginning of modernization.
8. Therborn (Therborn 1995: 131, 135-137) writes about two vehicles through modernity: individualism linked to liberalism, and association related to nationalism and socialism.
9. Anderson 1987. This community is "imagined" because most of its members are unknown to each single individual.
10. On the question of what created what - the nation or the state - and their relations with the industrial revolution, there are considerable differences of opinion.
11. See Beyer 1994: 33-41 drawing especially on Luhmann, N., *Soziale Systeme: Grundriss einer Allgemeinen Theorie*, Frankfurt, Suhrkamp, 1984, and Luhmann, N., *Essays on Self-Reference*, New York, Columbia University, 1990.
12. See Van der Loo, Van Reijen 1993: 88-91, drawing on Durkheim, E., *De la division du travail social*, Paris, 1893.
13. Bourdieu, Wacquant 1992: 97; Beyer 1994: 33-41 drawing especially on Luhmann.
14. Not only Marx's class society is a case in point here. Weber points to the role of economic possessions and prestige as two sources of social inequality. See Van der Loo, Van Reijen 1993: 101-107.
15. See Beyer 1994: 33-41 drawing on Luhmann.
16. Robertson writes about fundamentalism as a culturally protectionist strategy (Robertson 1992: 69, 170). I use this term in a similar way without implying any theological or normative connotations.
17. Races or languages. See Hannerz 1992.

18. Things modern categories are supposed to keep apart, such as nature and culture. See Latour 1993.
19. Practices and meanings stemming from different religions. See Droogers 1989.
20. At least e.g. P. Berger, N. Luhmann, B. Wilson, and P. Bourdieu think it does, Th. Luckmann is sceptical about this idea. P. Beyer says that only Christianity has been partially successful in this respect. See Beyer 1994: 101-106.
21. Bourdieu 1971a: 295-334; Bourdieu 1971b: 3-21. Bourdieu draws heavily on Weber in his discussion of the religious field.
22. The term "popular religion" has an ambiguous character because it may refer both to the religion of the laity in relation to official religion and to the religion of subordinated groups and classes in relation to the religion of the ruling groups and classes. The two meanings of the term need not coincide.
23. Hervieu-Léger 1989: 71, 75, 76, drawing especially on Luckmann.
24. For a discussion of group-wise labour see Chapter Seven.

Chapter two

1. According to a Spanish source of 1637 there were ten or twelve of these confraternities in each town with no more than a hundred Indians: cited in Oss, van 1986: 89.
2. The department of Alta Verapaz covered almost all the Q'eqchi'es at that time, and had a limited number of *Poqomchi'* inhabitants. Wagner 1991: 204, 212.
3. Smith 1990c: 72-95. Usually the word *ladino* is used to identify someone who does not belong to one of the various Indian or Afro-Caribbean cultures in Guatemala. It is primarily a cultural and not a racial category.
4. AVANCSO n.d.(b): 27; Cabarrús 1979: 113; Sapper 1936: 44; Wagner 1991: 186.
5. Jonas 1991: 24. The abolition of the forced labour laws was one of the few reforms of the progressive governments of Arévalo and his successor Jácobo Arbenz Guzmán that were not turned back after the coup of 1954.
6. Wagner 1991: 173; Adams 1965: 31. For several decades population growth in Alta Verapaz remained considerably lower than the national average. Between 1950 and 1964 the population of Alta Verapaz increased by 2.4 per cent per annum, whereas the national yearly growth rate reached 3.1 per cent (Carter 1969: 2).
7. The *quetzal* is the local Guatemalan currency, at that time it equaled the US dollar.
8. For strategic reasons supported by the army who wanted to destroy the hiding places of guerrilla movement.
9. This conclusion is based on the findings of Pedroni (Pedroni 1991) and is confirmed by my own interviews with respondents in the villages in the settlement areas.
10. AVANCSO n.d.(b): 45; Adams 1965: 10, 15. It is impossible to give an indication of numbers of people involved in this kind of experiences, but in all the settlement areas the priests and religious women were able to mention a great number of such stories.
11. Information provided by the priest who was in charge of the parish of Panzós at that time.
12. Several sources estimate the number of deaths at the beginning of the 1980s at 50,000 to 70,000, the number of destroyed communities at 440, the number of people who had to leave their places of origin at about one million and the number of refugees who fled to Mexico at more than 100,000. These sources include: Washington Office on Latin America 1985; Manz 1986; Amnesty International 1981.
13. See for example Black 1984, Arias 1985, Jiménez 1985 and Jonas 1991.
14. This is the general picture that emerges from the statements of many respondents within and outside of the Catholic church. See also AVANCSO 1992: 173.
15. These sources include AVANCSO 1990; AVANCSO 1992; CEIDEC 1990.

16. For an elaboration on the restoration of the Catholic church see Samandú, Siebers, Sierra 1990: 27-36, 34, 43-45. The bishopric of Verapaz covers the departments of both Alta and Baja Verapaz.
17. An excellent account of these conflicts is presented by Falla 1978.
18. The data of this section consist of estimations based on several sources including the National Institute of Statistics INE in the capital, the department of statistics of the departmental government in Cobán, the various municipalities and the priests and religious women in the various parishes. These data refer to 1992.
19. This text on identity constructions is mainly based on the conversations I had with my respondents in the local communities I studied in detail (see next section). In these conversations we did not focus very much on identity aspects such as gender and age, which subsequently do not appear in this text.
20. For an overview of the relevant literature see Smith 1990b: 26*ff*.
21. For the super-exploitation thesis see Martínez Peláez 1971; for the culture of resistance interpretation see Guzmán Böckler, Herbert 1970.
22. Good examples are presented by Smith 1991, Watanabe 1992, Warren 1992, 1993, 1995, 1996, 1997a and 1997b.
23. See Fischer, McKenna Brown 1996 and *Cultura de Guatemala* 1997.
24. Concerning Guatemalan Indian communities in general Carol Smith writes that the desire to retain their local autonomy is central to their strategies (Smith 1990a: 263).
25. Formulations such as "at present" or "now" in the following part of this book refer to the time when fieldwork was done, i.e. in 1991 and 1992.

Chapter three

1. The terms "ritual" and "religious practice" will be used interchangeably. Of course, there is considerable debate about questions concerning the enforced or voluntary character of rituals, their rational or non-rational features, their emphasis on performance instead of meaning, their implicit or explicit character and their role in social integration. All these issues are interesting and important, but I consider them to be relevant to religious practices in general and not just to a specific category of religious practices called rituals. For an excellent discussion of these debates see Boudewijnse 1995.
2. In this book I use the term "religion" in the general sense of practices and representations referring to a world of gods and spirits, regardless of the quetion whether they stem from customary or ecclesiastical sources.
3. The concept of intervening agencies will be used in line with Long 1992: 16-43. However, Long uses the term mainly referring to development agencies, while here the concept is enlarged and linked to the concept of field so as to include e.g. churches in the religious field
4. It is more polite to use the word "religious women" than the term "nuns".
5. The New Testament has been translated into the Q'eqchi' language.
6. For a discussion of the policies on pastoral work within the Catholic church in Guatemala see L. Samandú, H. Siebers, O. Sierra 1990: 46-49.
7. Even in a Western metropolis it is hard to find an advocate of modernity as virulent as this Salesian priest these days.
8. Only in the neighbourhoods of Cobán, San Martín parish, there are five communities that come close to the concept of Base Communities.
9. Little pancake made of maize: an indispensable ingredient of every meal.
10. Copal pom is made of resin and is usually burned on ceremonial occasions.
11. Sacrifice ritual addressing the mountain, see next chapter.
12. Local liquor made of sugar cane.

13. The conflict between catechists and customary leaders at the beginning of the 1970s has been well documented by Cabarrús 1979: 120-128.
14. It goes much too far to say that these catechists have become independent from the institutional hierarchy and have formed a "movement", as Wilson does (Wilson 1995: 303). In general, catechists remain quite obedient to the clergy and only reluctantly develop activities outside of the framework of the church.
15. Parents and godfathers of a child call each other *compadres*.

Chapter four

1. The quote at the beginning of Chapter Three refers to this occasion.
2. Drink made out of maize flour.
3. Little mat used to sleep upon.
4. A similar argument has been put forward by Ricardo Falla explaining the "conversion" to the Catholic lay movement *Acción Católica* by young industrious members of the community of San Antonio Ilotenango, El Quiché: Falla 1978. Apparently, some of the reasons for indigenous people to turn to an evangelical church coincide with those of Catholics who become active members of their church.
5. Evangelicals criticise Catholics for drinking abuses while Catholics criticise those who perform customary rituals for the same reason. All this opens up the question of what the facts concerning alcohol abuse really are. I do not want to make any conclusion on this highly controversial issue because the respondents' statements are biased in this respect.
6. Most of the settlement areas are flat. There the idea of the Tzuultaq'a is related both to the central mountains in the heartland and to the landscape or natural environment as such.
7. Carlson, R., Eachus 1978: 50-52. Here the terms *xwiinkul* and *xdiosil* are written according to the new spelling rules.
8. The Q'eqchi' words *Qana'* and *Qawa'* are respectful designations for a woman and a man respectively.
9. Of course, harmony of the community constitute the norm, reality is often different. No community that I studied in detail was free from serious internal conflicts and rivalries.
10. Jon Schackt provides an excellent example of the revival of mayejak rituals in a Belizean Q'eqchi' village after it was struck by famine and a hurricane, which were interpreted as as a result of the wrath of the Tzuultaq'a: Schackt 1984: 16-29.
11. Cabarrús emphasizes the context of fear created by all the things God requires the Q'eqchi'es to do which makes it impossible to avoid committing sins: Cabarrús 1979: 37-38.
12. Karl Sapper holds that in his time - the end of the previous century - the Q'eqchi'es had a rather concrete view of God. They related Him to a specific territory (the territory effectively controlled by the whites) and in their eyes God preferred the whites: Sapper 1904: 462, 467. At present, God has lost this territorial link and both whites, Kastii and Q'eqchi'es are considered as His children.
13. *El dios de lo concreto*: Cabarrús 1979: 41-42.
14. Of course, talking to me as an outsider is not just a private matter. Within the protection of their own house the villagers told me about customary practices that are celebrated at the level of the household and about customary meanings, something they were not willing to admit in meetings with other villagers.
15. Of course, italics are mine.
16. Samandú uses the term *transacción* here.

Notes 181

Chapter five

1. My conclusions are in line with Rostas and Droogers who write about the mixing and mingling of beliefs and practices from different religious sources in a long-term process of ever-evolving bricolage marking the popular use of popular religion in Latin America (Rostas, Droogers 1993: 10-11).
2. It is certainly permissable to inscribe these conclusions in a Giddensian vein. He would classify the articulation of pre-modern (customary) and modern (Bible-oriented) elements as typical of a rather early phase of modernity, not of a more contemporary or radicalized form of modernity. See Giddens 1990: 48-51.

Chapter six

1. Information on landlords and the ways they run their estates was collected by interviewing respondents who have knowledge of these issues in a specific area, such as catechists, priests and employees of state agencies. I have visited several of these estates.
2. One caballería equals 45.1 hectares.
3. Source: a team of the research institute AVANCSO which has compared the levels of investment on fincas in various parts of the country.
4. A manzana equals 6987.2 square metres. 64.6 Manzanas make up one caballería and 16 *cuerdas* equal one manzana. A cuerda is 436.7 square metres.
5. At the time fieldwork was done the US dollar was worth more or less five quetzales.
6. This part on merchants is based on information provided by spokesmen and spokeswomen with a regional overview and on interviews in the local communities.
7. Price differences of a quintal of maize between El Petén and Cobán can be as high as 15 to 20 quetzales.
8. INTA has offices in Cobán, La Tinta, Fray Bartolomé de Las Casas, Modesto Mendez, Poptún, San Luís Petén and Sayaxché. I have interviewed senior officials in almost all of these offices and collected relevant INTA documents.
9. This part on DIGESA is based on interviews with DIGESA employees in 14 different areas. DIGESEPE employees have been interviewed in five different areas.
10. Estimate based on the information provided by the extension workers I interviewed.
11. In the next chapter the economic strategies, indigenous knowledge and technology of the Q'eqchi'es and their ways of dealing with DIGESA technology will be discussed.
12. Based on an interview with a DIGESEPE staff member and on AVANCSO 1992: 217.
13. Information concerning these agencies has been gathered through interviews with several of their officials and by asking other respondents with a regional overview.
14. Data of 1991 provided by a FEDECOVERA spokesman.
15. Information on INACOP was collected by conducting interviews with INACOP spokesmen in three areas.
16. Information based on an interview with the director of the Cobán office of INTECAP.
17. Figures referring to 1997.
18. For a discussion on this and other letters of the bishops on social matters and the reactions of various social organizations see Samandú, Siebers, Sierra 1990: 146-158.
19. A cuerda equals 436.7 square metres.

Chapter nine

1. Originally the term creolization refers to racial categories or to the mixing of two different languages from which a third language arises. This linguistic analogy has

subsequently been used to characterize cultural mixing in a more general sense and the construction of new identities drawing on various cultural sources, especially in polyethnic societies (Drummond 1980). Next, Hannerz has applied the term in globalization theory (Hannerz 1992: 261-267; Hannerz 1996).

In linguistic theory occasionally a difference is made between creolization and hybridization pointing to various degrees of merging and mixing of languages. I do not adopt this difference of terminology. Moreover, I want to call attention to the difference between the general way in which Hannerz uses the term creolization and the specific meanings attributed to the English word "Creole" and the Spanish term "*Criollo*". I use the term creolization in this general sense without implying these specific connotations.

2. I draw on Strauss & Quinn 1994; D'Andrade 1995; D'Andrade & Strauss 1992; Holland & Quinn 1987. See also Bruner 1990; Sperber, Wilson 1986; and Bouwhuijsen 1996.
3. There is an obvious parallel with Bourdieu's concept of habitus pointing to the inculcation of experiences in the context of social structure and producing dispositions which guide further action. Nevertheless, connectionism differs from Bourdieu in various respects. It not only talks about practices, dispositions and knowledge, but also about emotions, desires and intentions. Next, connectionism emphasizes the often ambiguous nature of past experiences and their processing which leads to contradictory meanings and emotions. Finally, it emphasizes the possibility of actors making a 'deliberate cognitive effort' to create new associations and partially transcend existing networks of association (Strauss, Quinn 1994: 294-295).
4. I do not want to suggest here that a rational mode of reflexivity would be typically Western or that an associative mode of reflexivity would characterize non-Western actors. Both modes of reflexivity can probably be found in both Western and non-Western areas alike. What I do want to point to here is the fact that especially professionalized discourses reach the Q'eqchi'es from other parts of the world, which tend to be rationalized and systematized.
5. The most notable exception are those boys who receive their education in the boarding schools run by the Salesian priests. Isolated from their local communities they are continuously confronted with and influenced by the priests' rationalizing discourse.
6. Referring to religion see Rostas, Droogers 1993: 10.
7. The thesis that Western culture would destroy cultural particularities in non-Western areas portrays Western culture itself as a homogeneous phenomenon, the adoption of which would create cultural homogeneity all over the world. This idea becomes ever more problematic as post-modernists and others draw attention to the fact that cultural homogeneity, even at the level of the individual, is an issue that causes serious trouble, let alone at large-scale levels such as a supposed Western culture.

Bibliography

Adams, R.N., (1965), *Migraciones internas en Guatemala. Expansión agraria de los indígenas kekchíes hacia El Petén, Estudios Centroamericanos No.1*, Guatemala, Seminario de Integración Social Guatemalteca.
Adams, R.N., (1990), 'Ethnic Images and Strategies in 1944', in: Smith, C.A. (ed.), *Guatemalan Indians and the State: 1540 to 1988*, Austin Texas, University of Texas Press, pp. 141-162.
Amnesty International, (1981), *Guatemala: a Government Program of Political Murder*, New York, Amnesty International.
Anderson, B., (1987), *Imagined Communities. Reflections on the Origin and Spread of Nationalism*, London-New York, Verso.
Annis, Sh., (1987), *God and Production in a Guatemalan Town*, Austin, Univ. of Texas Press.
Appadurai, A., (1990), 'Disjuncture and Difference in the Global Cultural Economy', in: Featherstone, M. (ed.), *Global Culture: Nationalism, Globalization and Modernity*, London-Newbury Park-New Delhi, SAGE, pp. 295-310.
Appadurai, A., (1996), *Modernity at Large. Cultural Dimensions of Globalization*, Minneapolis/London, University of Minnesota Press.
Arias, A., (1985), 'El movimiento indígena en Guatemala: 1970-1983', in: Camacho, D., Menjívar, R., (eds.), *Movimientos populares en Centroamérica*, San José, Costa Rica, EDUCA, pp. 62-119.
Arnason, J., (1990), 'Nationalism, Globalization and Modernity', in: Featherstone, M. (ed.), *Global Culture: Nationalism, Globalization and Modernity*, London-Newbury Park-New Delhi, SAGE, pp. 207-236.
AVANCSO, (1990), *Política institucional hacia el desplazado interno en Guatemala, Cuaderno de Investigación no. 6*, Guatemala.
AVANCSO, (1992), *¿Dónde está el futuro? Procesos de reintegración en comunidades de retornados. Cuaderno de Investigación no. 8*, Guatemala.
AVANCSO, (n.d.:a), Tema: Las Verapaces, una visión de su geografía, manuscript, Guatemala.
AVANCSO, (n.d.: b), Relaciones históricas del Estado y la región de las Verapaces, manuscript, Guatemala.
Barth, F. (ed.), (1969), *Ethnic Groups and Boundaries. The Social Organization of Cultural Difference*, London, Allen & Unwin.
Bauman, Z., (1990), 'Modernity and ambivalence', in: Featherstone, M. (ed.), *Global Culture: Nationalism, Globalization and Modernity*, London-Newbury Park-New Delhi, SAGE, pp. 143-169.
Bauman, Z., (1991), *Modernity and Ambivalence*, Cambridge, Polity Press.
Bauman, Z., (1993), *Postmodern Ethics*, Oxford-Cambridge Mass., Blackwell.
Bauman, Z., (1995), *Life in Fragments. Essays in Postmodern Morality*, Oxford, Blackwell.
Beyer, P., (1994), *Religion and Globalization*, London-Thousand Oaks-New Delhi, SAGE.
Black, G., (1984), *Garrison Guatemala*, London, Zed Books.
Boudewijnse, B., (1995), 'The Concept of Ritual. A History of its Problematic Aspects", in: *Jaarboek voor liturgie-onderzoek*, Vol. 11, pp. 31-56.

Bourdieu, P., (1971a), 'Genèse et structure du champ religieux', in: *Revue Française de Sociologie*, Vol. XII, No. 3, Juillet-Sept. 1971, pp. 295-334.
Bourdieu, P., (1971b), 'Une interpretation de la théorie de la religion selon Max Weber', in: *Archives Européennes de Sociologie*, Vol. XII, No. 1, 1971, pp. 3-21.
Bourdieu, P., (1972), *Esquisse d'une Théorie de la Pratique*, Genève, Droz.
Bourdieu, P., Wacquant, L.J.D., (1992), *An Invitation to Reflexive Sociology*, Cambridge, Polity Press.
Bouwhuijsen, H. van den, (1996), *Playfellows of God. Towards an Anthropology of Science*, Utrecht, ISOR.
Bruner, J., (1990), *Acts of Meaning*, Cambridge (Mass.), Harvard University Press.
Cabarrús, C.R., (1979), *La cosmovisión K'ekchi' en proceso de cambio*, San Salvador, UCA.
Carlson, R., Eachus, F, (1978), 'El mundo espiritual de los Kekchies', in: *Guatemala Indígena*, Vol. XIII, No. 1-2, Enero-Junio de 1978, pp. 37-73.
Carter, W.E., (1969), *New Lands and Old Traditions. Kekchi Cultivators in the Guatemalan Lowlands*, Gainesville, University of Florida Press.
CEIDEC, (1990), *Guatemala. Polos de Desarrollo. El caso de la desestructuración de las comunidades indígenas*, Mexico, CEIDEC/Editorial Praxis.
Cultura de Guatemala. Primer Congreso de Estudios Mayas, 7-9 de Agosto de 1996, Año 18., Vol. 1 (Segunda Epoca), Enero-Abril 1997
D'Andrade, R., (1995), *The Development of Cognitive Anthropology*, Cambridge, Cambridge University Press.
D'Andrade, R., Strauss, C. (eds.), (1992), *Human Motives and Cultural Models*, Cambridge, Cambridge University Press.
Dirección General de Estadísticas, Ministerio de Economía, República de Guatemala, (1982), *III. Censo Nacional Agropecuario 1979*. Vol. I, Tomo I, Guatemala.
Dominguez, E., (1994), 'The Great Commission', in: *North American Congress on Latin America, NACLA Report on the Americas*, Vol. 18, No. 1, Jan.-Febr. 1994, pp. 12-22.
Droogers, A., (1989), 'Syncretism: The Problem of Definition, the Definition of the Problem', in: Gort, J., Vroom, H., Fernhout, R., Wessels, A. (eds.), *Dialogue and Syncretism. An Interdisciplinary Approach*, Grand Rapids-Amsterdam, Eerdmans-Rodopi, pp. 7-25.
Droogers, A., Siebers, H., (1991), 'Popular Religion and Power in Latin America: An Introduction', in: Droogers, A., Huizer, G., Siebers, H. (eds.), *Popular Power in Latin American Religions*, Saarbrücken/Fort Lauderdale, Breitenbach, pp. 1-25.
Drummond, L., (1980), 'The Cultural Continuum: A Theory of Intersystems', in: *Man. The Journal of the Anthropological Institute*, Vol. 15, pp. 352-374.
Falla, R., (1978), *Quiché Rebelde. Estudio de un movimiento de conversión religiosa, rebelde a las creencias tradicionales, en San Antonio Ilotenango Quiché (1948-1970)*, Guatemala, Editorial Universitaria de Guatemala.
Falla, R., (1979), *El indio y las clases sociales. El indígena panameño y la lucha de clases/pista para la intelección de los grupos étnicos*, Panamá, Centro de Capacitación Social.
Featherstone, M. (ed.), (1990), *Global Culture: Nationalism, Globalization and Modernity*, London-Newbury Park-New Delhi, SAGE.
Fischer, E.F., McKenna Brown (eds.), (1996), *Maya Cultural Activism in Guatemala*, Austin, University of Texas Press.
Friedman, J., (1995), 'Global System, Globalization and the Parameters of Modernity', in: Featherstone, M., Lash, S., Robertson, R., (eds.), *Global Modernities*, London-Thousand Oaks-New Delhi, Sage, pp. 69-90.
Garrard, V.C., (1986), *A History of Protestantism in Guatemala*, Ph.D. Thesis, Austin/Texas.
Gellner, E., (1992), *Postmodernism, Reason and Religion*, London-New York, Routledge.
Giddens, A, (1990), *The Consequences of Modernity*, Cambridge, Polity Press.
Godelier, M., (1977), *Horizon, trajets marxistes en anthropologie*, Tome II, Paris, Maspero.
Godelier, M., (1978), 'Infrastructures, Societies, and History', in: *Current Anthropology*, Vol. 19, No. 4, December 1978, pp. 763-768.

Gómez Lanza, H., (1983), *Desarrollo histórico de la Verapaz y la conquista pacífica*, Guatemala, Instituto Indigenísta Nacional.
Guzmán Böckler, C., Herbert, J.-L., (1970), *Guatemala: una interpretación histórico-social*, Mexico-Madrid-Buenos Aires, Siglo XXI.
Hall, St., (1991), 'The Local and the Global: Globalization and Ethnicity', in: King, A.D. (ed.), *Culture, Globalization and the World-System. Contemporary Conditions for the Representation of Identity*, Houndmills-Basingstoke-London, MacMillan, pp. 19-39.
Hamelink, C., (1983), *Cultural Autonomy in Global Communications*, New York, Longman.
Hannerz, U., (1992), *Cultural Complexity. Studies in the Social Organization of Meaning*, New York, Columbia University Press.
Hannerz, U., (1996), *Transnational Connections. Culture, People, Places*, London/New York, Routledge.
Hervieu-Léger, D., (1989), 'Tradition, Innovation and Modernity: Research Notes', in: *Social Compass*, Vol. 36, Nr. 1, 1989, pp. 71-81.
Hettne, B., (1990), *Development Theory and the Three Worlds*, Harlow/New York, Longman.
Hobsbawm, E., Ranger, T. (eds.), (1983), *The Invention of Tradition*, Cambridge, Cambridge University Press.
Holland, D., Quinn, N. (eds.), (1987), *Cultural Models in Language and Thought*, Cambridge, Cambridge University Press.
Hopkins, T.K., Wallerstein, I., (1982), *World-System Analysis. Theory and Methodology*, Beverly Hills-London- New Delhi, SAGE.
Huntington, D., (1994), 'God's Saving Plan', in: *North American Congress on Latin America, NACLA Report on the Americas*, Vol. 18, No. 1, Jan.-Febr. 1994, pp. 23-33.
Inforpress Centroamericana, (1988), *Centro América 1988. Análisis económicos y políticos sobe la región. Centro América, Belice, Guatemala, El Salvador, Honduras, Nicaragua, Costa Rica, Panamá*, Guatemala, Inforpress Centroamericana.
Instituto Nacional de Estadística, (1988), *Encuesta Nacional Socio-demográfica 1986-1987, región norte*, Guatemala, INE.
Instituto Nacional de Estadística, (1990), *Encuesta nacional socio-demográfica 1989, región norte*, Guatemala, INE.
Inter-American Development Bank, (1993), *1992. Annual Report*, Washington.
Jiménez, D., (1985), 'El movimiento campesino en Guatemala: 1969-1980', in: Camacho, D., Menjívar, R., (eds.), *Movimientos populares en Centroamérica*, San José, Costa Rica, EDUCA, pp. 293-343.
Jonas, S., (1991), *The Battle for Guatemala. Rebels, Death Squads, and U.S. Power*, Boulder-San Francisco-Oxford, Westview Press.
Knippenberg, L., Schuurman, F., (1996), 'Stripped: A critical phenomenology of progress and development', in: Köhler, G., Gore, Ch., Reich, U-P., Ziesemer, T. (eds.), *Questioning Development. Essays in the theory, policies and practice of development interventions*, Marburg, Metropolis-Verlag, pp. 45-70.
Laclau, E., (1985), 'New Social Movements and the Plurality of the Social', in: Slater, D. (ed.), *New Social Movements and the State in Latin America*, Amsterdam, CEDLA, pp. 27-42.
Latour, B., (1993), *We Have Never Been Modern*, New York, Harvester Wheatsheaf.
Laughlin, Ch., Brady, J. (eds.), (1978), *Extinction and Survival in Human Populations*, New York-Guildford, Columbia University Press.
Lévi-Strauss, C., (1962), *La pensée sauvage,* Paris, Plon.
Long, N., (1992), 'From paradigm lost to paradigm regained?', in: Long, N., Long, A. (eds.), *Battlefields of Knowledge. The interlocking of theory and practice in social research and development*, London-New York, Routledge, pp. 16-43.
Loo, H. van der, Reijen, W. van, (1993), *Paradoxen van modernisering. Een sociaalwetenschappelijke benadering*, Muiderberg, Coutinho.
Luckmann, Th., (1991), 'The New and the Old in Religion', in: Bourdieu, P., Coleman, J.S. (eds.), *Social Theory for a Changing Society*, Oxford, Westview Press, pp. 167-182.

Lutz, Ch.H., Lovell, W.G., (1990), 'Core and Periphery in Colonial Guatemala', in: Smith, C.A. (ed.), *Guatemalan Indians and the State: 1540 to 1988*, Austin Texas, University of Texas Press, pp. 35-51.
Lyotard, J.-F., (1984), *The Postmodern Condition: A Report on Knowledge*, Minneapolis, University of Minnesota Press.
Manz, B., (1986), *Guatemala: cambios en la comunidad, desplazamientos y repatriación*, Mexico, Editorial Praxis.
Martínez, A., Samandú, L., (1990), 'Acerca del desafío pentecostal en Centroamérica', in: Samandú, L., (ed.), *Protestantismos y procesos sociales en Centroamérica*, San José, EDUCA, pp. 41-65.
Martínez Peláez, S., (1971), *La patria del criollo. Ensayo de interpretación de la realidad colonial guatemalteca*, Guatemala, Editorial Universitaria.
McCreery, D., (1990), 'State Power, Indigenous Communities, and Land in Nineteenth-Century Guatemala, 1820-1920', in: Smith, C.A. (ed.), *Guatemalan Indians and the State: 1540 to 1988*, Austin Texas, University of Texas Press, pp. 96-115.
Morrison, K., (1995), *Marx, Durkheim, Weber. Formations of Modern Social Thought*, London-Thousand Oaks- New delhi, SAGE.
Opazo Bernales, A., (1990), 'El movimiento protestante en Centroamérica. Una aproximación cuantitativa', in: Samandú, L., (ed.), *Protestantismos y procesos sociales en Centroamérica*, San José, EDUCA, pp. 13-38.
Oss, A. van, (1986), *Catholic Colonialism. A parish history of Guatemala 1524-1821*, Cambridge a.o., Cambridge University Press.
Pacay Coy, E., (1987), Aproximación a la cosmovisión Maya y la concepción K'ekchi' del mu, unedited manuscript.
Pacheco, L., (1988), *Tradiciones y costumbres del pueblo Maya Kekchi. Noviazgo, matrimonio, secretos, etc.*, San José, Costa Rica, Ed. Ambar.
Palma, D., (1991), Los Qu'ekchis, unedited manuscript, Guatemala.
Pedroni, G., (1991), *Territorialidad Kekchi. Una aproximación al acceso a la tierra: La migración y la titulación*, Guatemala, FLACSO.
Robertson, R., (1992), *Globalization: Social Theory and Global Culture*, London-Newbury Park-New Delhi, SAGE.
Robertson, R., (1994), 'Religion and the Global Field', in: *Social Compass*, Vol. 41, No. 1, 1994, pp. 121-135.
Robertson, R., (1995), 'Glocalization: Time-Space and Homogeneity-Heterogeneity', in: Featherstone, M., Lash, S., Robertson, R., (eds.), *Global Modernities*, London-Thousand Oaks-New Delhi, SAGE, pp. 25-44.
Roosens, E., (1989), *Creating Ethnicity: the Process of Ethnogenesis*, Newbury Park, Sage.
Rostas, S., Droogers, A. (eds), (1993), 'The Popular Use of Popular Religion in Latin America: Introduction', in: Rostas, S., Droogers, A. (eds.), *The Popular Use of Popular Religion in Latin America*, Amsterdam, CEDLA, pp. 1-16.
Rostow, W.W., (1960), *The Stages of Economic Growth. A Non-Communist Manifesto*, Cambridge-London-NewYork, Cambridge University Press.
Samandú, L., (1989), 'La Iglesia del Nazareno en Alta Verapaz: Su historia y presencia en el mundo Kekchí', in: *El Protestantismo en Guatemala. Cuadernos de Investigación. Dirección General de Investigaciones*, Univesidad de San Carlos de Guatemala, No. 2-89, pp. 17-47.
Samandú, L. (1990), 'Estrategias evangélicas hacia la población indígena de Guatemala', in: Samandú, L., (ed.), *Protestantismos y procesos sociales en Centroamérica*, San José, Costa Rica, EDUCA, pp. 69-110.
Samandú, L., Siebers, H., Sierra, O., (1990*), Guatemala: Retos de la Iglesia Católica en una sociedad en crisis*, San José, Costa Rica, DEI.
Samandú, L., Van Nieuwenhove J., Siebers, H., Klein Goldewijk, B., (1986), *Life and Death in Central America. A Sociological, Theological and Political Interpretation of the Irruption of the New Subject*, Exchange Vol. XV, Leiden, IIMO.

Sapper, K., (1904), 'Religiöse Gebräuche und Anschauungen der Kekchi-Indianer', in: *Archiv für Religions Wissenschaft*, Nr. 7, 1904, pp. 453-470.
Sapper, K., (1936), *Die Verapaz im 16. und 17. Jahrhundert. Ein Beitrag zur historischen Geographie und Ethnographie des nordöstlichen Guatemala*, München, Verlag der Bayerischen Akademie der Wissenschaften.
Schackt, J., (1984), 'The Tzuultak'a: Religious Lore and Cultural Processes among the Kekchi', in: *Belizean Studies*, Vol. 12, no. 5, 1984, pp. 16-29.
Séguy, J., (1989), 'Introduction', in: *Social Compass*, Vol. 36, Nr. 1, 1989, pp. 3-12.
Siebers, H., (1991), 'Indian religion and the Catholic Church in Guatemala', in: Droogers, A., Huizer, G., Siebers, H., (eds.), *Popular Power in Latin American Religions*, Breitenbach, Saarbrücken/Fort Lauderdale, pp. 82-105.
Siebers, H., (1994), 'On the Crossroads between Tradition and Modernity: Religious and Economic Development of the Q'eqchi'es of Guatemala', in: Schuurman, F. (ed.), *Current Issues in Development Studies. Global Aspects of Agency and Structure*, Saarbrücken/Fort Lauderdale, Breitenbach, pp. 209-245.
Siebers, H., (1996), 'Popular Culture and Development: Religion, Tradition and Modernity Among the Q'eqchi'es of Guatemala', in: Salman T. (ed.), *The Legacy of the Disinherited. Popular Culture in Latin America: Modernity, Globalization, Hybridity and Authenticity*, Amsterdam, CEDLA, pp. 137-158.
Siebers, H., (1997a), 'Mixing and Mingling in a Globalizing World: Identity Constructions of the Q'eqchi'es of Guatemala', in: Staring, R., Land, M. van der, Tak, H. (eds.), *Globalization/localization: Paradoxes of Cultural Identity. Focaal. Tijdschrift voor Antropologie*, Nrs. 30/31, 1997, pp. 179-192.
Siebers, H., (1997b), 'Zwischen Fragmentierung und Reflexivität: Gibt es eine Zukunft für Identität und Ethnizität?', in: *Peripherie. Zeitschrift für Politik und Ökonomie in der Dritten Welt*, Jrg. 17, Nr. 67, August 1997, pp. 46-66.
Siebers, H., (1998), 'Globalization and Religious Creolization among the Q'eqchi'es of Guatemala', in: Smith, Chr., Prokopy, J. (eds.), *Latin American Religion in Motion:Tracking Innovation, Complexity and Unexpected Change*, London, Routledge.
Similox Salazar, V., (1991), Los protestantismos en Guatemala, unedited manuscript, Guatemala.
Smith, C.A., (1990a), 'Conclusion: History and Revolution in Guatemala', in: Smith, C.A. (ed.), *Guatemalan Indians and the State: 1540 to 1988*, Austin Texas, University of Texas Press, pp. 258-285.
Smith, C.A., (1990b), 'Introduction: Social Relations in Guatemala over Time and Space', in: Smith, C.A. (ed.), *Guatemalan Indians and the State: 1540 to 1988*, Austin Texas, University of Texas Press, pp. 1-30.
Smith, C.A., (1990c), 'Origins of the National Question in Guatemala: A Hypothesis', in: Smith, C.A. (ed.), *Guatemalan Indians and the State: 1540 to 1988*, Austin Texas, University of Texas Press, pp. 72-95.
Smith, C.A., (1991), 'Destrucción de las bases materiales de la cultura indígena: cambios económicos en Totonicapán', in: Carmack, R. (ed.), *Guatemala: cosecha de violencias*, San José, Costa Rica, FLACSO, pp. 341-381.
Sperber, D., Wilson, D., (1986), *Relevance: Communication and Cognition*, Oxford, Blackwell.
Stoll, D., (1990), *Is Latin America Turning Protestant? The Politics of Evangelical Growth*, Berkeley-Los Angeles-Oxford, University of California Press.
Strauss, C., Quinn, N., (1994), 'A Cognitive/Cultural Anthropology', in: Borofsky, R. (ed.), *Assessing Cultural Anthropology*, New York, McGraw-Hill, pp. 284-297.
Therborn, G., (1995), 'Routes to/through Modernity', in: Featherstone, M., Lash, S., Robertson, R., (eds.), *Global Modernities*, London-Thousand Oaks-New Delhi, SAGE, pp. 124-139.
Tönnies, F., (1957), *Community and Society*, New York, Harper and Row.

Tomlinson, J., (1991), *Cultural Imperialism: A Critical Introduction*, London, Pinter Publishers.

Wagner, R., (1991), *Los Alemanes en Guatemala 1828-1944*, Guatemala, Editorial IDEA.

Wallerstein, I., (1990), 'Culture as the Ideological Battleground of the Modern World-System', in: Featherstone, M. (ed.), *Global Culture*: Nationalism, Globalization and Modernity, London-Newbury Park-New Delhi, SAGE, pp. 31-55.

Warren, K, (1978), *The Symbolism of Subordination: Indian Identity in a Guatemalan Town*, Austin, University of Texas Press.

Warren, K., (1992), 'Transforming Memories and Histories: The Meaning of Ethnic Resurgence for Mayan Indians', in: Stepan, A. (ed.), *Americas: New Interpretive Essays*, Oxford, Oxford University Press, pp. 189-219.

Warren, K., (1993), 'Interpreting La Violencia in Guatemala: Shapes of Mayan Silence and Resistance', in: Warren, K.B. (ed.), *The Violence Within: Cultural and Political Opposition in Divided Nations*, Boulder (Col.), Westview Press, pp. 25-56.

Warren, K., (1995), 'Each Mind is a World. Dilemmas of Feeling and Intention in a Kaqchikel Maya Community', in: Rosen, L. (ed.), *Other Intentions. Cultural Contexts and the Attribution of Inner States*, Santa Fe (New Mexico), School of American Research Press, pp. 47-67.

Warren, K., (1996), 'Mayan History as Practice. Chronicles, Translations, and Self-Discovery', in: Fischer, E., McKenna Brown, R. (eds.), *Mayan Cultural Activism in Guatemala*, Austin (Texas), University of Texas Press.

Warren, K., (1997a), 'Narrating Cultural Resurgence: Genre and Self-Representation for Pan-Mayan Writers', in: Reed-Danahay, D. (ed.), *Auto/Ethnography. Rewriting the Self and the Social*, Oxford/New York, Berg, pp. 21-45.

Warren, K., (1997b), 'Tensiones persistentes e identidades cambiantes: luchas de la familia maya en Guatemala', in: *Cultura de Guatemala. Primer Congreso de Estudios Mayas, 7-9 de Agosto de 1996*, Año 18., Vol. 1 (2a Epoca), Enero-Abril 1997, pp. 271-296.

Washington Office on Latin America, (1985), *Security and Development in the Guatemalan Highlands*, Washington, WOLA.

Watanabe, J., (1992), *Maya Saints and Souls in a Changing World*, Austin, University of Texas Press.

Weber, M., (1958), *The Protestant Ethic and the Spirit of Capitalism*, New York, Scribner.

Wilk, R.R., (1987), 'The Search for Tradition in Southern Belize: A Personal Narrative', in: *América Indígena*, Vol. XLVII, No. 1, Enero-Marzo de 1987, pp. 77-95.

Wilson, R., (1990), *Mountain Spirits and Maize: Catholic Conversion and the Renovation of Traditions Among the Q'eqchi' of Guatemala*, PhD thesis, University of London.

Wilson, R., (1991), 'Machine Guns and Mountain Spirits. The cultural effects of state repression among the Q'eqchi' of Guatemala', in: *Critique of Anthropology*, Vol. 11, No. 1, 1991, pp. 33-61.

Wilson, R., (1993), 'Anchored Communities: Identity and History of the Maya-Q'eqchi'', in: *Man. The Journal of the Royal Anthropological Institute*, Vol. 28, No. 1, March 1993, pp. 121-138.

Wilson, R., (1995), *Maya Resurgence in Guatemala: Q'eqchi' Experiences*, Norman-London, University of Oklahoma Press.

Wolf, E., (1957), 'Closed Corporate Communities in Mesoamerica and Central Java', in: *Southwestern Journal of Anthropology*, Vol. 13, No. 1, pp. 1-18.

Wolf, E., (1986), 'The Vicissitudes of the Closed Corporate Peasant Community', in: *American Ethnologist*, Vol. 13, No.2, pp. 325-329.

Woodward, R.L., (1990), 'Changes in the Nineteenth-Century Guatemalan State and Its Indian Policies', in: Smith, C.A. (ed.), *Guatemalan Indians and the State: 1540 to 1988*, Austin Texas, University of Texas Press, pp. 52-71.

Glossary

(C): word in Castilian or Spanish.
(Q): word in Q'eqchi' or other Guatemalan indigenous language.

Acción Católica (C)	Catholic Action, Catholic lay movement
Agentes multiplicadores de pastoral social (C)	Representatives of the Department of Social Pastoral Work, bishopric of Verapaz
Akala'es (Q)	Name of an ethnic group
Alcalde Auxiliar (C)	Auxiliary mayor, representative of the mayor in the local community
Alcalde Mayor (C)	Spanish colonial administrator
Aldea (C)	Village, local community not situated on a finca or hacienda
Atol (C)	Drin made of maize flour
Awas (Q)	Taboo, prescription of how to deal with "persons" and objects, disease caused by maltreating "persons" or objects
B'antioxink (Q)	Thanksgiving at the moment of harvesting maize
B'oj (Q)	Local liquor made of sugar cane
Baldío (C)	Piece of land that has no private owner and consequently belongs to the state
Caballería (C)	Area measure, 45.1 hectares, 64.6 manzanas
Cacique (C)	Local indigenous leader in the colonial period
Camionero (C)	Merchant with truck
Castellano (C)	Spanish
Ch'oles (Q)	Name of an ethnic group
Chi junil (Q)	'It is all the same', Q'eqchi' expression indicating that they do not care about contradictions
Chinam (Q)	Member of rural confraternity
Chirimía (C)	Kind of flute
Cofradía (C)	Kind of confraternity, urban religious brotherhood dedicated to a special saint
Comisionado Militar (C)	Military commissioner representing the army in the local community
Comité de Desarrollo Local (C)	Local Development Committee in the local communities
Comité Pro Mejoramiento (C)	Improvement Committee in the local communities
Compadre (C)	Name parents give to the godparents of their child
Copal pom (Q)	Substance made of resin and used on ceremonial occasions

Costumbre (C)	Custom, in its plural form used to designate indigenous culture
Cuerda (C)	Area measure, 436.7 square metres
Dirección General de Servicios Agrícolas (DIGESA) (C)	Sub-division of ministry of agriculture promoting agrarian production among small and medium sized farmers
Dirección General de Servicios Pecuarios (DIGESEPE) (C)	Sub-division of ministry of agriculture promoting livestock raising among small and medium sized peasants and farmers
Ejército Guerrillero de los Pobres (EGP) (C)	Armed revolutionary organization
Empresa de Fomento y Desarrollo del Petén (FYDEP) (C)	Official development organization of the department of El Petén until 1990
Encomienda (C)	Colonial system granting individual Spaniards the right to collect tribute from a certain number of Indians
Faenas (C)	Communitarian tasks which all the community members are supposed to perform
Federación de Cooperativas de las Verapaces (FEDECOVERA) (C)	Federation of production co-operatives in Alta and Baja Verapaz
Finca (C)	Large privately owned estate dedicated to agrarian production
Finca nacional (C)	Large state owned estate dedicated to agrarian production
Finquero (C)	Large landowner
Garífunas (C)	Afro-Caribbean ethnic group living in Lívingston and Puerto Barrios, Honduras and Belize
Gramoxone (C)	Chemical product used to disinfect the land
Guerrilleros (C)	Armed resistance fighters
Habilitación (C)	Hereditary labour recruitment system in which workers receive payment in advance and pay off their debt with interest by working on a finca, debt peonage
Hacienda (C)	Large privately owned estate dedicated to livestock raising
Hermandad (C)	Urban religious brotherhood organizing religious ceremonies in the Holy Week
Huipil (C)	Typical white blouse worn by Q'eqchi' women
Ilonel (Q)	Customary healer
Indígena (C)	Indian, indigenous
Instituto Nacional de Transformación Agraria (INTA) (C)	State organization responsible for giving out land titles in settlement areas
Intendente (C)	Loca ruler appointed by the government in the 1930s
Itza'es (Q)	Name of an ethnic group
Jornaleros (C)	Day labourers
K'anjel (Q)	Work, (moral) effort
K'iche'es (Q)	Name of an ethnic group
Kastii (Q)	Name the Q'eqchi'es use to designate non-Q'eqchi'es, those who speak Castilian

Ladino (C)	Guatemalan not belonging to an indigenous or Afro-Caribbean group, speaking Castilian
Lakandones (Q)	Name of an ethnic group
Latifundio (C)	Large estate
Libra (C)	Weight measure, 453 grams
Lote (C)	Piece of land reserved for house building
Ma'us (Q)	Bad spirit
Manzana (C)	Area measure, 6987.2 square metres, 16 cuerdas
Marimba (C)	Musical instrument
Maya-Mopanes (Q)	Name of an ethnic group living in San Luís Petén and Belize
Mayejak (Q)	Sacrifice ritual dedicated to the mountain spirit, community rituals just before clearing the land
Mayordomo (C)	Office holder in religious brotherhood, elders
Mertom (Q)	Assistant of chinam
Minifundio (C)	Small estate
Ministro (C)	Catholic lay leader receiving his orders directly from a Salesian priest and offering communion
Mozos colonos (C)	Permanent labourers living on a finca or hacienda
Na'leb' (Q)	Culture, knowledge
Padrino (C)	Godfather
Parcelamiento (C)	Individual land title
Pasawinq (Q)	Man and woman who have served as chinam, elders
Patrimonio agrario colectivo (C)	Land title of a mixed communitarian and individual character
Patrón (C)	Landlord, employer
Petate (C)	Small mat used to sleep on
Poqomchi'es (Q)	Name of an ethnic group living in the southwestern part of the department of Alta Verapaz
Posadas (C)	Religious rituals performed in the nine days preceding Christmas
Promotores pecuarios (C)	Livestock raising promoters
Qana' (Q)	Lady, respectful term used to address a woman
Qawa' (Q)	Lord, sir, mister, respectful term used to address a man
Quetzal (C)	Famous tropical bird, national Guatemalan currency, at the time of fieldwork five quetzales equaled one US dollar
Quintal (C)	Weight measure, 45.3 kilos
Rab'inal Achi'es (Q)	Name of ethnic group living in Baja Verapaz
Reducciones (C)	Indian population concentrated in towns by the Spaniards
Representantes agrícolas (C)	Representatives of the ministry of agriculture in the local rural communities
Rilomil tzuul (Q)	'Seen by the mountain', customary disease
Roxil (Q)	Third couple in the hierarchy of chinames

Tierra caliente (C)	'Warm land', lowlands
Tierra fría (C)	'Cold land', land on high altitudes
Tierra templada (C)	'Moderate land', land situated between highlands and lowlands
Tortilla (C)	Pancake made of maize flour
Túnica Blanca (C)	Name of a confraternity in San Pedro Carchá
Túnica Morada (C)	Name of a confraternity in San Pedro Carchá
Tuul (Q)	Witch, sorcerer
Tzuultaq'a (Q)	Mountain spirit, mountain and valley, sacred landscape
Violencia (C)	'Violence', name given to the period marked by massive violations of human rights in the late 1970s and early 1980s
Wa'tesink re li kab'l (Q)	'Feeding the house' rituals at the time of entering a new house
Xb'enil (Q)	First couple in the hierarchy of chinames
Xiw (Q)	'Spirit loss', customary disease
Xkab'il (Q)	Second couple in the hierarchy of chinames
Yo'lek (Q)	Ritual of keeping vigil while addressing all that abide in the universe
Yuca (C)	Kind of vegetable
Yuwa' ch'och (Q)	'Chief of the land', customary leader in charge of allocating household lands

Index

articulation 46; 101; 105; 108; 150; 159; 162; 164; 166; 168; 172; 181
Asamblea de Dios 38; 49; 60; 61; 68; 73; 79; 80; 83; 96
association 59; 160; 162; 163; 164; 168; 177; 182
auxiliary mayor 29; 34
awas 57; 189
b'antioxink 63; 71; 73; 87; 93; 145
Bible-oriented 77; 83; 88; 89; 90; 91; 92; 93; 94; 95; 96; 97; 98; 100; 101; 102; 105; 107; 108; 141; 142; 143; 146; 148; 150; 151; 157; 159; 162; 181
brokers 29; 32; 105; 154; 163; 168; 174; 175
catechists 26; 27; 29; 38; 39; 40; 41; 42; 44; 48; 53; 54; 56; 58; 59; 60; 61; 69; 74; 75; 76; 81; 82; 83; 91; 93; 94; 104; 105; 106; 107; 108; 142; 148; 154; 161; 162; 167; 168; 174; 175; 179; 181
Catholic vii; viii; ix; 20; 25; 26; 27; 33; 36; 37; 38; 39; 40; 41; 42; 43; 44; 46; 48; 49; 51; 52; 53; 58; 59; 61; 62; 63; 66; 68; 69; 70; 71; 73; 74; 75; 76; 78; 79; 80; 82; 83; 88; 89; 93; 95; 96; 97; 101; 102; 103; 104; 105; 106; 107; 108; 119; 148; 154; 167; 168; 169; 176; 178; 179; 180; 186; 187; 188; 189; 191
celebration of the Word 27; 41; 43; 44; 56; 58; 59; 66; 67; 74; 75; 76; 77; 78; 97; 108; 167
chinam 29; 38; 39; 53; 54; 55; 56; 58; 59; 60; 61; 64; 65; 66; 67; 81; 91; 94; 105; 106; 107; 166; 167; 175; 191; 192
Claretians 42
cofradía 20; 22; 27; 29; 39; 53; 54; 55; 103; 106; 107; 166
commoditization 129; 144; 145
commodity 14; 125; 143; 144; 145; 146; 150
conversion 19; 20; 27; 49; 52; 79; 80; 81; 82; 108; 161; 180
creolization viii; 11; 100; 101; 102; 108; 150; 157; 159; 162; 164; 165; 166; 167; 168; 170; 171; 172; 176; 181; 182
creole 11; 20
customary vii; 19; 32; 38; 40; 44; 45; 46; 47; 48; 49; 50; 53; 54; 55; 56; 58; 59; 60; 61; 62; 63; 64; 65; 66; 68; 70; 71; 72; 73; 74; 75; 76; 77; 78; 79; 83; 84; 85; 86; 87; 88; 89; 90; 91; 92; 93; 94; 95; 96; 97; 98; 99; 100; 101; 102; 103; 104; 105; 106; 107; 108; 141; 142; 143; 144; 145; 146; 148; 150; 151; 162; 163; 164; 166; 167; 168; 175; 179; 180; 181; 191; 192
Department of Social Pastoral Work viii; ix; 47; 118; 125; 138; 154; 164

development vii; viii; 2; 3; 7; 26; 29; 32; 52; 61; 116; 119; 120; 123; 127; 153; 158; 161; 164; 177; 179; 185; 190
differentiation 9; 15; 21; 59; 83; 140; 147; 152; 163
DIGESA 114; 115; 116; 122; 129; 135; 136; 137; 143; 153; 158; 161; 171; 181; 189
DIGESEPE 114; 115; 116; 122; 127; 135; 136; 142; 153; 158; 181; 190
disembedding 5
Dominicans 18; 19; 21; 42; 45; 48
evangelical 26; 27; 29; 33; 36; 37; 38; 39; 40; 41; 43; 47; 48; 49; 50; 51; 52; 53; 54; 59; 60; 61; 62; 63; 65; 68; 69; 70; 71; 73; 76; 78; 79; 80; 81; 82; 83; 88; 89; 90; 94; 95; 96; 97; 103; 104; 105; 106; 107; 108; 118; 120; 142; 148; 154; 161; 162; 167; 168; 169; 174; 180
extension worker 34; 114; 115; 138; 143; 174; 181
external inputs 123; 125; 130; 131; 134; 135; 136; 137; 142; 143; 150; 151; 153; 154; 156
fundamentalism 171; 172; 177
fundamentalist 11; 16; 171; 172
globalization vii; viii; 2; 4; 5; 6; 7; 8; 10; 14; 16; 159; 168; 171; 177; 181
global flows vii; viii; 4; 159; 161; 162; 168; 169
God 9; 12; 13; 15; 27; 33; 43; 44; 45; 46; 49; 50; 57; 58; 61; 64; 65; 66; 67; 68; 69; 70; 71; 72; 73; 74; 75; 77; 79; 80; 81; 82; 83; 84; 86; 88; 89; 90; 92; 95; 96; 97; 100; 101; 103; 104; 105; 143; 144; 145; 148; 151; 157; 169; 180; 183; 184; 185; 191

gross product 131; 132; 133; 134; 137
hermandad 53; 54; 55; 77; 78; 106; 107
hybrid 11; 114; 137; 142; 143; 159; 161; 182
hybridization 159; 182
Iglesia de Dios del Evangelio Completo 49
Iglesia del Nazareno (Nazarene church) 38, 48, 49; 50; 51; 52; 60; 79; 118; 186
imagined community 8; 32; 168
indigenous knowledge 9; 45; 47; 115; 118; 153; 154; 181
intervening agencies 18; 36; 40; 120; 122; 151; 152; 153; 155; 159; 161; 162; 164; 165; 170; 171; 179
jornaleros 110; 152
Kastii 32; 33; 34; 45; 51; 55; 109; 111; 112; 113; 115; 126; 135; 136; 137; 141; 142; 143; 149; 151; 161; 164; 168; 170; 180
knowledge viii; 2; 5; 6; 9; 10; 15; 34; 41; 44; 47; 56; 107; 114; 115; 118; 134; 153; 154; 157; 162; 168; 174; 175; 181; 182; 191
labour 5; 7; 8; 9; 14; 15; 17; 19; 20; 21; 22; 23; 25; 28; 37; 43; 55; 69; 75; 89; 110; 111; 116; 117; 118; 123; 126; 127; 128; 129; 131; 132; 133; 134; 135; 143; 144; 145; 146; 147; 148; 150; 151; 152; 153; 154; 156; 157; 165; 167; 170; 171; 175; 178; 190; 191
individual labour 128; 144; 150; 153
group-wise labour 15; 127; 128; 129; 144; 145; 146; 150; 151; 170; 178
wage labour 7; 14; 15; 22; 89;

111; 127; 128; 129; 131;
  133; 134; 135; 143; 147; 148;
  153; 175
communitarian labour 127; 154
ladino 20; 21; 24; 27; 28; 32; 33;
  34; 35; 37; 50; 166; 178
land conflicts 24; 25; 27; 46; 78;
  110; 119; 126; 153; 154; 165;
  170
land titles 112; 113; 114; 116; 120;
  124; 190
landlords 47; 86; 109; 110; 111;
  119; 152; 153; 158; 165; 170;
  181
liberating pastoral work 45; 46;
  47; 48; 54; 59; 60; 61; 62; 64;
  77; 103; 104; 105; 107; 118;
  154; 158; 161; 169
liberation theology 27; 45
Local Development Committee 29;
  112; 120; 146; 147; 148; 155;
  189
localization vii; 4; 5; 6; 16; 186;
  187
ma'us 190
market-oriented activities 37; 112;
  126; 127; 131; 132; 133; 135;
  140; 141; 142; 144; 147; 148;
  149; 151
market-oriented production 14;
  131; 135; 138; 141; 152; 153;
  157
Maya ix; 18; 19; 24; 28; 32; 46;
  48; 168; 184; 186; 188; 191
mayejak 47; 63; 65; 66; 67; 68; 69;
  72; 77; 83; 84; 85; 86; 87; 91;
  92; 93; 94; 97; 98; 99; 108; 141;
  144; 145; 146; 163; 167; 175;
  180
merchants 18; 22; 32; 33; 35; 37;
  57; 111; 112; 127; 134; 135;
  137; 152; 153; 158; 165; 181
military commissioner 29
ministro 59; 93; 94; 148

modernity
  pre-modern vii; viii; 3; 5; 6; 7;
    14; 15; 103; 156; 158; 159;
    166; 171; 175; 177; 179; 181
  originally modern vii; viii; 3; 5;
    6; 7; 14; 15; 103; 156; 158;
    159; 166; 171; 175; 177; 179;
    181
  contemporary modern vii; viii;
    3; 5; 6; 7; 14; 15; 103; 156;
  post-modern vii; viii; 3; 5; 6; 7;
    14; 15; 103; 156; 158; 159;
    166; 171; 175; 177; 179; 181
    158; 159; 166; 171; 175; 177;
    179; 181
modernization vii; viii; 3; 5; 6;
  7; 14; 15; 103; 156; 158; 159;
  166; 171; 175; 177; 179; 181
mozos 110; 111; 117; 128; 133;
  152; 167
net income 131; 132; 133; 134;
  137; 138; 139; 140; 147; 148;
  155
pasawink 67; 98; 101; 175
patron saint 39; 53; 54; 63; 64; 65;
  66; 68; 77; 85; 86; 91; 94; 99;
  108; 163; 166
Pentecostal 13; 49; 50; 51; 52; 62;
  79; 81; 96; 103; 104; 106; 151;
  169
periphery 169
planting rituals 63; 69; 70; 71; 72;
  87; 93; 96; 143; 145
prayer healing 79; 80; 81; 96
Príncipe de Paz 50
rationalization/rational 10; 160
reflexivity 13; 102; 162; 163; 164;
  175; 182
  reflexive 13; 102; 162; 163;
    164; 175; 182
relativization 4; 11; 13; 16; 101;
  104; 171
rilomil tzuul 57; 86; 96

sacramentalist 43; 48; 61; 103; 104; 154
sacramentalist pastoral policy 61; 104
sacramentalist pastoral work 43; 48; 104; 154
sacraments 19; 41; 43; 49; 62; 74; 75; 103; 106
saint 20; 29; 39; 53; 54; 55; 57; 62; 63; 64; 65; 66; 68; 70; 72; 74; 75; 76; 77; 80; 82; 84; 85; 86; 90; 91; 92; 94; 95; 96; 99; 108; 163; 166; 189
Salesians 42; 43; 44; 45; 47; 48; 55; 56; 59; 62; 66; 81; 104; 105; 118; 119; 161; 164; 175
secularization 12; 13
strategies viii; 27; 33; 45; 47; 95; 97; 109; 115; 123; 140; 141; 142; 143; 147; 148; 149; 151; 152; 153; 154; 155; 156; 160; 164; 165; 171; 179; 181
stratification 14; 15; 53; 82; 123; 138; 139; 147; 148; 150; 151; 156
subsistence crops 71; 89
subsistence production 14; 15; 37; 123; 129; 130; 131; 132; 137; 138; 140; 162; 175
Tzuultaq'a 66; 67; 68; 69; 70; 71; 72; 73; 84; 85; 86; 87; 88; 89; 90; 91; 92; 93; 94; 95; 96; 97; 98; 99; 100; 101; 141; 143; 144; 145; 146; 157; 161; 167; 170; 180; 192
violence 8; 24; 25; 26; 27; 33; 35; 37; 38; 47; 51; 52; 60; 61; 68; 80; 81; 82; 89; 90; 105; 114; 117; 118; 154; 165; 167; 173; 174; 175; 176
wa'tesink 63; 72; 73; 85; 93; 99
xiw 57; 86
yo'lek 64; 65; 66; 67; 74; 84; 87; 90; 92

CEDLA PUBLICATIONS

CEDLA LATIN AMERICA STUDIES (CLAS) series

Pitou van Dijck (ed.), *The Bolivian Experiment: Structural Adjustment and Poverty Alleviation*
CLAS 84, 1998, pp. 312   NLG 42,50/Gbp 16.95/US$ 28.00
ISBN 90 70280 37 X

Ruerd Ruben, *Making Cooperatives Work, Contract Choice and Resource Management within Land Reform Cooperatives in Honduras*
CLAS 83, 1998   NLG 40,00/Gbp 15.95/US$ 26.50
ISBN 90 70280 27 2

Hans Siebers, *'We Are Children of the Mountain', Creolization and Modernization among the Q'eqch'es.*
CLAS 82, 1998   NLG 37,50/Gbp 14.95/US$ 25.00
ISBN 90 70280 17 5

Daniel Míguez, *Spiritual Bonfire in Argentina: Confronting Current Theories with an Ethnographic Account of Pentecostal Growth in a Buenos Aires Suburb*
CLAS 81, 1998, pp. 216   NLG 37,50/Gbp 14.95/US$ 25.00
ISBN 90 70280 96 5

Veronica Montecinos, *Economists, Politics and the State: Chile 1958-1994.*
CLAS 80, 1998, pp. 160   NLG 35,00/Gbp 12.95/US$ 23.50
ISBN 90 70280 85 X

Susana Menéndez, *En búsqueda de las mujeres. Percepciones sobre género, trabajo y sexualidad, Buenos Aires 1900-1930.*
CLAS 79, 1997, pp. 216   NLG 35,00/Gbp 13.95/US$ 23.50
ISBN 90 70280 86 8

Pieter de Vries, *Unruly Clients in the Atlantic Zone of Costa Rica. A Study of How Bureaucrats Try and Fail to Transform Gatekeepers, Communists and Preachers into Ideal Beneficiaries*
CLAS 78, 1997, pp. 264   NLG 37,50/Gbp 14.95/US$ 25.00
ISBN 90 70280 66 3

Kevin Gosner & Arij Ouweneel (eds), *Indigenous Revolts in Chiapas and the Andean Highlands*
CLAS 77, 1996, pp. 296   NLG 37,50/Gbp 14.95/US$ 25.00
ISBN 90 70280 56 6

Ton Salman (ed.), *The Legacy of the Disinherited. Popular Culture in Latin America: Modernity, Globalization, Hybridity and Authenticity*
CLAS no 76, 1996, pp. 288   NLG 37,50/Gbp 14.95/US$ 25.00
ISBN 90 70280 46 9

C.F.G. de Groot, *Brazilian Catholicism and the Ultramontane Reform, 1850-1930*
CLAS no 75, 1996, pp. 220   NLG 35,00/Gbp 13.95/US$ 23.50
ISBN 90 70280 36 1

Gerrit Burgwal, *Struggle of the Poor: Neighborhood Organization and Clientelist Practice in a Quito Squatter Settlement*
CLAS no 74, 1995, pp. 276   NLG 37,50/Gbp 12.95/US$ 25.00
ISBN 90 7028026 4

Prices are given in Netherlands guilders (NLG), British pounds sterling (Gbp) and US dollars.

Jan M.G. Kleinpenning, *Peopling the Purple Land: A Historical Geography of Rural Uruguay, 1500-1915*
    CLAS no 73, 1995, pp. 376   NLG 47,50/Gbp 19.95/US$ 32.00
    ISBN 90 70280 06 X

Simon Miller, *Landlords & Haciendas in Modernizing Mexico: Essays in Radical Reappraisal*
    CLAS no 72, 1995, pp. 208   NLG 35,00/Gbp 11.95/US$ 23.50
    ISBN 90 70280 95 7

Ton Salman, *De verlegen beweging: desintegratie, inventiviteit, en verzet van de Chileense 'pobladores' – 1973-1990*
    CLAS no. 71, 1993, pp. 380   NLG 45,00/Gbp 17.95/US$ 30.00
    ISBN 90 70280 55 8

Susanna Rostas & André Droogers (eds), *The Popular Use of Popular Religion in Latin America*
    CLAS no. 70, 1993, pp. 240   NLG 42,50/Gbp 16.95/US$ 28.00
    ISBN 90 70280 65 5

Rik Hoekstra, *Two Worlds Merging: The Transformation of Society in the Valley of Puebla, 1570-1640*
    CLAS no. 69, 1993, pp. 296   NLG 40,00/Gbp 15.95/US$ 26.50
    ISBN 90 70280 25 6

Roelie Lenten, *Cooking under the Volcanoes: Communal Kitchens in the Southern Peruvian City of Arequipa*
    CLAS no. 68, 1993, pp. 232   NLG 35,00/Gbp 13.95/US$23.50
    ISBN 90 70280 15 9

Frans Papma, *Contesting the Household Estate: Southern Brazilian Peasants and Modern Agriculture*
    CLAS no. 67, 1992, pp. 280   NLG 40,00/Gbp 14.95/US$ 26.50
    ISBN 90 70280 84 1

Jan J.G. Kleinpenning, *Rural Paraguay, 1870-1932*
    CLAS no. 66, 1992, pp. 548   NLG 55,00/Gbp 22.95/US$ 36.50
    ISBN 90 70280 64 7

For information, contact:
C E D L A
Keizersgracht 395-397
NL-1016 EK Amsterdam
Países Bajos/The Netherlands

Fax 31 20 6255127. E-mail: secretariat@cedla.uva.nl

Prices are given in Netherlands guilders (NLG), British pounds sterling (Gbp) and US dollars.